EAST ANGLIAN ARCHAEOLOGY

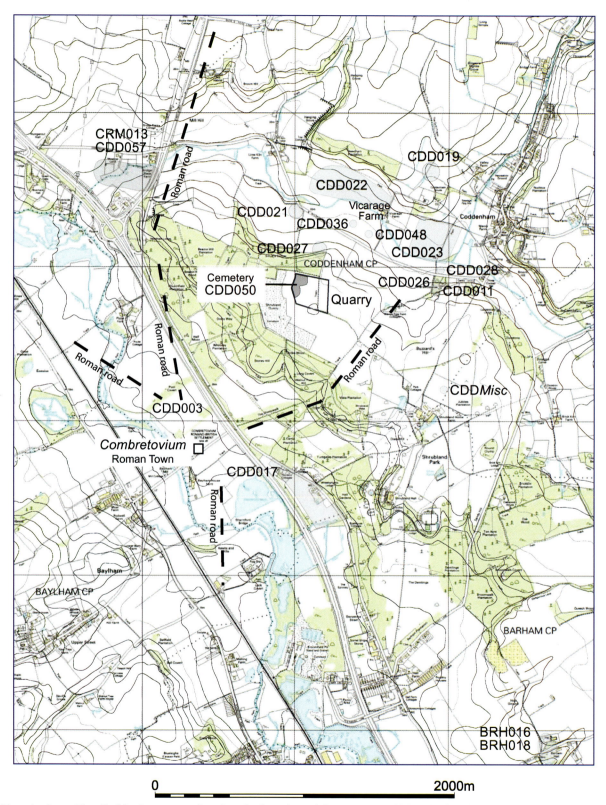

Frontispiece The Coddenham area, showing the location of the cemetery (CDD 050), other sites mentioned in the text (CDD 003, 013, 017, 019, 021–3, 027, 057, CRM 013) and Roman town of *Combretovium*

The Anglo-Saxon Cemetery at Shrubland Hall Quarry, Coddenham, Suffolk

by Kenneth Penn

with contributions from
Sue Anderson, Birte Brugmann, Dylan Cox, Val Fryer, Karla Graham, John Hines, Michael Metcalf, Sarah Paynter, Ian Riddler, Penelope Walton Rogers, Alan Vince and Jacqui Watson

illustrations by
Jason Gibbons, with Julie Curl, David Dobson, Chris Evans and Mike Feather

photographs by
Suffolk County Council Archaeological Service, Penelope Walton Rogers and Jacqui Watson

East Anglian Archaeology
Report No.139, 2011

Archaeological Service
Suffolk County Council

EAST ANGLIAN ARCHAEOLOGY
REPORT NO. 139

Published by
Suffolk County Council Archaeological Service
Economy, Skills and Environment
9–10 The Churchyard
Shire Hall
Bury St Edmunds
Suffolk IP33 2AR

in conjunction with
ALGAO East
http://www.algao.org.uk/cttees/Regions

Editor: Keith Wade
EAA Managing Editor: Jenny Glazebrook

Set in Times Roman by Jenny Glazebrook using Corel Ventura™
Printed by Henry Ling Limited, The Doset Press

This volume was published with the aid of funding from English Heritage

East Anglian Archaeology was established in 1975 by the Scole Committee for Archaeology in East Anglia. The scope of the series expanded to include all six eastern counties and responsibility for publication passed in 2002 to the Association of Local Government Archaeological Officers, East of England (ALGAO East).

For details of *East Anglian Archaeology*, see last page

Cover illustration: The bed burial in Grave 30. An artist's reconstruction of the burial (*Chris Evans, English Heritage Centre for Archaeology*)

Contents

List of Plates

List of Figures

List of Tables

Contributors

Sue Anderson
formerly Finds Manager, Suffolk County Council
Archaeological Service

Dr Birte Brugmann
freelance Anglo-Saxon specialist and heritage
consultant, Mannheim, Germany

Dylan Cox
English Heritage Centre for Archaeology, Fort
Cumberland, Eastney, Portsmouth PO4 9LD

Julie Curl
formerly Graphics Assistant, NAU Archaeology,
Scandic House, 85 Mountergate, Norwich NR1 1PY

David Dobson
Senior Illustrator, NAU Archaeology, Scandic House, 85
Mountergate, Norwich NR1 1PY

Mike Feather
formerly Graphics Assistant, NAU Archaeology,
Scandic House, 85 Mountergate, Norwich NR1 1PY

Jason Gibbons
freelance illustrator, c/o Norfolk Landscape
Archaeology, Union House, Gressenhall, Dereham,
Norfolk NR20 4DR

Karla Graham
English Heritage Centre for Archaeology, Fort
Cumberland, Eastney, Portsmouth PO4 9LD

Dr Michael Metcalf
Ashmolean Museum, Beaumont Street, Oxford OX1
2PH

Sarah Paynter
English Heritage Centre for Archaeology, Fort
Cumberland, Eastney, Portsmouth PO4 9LD

Kenneth Penn
formerly Senior Project Officer, NAU Archaeology,
Scandic House, 85 Mountergate, Norwich NR1 1PY

Ian Riddler
Freelance Consultant, Tatra, Diddies Road, Stratton, Nr
Bude, Cornwall, EX23 9DW

the late Dr Alan Vince
Archaeological Consultant, 25 West Parade, Lincoln
LN1 1NW

Penelope Walton Rogers
The Anglo-Saxon Laboratory, 8 Bootham Terrace, York
YO30 7DH

Jacqui Watson
English Heritage Centre for Archaeology, Fort
Cumberland, Eastney, Portsmouth PO4 9LD

Acknowledgements

Excavation of the site was undertaken in several stages, beginning with evaluation and moving on to trial trenching, carried out by Stuart Boulter, and then excavation, carried out by Chris Topham-Smith. Stuart Boulter reported on the first two stages of work. Metal-detecting was carried out by Dave Cummings. A Project Design for Assessment was compiled by Sue Anderson with a number of specialist contributors: Michael Metcalf, Ian Riddler, Penelope Walton Rogers, Karla Graham and Dylan Cox, Alexis Willett, Cathy Tester, Jane Cowgill and Val Fryer; and submitted to English Heritage by Suffolk County Council.

The evaluation and excavation was funded by Wildings Aggregates Ltd, with supplementary funds generously granted by English Heritage so that complete excavation and analysis could be undertaken; special thanks are due to Mr P. McCartney of Wilding Aggregates Ltd, their consultant, Stephen Daw ARICS, and to quarry staff for their help on site. At English Heritage, Chris Scull, Philip Walker and Tom Cromwell ensured support for the assessment and analysis phase of the project, which had become a challenge to the available resources.

We are grateful to Lord and Lady de Saumarez of Shrubland Hall, owners of the site, for their interest in the discoveries at Coddenham and their help at an early stage of work. They have also most generously donated the finds to Ipswich Museum following the reporting of the relevant gold and silver finds under the Treasure Act 1996 thereby removing any need to proceed to inquest.

Excavation of Graves 1 and 30, in particular, presented many challenges to the excavators and to the conservation team. At English Heritage Centre for Archaeology, Fort Cumberland (EHCfA), Karla Graham and Dylan Cox also provided a Conservation Assessment of the Coddenham material (April 2001), with advice on mineral- preserved organic material from Glynis Edwards and Dylan Cox.

Post-excavation conservation was carried out at EHCfA by Karla Graham and Jacqui Watson, who also provided X-rays of objects submitted to her, and supervised excavation of soil blocks. The Centre also holds the Conservation Records and photographs taken during conservation.

The bed burial in Grave 30 received special attention, and we are indebted to colleagues at EHCfA and to

Penelope Walton Rogers (Anglo-Saxon Laboratory, York) for their contributions. Remains of textiles were also examined by Penelope Walton Rogers.

At English Heritage, Chris Scull and Alex Bayliss kindly submitted a radiocarbon sample from Grave 30 to Queen's University, Belfast, and discussed the results.

Jacqui Watson (EHCfA), wishes to acknowledge the help given by Richard Darrah in their joint discussions over the bed construction, and especially his expertise on woodworking and the recognition that the bed must have been dismantled before placing in the grave. Several figures were produced by John Vallender from the original grave plan by Suffolk County Council Archaeological Services. Chris Evans translated Jacqui Watson's notes and sketches on the grave reconstruction into a watercolour of the burial.

The co-ordination of work on the finds and post-excavation schedules was in the initial stages in the hands of Sue Anderson, latterly, John Newman and Richenda Goffin. Individual classes of objects were kindly examined by a number of specialists, both in the assessment phase and for the final analysis presented here. Sue Anderson examined human skeletal remains, Early Saxon pottery and small finds generally, whilst Val Fryer analysed plant macrofossils from prehistoric and Early Saxon features. Other specialists to whom we remain grateful for their advice and contributions are Birte Brugmann (beads), Michael Metcalf (coins), Ian Riddler (combs), Penelope Rogers (textiles), and advice from Helen Geake, John Hines (Grave 1 shield), Keith Parfitt (information on Buckland cemetery), Barry Ager, Carol Neuman de Vegvar (drinking horns) and Sue Youngs, for much advice on the hanging bowl. Other advice and information was willingly given by Adrian Marsden, Stuart Brookes (boat burials), Phil Andrews and Mark Simmons, of Hartlepool Museums and Heritage Service, on the bed burial from Street House, Loftus, Yorks.

The pottery thin sections were prepared by Steve Caldwell of the Department of Earth Sciences, University of Manchester, and the chemical analysis was carried out at the Department of Geology, Royal Holloway College, London, under the supervision of Dr N. Walsh. Alan Vince is grateful to Sue Anderson for the opportunity to study the Coddenham and Hadleigh vessels and to the staff of the

Medieval and Modern Europe Department of the British Museum, in particular Barry Ager and Leslie Webster, for their help in allowing him to examine the imported pottery held by their department. Alan Vince also wishes to thank Mike Cowell, of the Department of Scientific Research, British Museum, for permission to re-analyse his data.

Erica Darch of Norfolk Landscape Archaeology and Roz Britton-Strong of the Ashmolean Museum, Oxford, kindly made arrangements for the transport of several finds. Caroline McDonald of Colchester and Ipswich Museums Service checked details of coins in their care.

The writer is grateful to Jason Gibbons, the illustrator, whose comments and advice were helpful in understanding the grave assemblages.

During preparation of this report, Colin Pendleton at Suffolk County Council Archaeology Service provided information from the Suffolk Historic Environment Record. Chris Scull and Keith Wade kindly provided the writer with a draft copy of the Buttermarket report, and finally, the writer is grateful to Jenny Glazebrook for her support.

Summary

The Anglo-Saxon cemetery at Shrubland Hall Quarry, Coddenham, was unknown until its discovery during investigation of an Iron Age site. The fifty Anglo-Saxon burials found were possibly the remains of a larger cemetery, extending an unknown distance to the west, the other graves being lost to earlier gravel extraction. While most of the fifty burials lacked grave-goods, or had modest accompaniments, several graves included elaborate grave-goods, some imported, and typical of the later 7th and early 8th century.

The cemetery lay around a probable prehistoric barrow, and barrows were raised over three of the burials. Coins found in two burials give a general date to the cemetery, placing it in the later 7th and early 8th centuries. The grave-goods are mostly typical of the mid-7th to early 8th century, when a distinct range of object types was deposited. Some of the grave-goods indicate access to objects drawn from overseas. The more lavishly provided burials included two in wooden chambers, one of them (Grave 30) a bed burial within a chamber, over which was placed a curved wooden cover, possibly a fragment of boat, the other (Grave 1), partly removed by earlier quarrying, containing a seax and imported bronze bowl.

Finds included wo seaxes (one with inlaid iron buckle) and a fauchard, two shields, some fragments of a hanging bowl, two other bronze bowls and the remains of three combs. Dress fittings included two silver 'safety pin' brooches, typical late 7th-century beads, and a pendant reusing a Frankish gold coin of Dagobert I. In particular, the affinities of the assemblage lie with contemporary cemeteries at Boss Hall and Buttermarket in Ipswich, at Harford Farm in Norfolk, at Burwell and Shudy Camps in Cambridgeshire, and further afield in Kent, Yorkshire and Frankish areas of the continent. Two of the three bronze bowls add to a corpus of distinctive imported vessels, whose distribution emphasizes the long-distance connections of contemporary material culture.

Local patterns of settlement also provide a context for the cemetery, which may be the burial place for a high-status community inhabiting a site in the valley below. Coddenham lies close to the Roman road system and to the site of the Roman town of *Combretovium*, in the Gipping valley to the west. Metal-detecting in the adjacent parish of Barham has recorded another 'productive' site, next to the medieval church, with finds similar to those from Coddenham.

The excavation is of importance in adding a cemetery to the known mortuary landscape at a time when accompanied burial was about to end. The graves illustrate the varied practices used in this period, including structures within graves and the use of barrows.

Résumé

C'est au cours de fouilles effectuées sur un site de l'âge du fer que l'on a découvert le cimetière anglo-saxon de Shrubland Hall Quarry à Coddenham, qui était jusqu'alors inconnu. Les cinquante tombes anglo-saxonnes qui ont été trouvées représentaient peut-être les restes d'un cimetière plus grand qui s'étendait vers l'ouest jusqu'à une distance inconnue. Quant aux autres tombes, elles n'ont pas été retrouvées en raison de l'extraction de gravier effectuée auparavant. Alors que la plupart des cinquante tombes étaient dépourvues d'objets funéraires ou étaient accompagnées d'ornements modestes, plusieurs d'entre elles possédaient des objets funéraires élaborés, importés pour certains, qui étaient représentatifs de la fin du septième et du début du huitième siècle.

Le cimetière encerclait un tumulus qui datait probablement de la période préhistorique. On a également trouvé des tumulus sur trois des tombes. Les pièces trouvées dans deux tombes permettent grosso modo d'attribuer au cimetière une date comprise entre la fin du 7ème siècle et le début du 8ème siècle. Les objets funéraires sont surtout représentatifs d'une période allant du milieu du 7ème au début du 8ème siècle, lorsqu'un ensemble particulier de types d'objets a été déposé dans les tombes. Certains des objets funéraires montrent que les habitants avaient accès à des produits venant de l'étranger. Les tombes contenant les objets les plus luxueux comportaient deux chambres en bois. La chambre de la tombe 30 comprenait un lit funéraire sur lequel était placé un couvercle arrondi en bois. Quant à l'autre chambre, qui est située dans la tombe 1, elle contenait un scramasaxe et un bol en bronze importé, même si elle fut partiellement détruite par l'exploitation d'une carrière.

Les fouilles ont permis de découvrir des pièces de monnaie, deux scramasaxes (dont l'un était pourvu d'une boucle en fer incrustée), un fauchard, deux boucliers, quelques fragments d'un bol suspendu, deux autres bols en bronze ainsi que les restes de trois peignes. Parmi les parures et accessoires vestimentaires, on a trouvé deux broches en argent de type « épingle de sûreté », des perles représentatives de la fin du 7ème siècle et un pendentif qui intégrait une pièce en or franque de Dagobert I. L'ensemble présente surtout des ressemblances avec des objets trouvés dans des cimetières de la même époque à Boss Hall et à Buttermarket dans l'Ipswich, à Harford Farm dans le Norfolk, à Burwell et à Shudy Camps dans le Cambridgeshire, dans des endroits plus éloignés du Kent et du Yorkshire et dans les zones franques du continent. Deux des bols de bronze s'ajoutent à un corpus particulier de récipients importés. Leur diffusion montre que les relations avec la culture matérielle s'établissaient sur de grandes distances.

Des configurations locales d'implantation fournissent également un contexte pour le cimetière, qui peut être le lieu d'inhumation d'une communauté d'un haut niveau social occupant un site dans la vallée située en contrebas. Coddenham se trouve près du réseau routier romain et du site de la ville romaine de *Combretovium*, dans la ville de Gipping en direction de l'ouest. Des opérations de détection de métal dans la paroisse voisine de Barham ont permis d'enregistrer un autre site « productif », près de l'église médiévale, avec des découvertes comparables à celles qui proviennent de Coddenham.

Les fouilles ont permis d'ajouter un cimetière au paysage mortuaire connu, à une époque où la pratique des morts d'accompagnement était sur le point de disparaître. Les tombes illustrent les pratiques variées utilisées pendant cette période, ce qui inclut la présence de structures dans les tombes et l'utilisation de tumulus.

(Traduction: Didier Don)

Zusammenfassung

Das angelsächsische Gräberfeld am Steinbruch von Shrubland Hall, Coddenham, war bis zur Untersuchung einer Stätte aus der Eisenzeit unbekannt. Die fünfzig zufällig gefundenen Gräber aus angelsächsischer Zeit deuten auf ein größeres Gräberfeld hin, dessen Ausdehnung in westliche Richtung nicht rekonstruiert werden konnte, da die restlichen Gräber aufgrund von Steinbrucharbeiten verloren gingen. Die meisten Gräber enthielten keine oder nur sehr schlichte Grabbeigaben, einige wiesen jedoch kunstvolle, zum Teil importierte und für die Zeit des späten 7. bzw. frühen 8. Jahrhunderts typische Grabbeigaben auf.

Das Gräberfeld war um einen vermutlich prähistorischen Grabhügel angelegt, wobei drei der Gräber eigene Grabhügel besaßen. Die in zwei Gräbern gefundenen Münzen erlauben eine Datierung des Gräberfelds auf die Wende vom 7. auf das 8. Jahrhundert. Die meisten Grabbeigaben sind für die Zeit von Mitte des 7. bis Anfang des 8. Jahrhunderts typisch, in der eine Reihe spezifischer Gegenstände deponiert wurde. Einige der Beigaben deuten darauf hin, dass Zugang zu ausländischen Waren bestand. Zwei der großzügiger ausgestatteten Gräber waren in hölzerne Grabkammern eingebettet. In einer Kammer (Grab 30) wurde eine Bettbestattung mit gewölbtem Holzdeckel gefunden, die andere (Grab 1), die durch frühere Steinbrucharbeiten teilweise zerstört war, enthielt einen Sax und eine importierte Bronzeschale.

Neben den Münzen wurden zwei Saxe (einer davon mit einem Eisenknauf mit Silbereinlage) sowie eine Hippe, zwei Schilde, Fragmente einer Hängeschale, zwei weitere Bronzeschalen und Reste von drei Kämmen gefunden. Das Kleidungszubehör umfasste zwei sicherheitsnadelähnliche silberne Gewandspangen, für das Ende des 7. Jahrhunderts typische Perlen und einen fränkischen Münzanhänger aus Gold mit dem Abbild Dagoberts I. Die Funde ähneln denen der zeitgleichen Gräberfelder von Boss Hall und Buttermarket in Ipswich, Harford Farm in Norfolk, Burwell und Shudy Camps in Cambridgeshire sowie von weiter entfernt gelegenen Gräberfeldern in Kent, Yorkshire und den fränkischen Gebieten in Kontinentaleuropa. Zwei der Bronzeschalen reihen sich in den Korpus besonderer Importgefäße ein, deren Verteilung die Fernverbindungen der damaligen materiellen Kultur belegen.

Die lokalen Siedlungsmuster liefern den Kontext für das Gräberfeld, das womöglich als Begräbnisstätte für eine hochgestellte Gruppe diente, die im Tal unterhalb der Stätte lebte. Coddenham liegt im Tal des Gipping, unweit mehrerer Römerstraßen und der Römerstadt *Combretovium* im Westen. Durch Metallortung wurde in der Nachbargemeinde Barham direkt neben der mittelalterlichen Kirche eine weitere ergiebige Stelle aufgespürt, die ähnliche Funde wie in Coddenham aufwies.

Die Ausgrabung fügt der bekannten Gräberlandschaft einer Zeit, in der sich die Deponierung von Grabbeigaben ihrem Ende zuneigte, ein weiteres Gräberfeld hinzu. Die Gräber verdeutlichen die verschiedenen Gepflogenheiten jener Zeit wie etwa Strukturen innerhalb von Gräbern und die Errichtung von Grabhügeln.

(Übersetzung: Gerlinde Krug

Chapter 1. Introduction

I. Background

The Suffolk village of Coddenham lies on a small tributary to the River Gipping, about 11km upstream from the town of Ipswich, and some 30km from the North Sea coast (Fig. 1). South-east Suffolk contains several other important early Anglo-Saxon sites, including the cemeteries at Hadleigh Road, Boss Hall and Buttermarket in Ipswich, besides the cemeteries at Sutton Hoo to the north-east. Urban beginnings at Ipswich and the beginnings of monastic development are broadly contemporary with the cemetery at Shrubland Hall Quarry.

The Anglo-Saxon cemetery (Suffolk Historic Environment Record CDD 050; TM 120 538) lies in an area of glacial gravels, on a ridge overlooking the village of Coddenham to the east, with the River Gipping 1km to the west. The cemetery was discovered in 1999 following routine evaluation and excavation of an Iron Age site by Suffolk County Council Archaeological Service (SCCAS) in advance of quarrying.

Following evaluation of the Iron Age site, commercial topsoil stripping was carried out under archaeological supervision. This revealed fifty graves of the Anglo-Saxon cemetery, which were then fully excavated, any to the west having been lost in earlier phases of quarrying. The excavated material was conserved for study by English Heritage Centre for Archaeology, and the structures of the bed in Grave 30 analysed.

II. Work Programme

Archaeological Phase 1

In December 1992 an initial archaeological evaluation of the proposed Shrubland Hall Quarry development area (involving field-walking, metal-detecting and shovel test-holes) was carried out by Suffolk County Council Archaeological Service (SCCAS). This was intended to assess the impact of any future planning application on archaeological features and deposits, and to decide whether any other survey or excavation might be necessary. The area for survey was some 22 hectares (quarry phases 1–4), mostly arable land, with a narrow access corridor to the old Norwich Road, on the ridge between the main Gipping Valley and a small tributary stream to the north-east (Fig. 2).

As part of the analysis, air photographs held by SCCAS and RCHME, English Heritage, were examined, but these revealed no features of archaeological interest in the area. Cropmarks were of post-medieval field boundaries, and an infilled pit, visible in photographs of 1946.

Fieldwork and metal-detecting were carried out over the 22 hectares, originally on 20m transects, but more intensively at the west end of the field after an Anglo-Saxon coin was found. Besides fieldwork, twenty-six shovel holes were dug at intervals across the survey area to record the soil sequence and character. This work produced a low-density scatter of prehistoric and Roman

finds, and one Saxon sceatta (Series G porcupine type, early 8th century) was found some 100m south of Grave 50, the most southerly burial identified in later excavations (Boulter 1993).

Archaeological Phase 2

In 1995 a planning application (MS/591/95) was made by Wilding and Smith Ltd (now Wilding Aggregates Ltd) for the extraction of gravel over the c.22 hectare plot. The area consisted of an irregular polygon of cultivated arable land bounded to the north, west and south by woodland.

A brief and specification was issued in December 1995 for further evaluation of the area. This second phase of archaeological works consisted of fifteen linear trial-trenches (equivalent to about 2.4 per cent of the site); seven additional trenches concentrated on the northern sector of the proposed area (phases 3 and 4 of the quarry development scheme), where the densest concentration of archaeological features was located. This site was recorded as CDD 050 on the county Historic Environment Record (HER), after which phases 1 and 2 of the quarry underwent extraction, but without archaeological monitoring.

Trenching in the second phase revealed features interpreted as a Late Iron Age occupation site, possibly surviving into the early Roman period (although this hypothesis depended on a single sherd of wheel-made pottery). Features identified included pits, ditches and post-holes, from which significant quantities of artefactual evidence were recovered; several elements of a field system were also identified.

While the evaluation trenching in 1995 located and characterised the area of Iron Age activity and the Roman field system in the northern part of the proposed quarry area, it did not reveal any evidence for the 7th-century cemetery subsequently found through open-area excavation. The failure to locate any graves was largely due to the difficulty of identifying them within the very mixed natural drift geology of sand, gravel and boulder clay but also due to the evaluation trenches, by chance, mostly running between rather than over graves.

Archaeological Phase 3

Phase 3 of the quarry was designated for extraction in 1999–2000, and in October–December 1999 a roughly rectangular area of about 31,000 square metres (also incorporating a section of quarry phase 4, located directly to the south) was fully excavated by SCCAS. This work was funded by contributions from Wilding Aggregates Ltd and English Heritage.

Archaeological work consisted of topsoil stripping under supervision, with archaeological features being marked. Stripping of a wide area revealed the Anglo-Saxon inhumation graves and ring-ditches, besides many Iron Age features (including a single cremation burial). With the discovery of the inhumation graves came the realisation that quarrying to the immediate west had removed any graves in that area (Frontispiece).

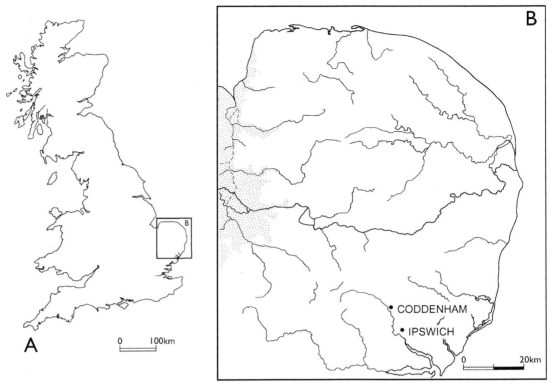

Figure 1 Location map

Since archaeological Phase 2 trenching had failed to locate any Anglo-Saxon graves, the resources agreed with Wildings Aggregates Ltd for Phase 3 of the archaeological work were inadequate for the excavation and analysis of the fifty graves found. Accordingly, English Heritage was approached for supplementary funding to complete the cemetery investigation (Newman 1999a). Additional funding was agreed in December 1999, with the contribution from English Heritage representing 32% of the archaeological fieldwork costs.

A project design for assessment was submitted to English Heritage (Topham-Smith and Anderson 2000) and included details of the post-excavation work which had been carried out up to that point. During the assessment phase of the project, the contextual database was checked and grave plans and inventories were prepared for specialists. Preliminary phasing of the site was carried out, but no attempt was made to define sub-phases within the Early Anglo-Saxon cemetery or the Iron Age site.

An updated project design (Anderson 2002) was presented to English Heritage and approved for support.

III. Results

The excavated area revealed features of Iron Age and Anglo-Saxon date, with very little intercutting of features. These features provided evidence of an Iron Age settlement with several regular boundary ditches, scattered hearths, a possible building and three shafts. There was also material of Roman date, possibly associated with one of the major boundary ditches.

Two ring-ditches (Graves 1 and 2) were of 'normal' size for Anglo-Saxon barrows (10–12m diameter), a third was very small, 4.25m diameter, and encircled the burial of an adolescent (Grave 17). The fourth ring-ditch

(context 219/220) was also quite large (*c*. 11m diameter) but enclosed no definable grave, and is therefore possibly prehistoric. Human skeletal survival was very variable across the site, depending on the soil environment.

The artefact assemblage was typical of many 'Final Phase' cemeteries, that is, only a few burials had much beyond a knife and buckle or a few beads, but these few were distinctively furnished. These furnishings included:

Grave 1	(ring-ditch), seax, spear, shield, bronze bowl, bucket
Grave 8	coins, comb, beads
Grave 11	two silver brooches
Grave 24	shield, spear, comb, pot, bronze bowl
Grave 30	('bed' and 'boat'?), hanging bowl, bronze bowl, comb, coins, pendant, beads, toilet sets and keys
Grave 48	seax, knife, Frankish buckle

Whilst a radiocarbon determination helps suggest a date for Grave 30 in the decade or so after AD 650, the grave-goods mostly indicate a date in the later 7th/early 8th century, with coins suggesting Grave 8, at least, belongs to the end of the century or a little later.

Conservation work was carried out at English Heritage Centre for Archaeology, reported in Cox (2001); Graham (2001a); Graham (2001b); Graham and Cox (2001); Watson (2006a); Watson (2006b).

IV. Site Phasing

The Shrubland Hall Quarry site produced significant evidence for three principal periods of activity, each with a varying degree of regional and national importance. The earlier phases of activity on the site will be reported separately. The significance of the Anglo-Saxon phase is outlined below. The site phases are:

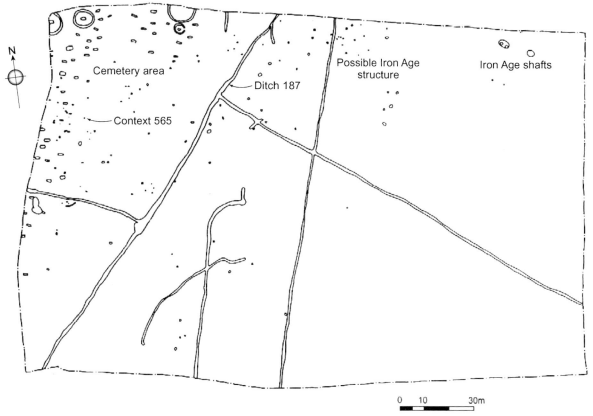

Figure 2 The excavated area, showing Anglo-Saxon cemetery, Iron Age shafts and structures, and probable Roman field boundaries

Prehistoric

About half of a circular ring-ditch, probably representing a ploughed-down barrow, was recorded at the north edge of the excavated area (Context 219/220). It was some 11.5m in diameter with a ditch just 0.60m wide, with a fill of gravelly sand. There were no finds.

Iron Age

The key features of the Iron Age site were three circular shafts in the north-east corner of the site; evidence for settlement on the edge of the Suffolk clays towards the end of the Iron Age.

Roman

A number of ditches were found, identified as part of a Roman field system within the hinterland of the Roman small town of *Combretovium*. One of the fills of ditch 187 produced the ferrule of a spear (SF 1194), probably Anglo-Saxon.

Anglo-Saxon

In the north-west corner of the stripped area were fifty inhumation burials, three of which (Graves 1, 2 and 17) were associated with ring-ditches marking ploughed-out barrows; a fourth ring-ditch failed to produce evidence for a burial and may be prehistoric (Fig. 3). These burials form part of a cemetery which clearly continued to the north and west of the excavation boundaries (although the steep slopes immediately to the north suggest a natural limit to the graveyard). Grave-goods present in about half the burials indicate a cemetery restricted in date to the 7th and early 8th centuries. Of particular interest are the association with ring-ditches of Graves 1, 2 and 17, the use of a chamber (Grave 1 and Grave 30), and the existence of well-furnished burials incorporating grave-goods that indicate overseas connections (seaxes, bowls, shields, buckle). In the two chamber burials, Grave 1 had a 'warrior burial' assemblage, while Grave 30 contained a woman buried on an iron-framed wooden bed. A large bronze bowl was recovered from each of these burials. Although Grave 1 may have had a chamber and canopy and Grave 30 was an elaborate bed burial in a chamber, there was no evidence for coffins.

A small pit (565) contained an iron object (SF 1224), possibly Early Anglo-Saxon, an iron ferrule (SF1194) came from the fill of a Roman ditch (187), and metal-detecting recovered Small Finds 1007 possibly Anglo-Saxon, and 1222, probably Roman.

There were no other features, but a stray surface find of a sceat was made 100m to the south of the cemetery. The graves lay in the extreme west edge of the excavated area, with the gravel quarry immediately to the west. The graves were laid out west to east, fairly spread out with no inter-cutting. Quarrying had removed any burials to the west, and truncated Grave 1, and almost removed Grave 34.

The cemetery appears to represent the first activity on the site after the Roman period. There is no obvious relationship between the burials and the network of field ditches, unless the position of six burials (Graves 45–50, effectively separated from the main cemetery by a shallow ditch) was deliberate. This must seem unlikely since three centuries or more separates these features.

During the excavation, minor intruder disturbance occurred, probably on a single occasion. Only Grave 30 suffered any degree of damage, and this was to artefacts visible under covers, possibly involving the bronze bowl (J. Newman pers. comm.).

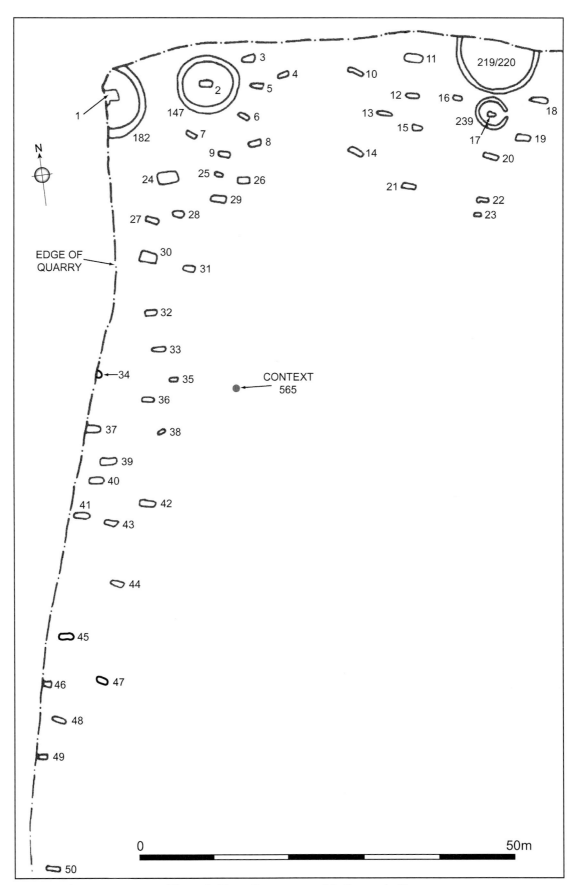

Figure 3 Plan of cemetery, with Graves 1–50

Post-cemetery features

Two graves were cut by pits but with no obvious disturbance to grave contents: Grave 45 was cut at the foot end by pit 289, and Grave 47 was cut at the west end by pit 295.

Chapter 2. The Site

I. Topography and geology

The cemetery site (Suffolk HER CDD050) lies just under 2km south-west of the village of Coddenham, centred about TM 120 538, on the northern side of a wide crest forming the watershed between valleys occupied by the River Gipping (to the south-west) and a small tributary stream (to the north-east) (Frontispiece). The excavation area lies between 50m and 55m OD, on the highest point of the crest; immediately to the north the land falls away sharply into the valley, while on the other sides the ground remains relatively flat for some distance before gradually sloping down towards the River Gipping.

Much of central Suffolk, away from the sandy coastal belt, is a great tract of Glacial Till, sometimes capped by glacial sands and gravels, with minor beds of silt and clay, especially associated with Suffolk's river systems. It is these superficial sands and gravels that are quarried at Shrubland Hall (British Geological Survey East Anglia Sheet 00 Quaternary 1991).

II. Previous work

Within East Anglia, south-east Suffolk has been a focus of intensive archaeological attention. This region appears to have been the heartland of the East Angles, and contained the royal cemetery at Sutton Hoo, several nearby royal vills including that mentioned by Bede at 'Rendlesham', a royal mausoleum at Blythburgh and a 'monastery' at Iken. Important later 6th- to early 7th-century cemeteries lay at Tranmer House (close to Sutton Hoo), Snape and at Hadleigh Road, Ipswich, overlooking the River Gipping. The mortuary landscape also included the cemetery at Buttermarket, Ipswich, in use from around AD 620 to 680 (a little earlier than Coddenham), and the single late 7th-century burial at Boss Hall, Ipswich (Fig. 4). Ipswich itself was a *wic*, a trading port with connections to the continent, besides having a pottery industry from the early 8th century, and an early monastery (probably a royal foundation).

Previously recorded archaeological material in the vicinity of Coddenham cemetery is extensive and includes the important Roman small town of *Combretovium*, some 700m to the south-west in the Gipping valley, and a probable Roman road about 500m to the south-east. Numerous Iron Age, Roman and Anglo-Saxon stray finds point to settlement along the river valleys, while 5th- and 6th-century artefacts indicate early Anglo-Saxon settlement and burial in the valley to the north and north-east.

At Vicarage Farm, in the valley to the north of the cemetery, lay a contemporary settlement (CDD022) a 'productive site' with a rich assemblage of metalwork found during metal-detecting over a number of years. This site was apparently occupied at the same time that people were being buried at Coddenham cemetery and both places ceased to be used in the early 8th century. Finds included coins, imported objects and items of gold (West 1998). Geophysical survey and trial excavations were carried out at Vicarage Farm in 2003, funded by the BBC

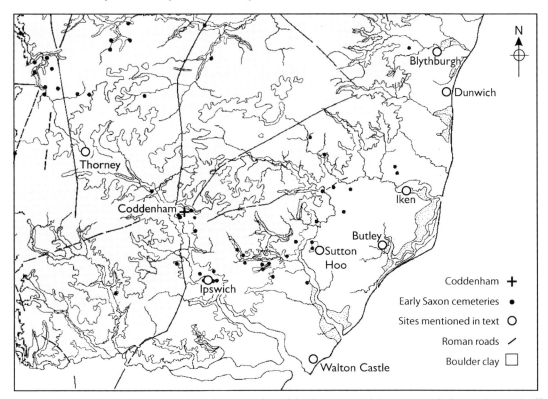

Figure 4 Early Saxon cemeteries, other sites mentioned in the text, and Roman roads in south-cast Suffolk

Hidden Treasures programme. This revealed occupation debris, a hall, and one or two possible sunken-featured buildings. There was also evidence for metalworking (Everett *et al.* 2003).

Other discoveries in Coddenham parish of 7th- to 8th-century date include a folding balance and imports, while in the adjacent parish of Barham, a site next to the medieval church has produced coins and metalwork of 7th- to 9th-century date. Both Coddenham and Barham contain important 'productive sites' of the 7th century and later, with foreign coins and other evidence for wide trading connections and high status. These two places should therefore be considered together; whilst there is evidence for occupation continuing around Coddenham church, there is evidence of significant activity continuing at Barham, possibly centred on an early church or high-status establishment. Both Coddenham and Barham are riverside parishes, and the River Gipping may have provided an inland link with the fenland basin to the north-west.

Most of the burials at Coddenham cemetery were either not provided with grave-goods or had a modest provision, but a few appear to have been of high status; one burial was lavishly provided and laid out on a bed.

III. The modern landscape

The cemetery lay towards the north-western end of a glacial ridge, within arable fields of the Shrubland Hall Estate, at a junction with the open heath and with modern woodland to north and west. In recent times, the west end of this ridge has been quarried for sand and gravel, the latest expansion of the quarry prompting evaluation of the site followed by more extensive excavation.

In the 1780s the estate was sold to John Middleton, who expanded the park a little to the west. An estate map of 1785 (SRO HD 1467, 2) shows a well-timbered park to the north-west of Shrubland Hall and a densely-treed area, marked 'Warren', once heathland and open fields, with the cemetery in an area then recorded as 'meadow and pasture'.

The next century saw the expansion of the estate along the ridge, and conversion of former arable fields to plantations, so that the whole ridge as far as Beacon Hill became wooded, including the fields to west and north of the cemetery (Frontispiece). The present landscape with its arable fields in the valley and extensive woodland and quarry on the high ground along the ridge has therefore altered considerably since the later 18th century, especially since quarrying began in the 1990s.

IV. Finds and archive

The finds were donated to Ipswich Museum by generous gift from the landowners, Lord and Lady de Saumarez, following reporting for Treasure Act 1996, therefore there was no need for inquest. The site archive is held by Suffolk County Council Archaeological Service.

V. A note on the report

This report presents the results of archaeological work undertaken at Shrubland Quarry as part of the planning conditions, but does not include the prehistoric and Roman phases of land-use (which will be reported elsewhere). This report on the Anglo-Saxon cemetery follows the conventional pattern of cemetery reports, with a catalogue of graves and burials, discussion of the objects and a report on the human skeletal remains. A final chapter presents Discussion and Conclusions.

Chapter 3. Catalogue of Graves

Context numbers of grave cuts are shown italicised in parentheses after grave numbers. Some objects are described according to their conventional typing, *i.e.* knives (Evison 1987, 113–6); buckles (Marzinzik 2005); seax (Böhner 1958); spearheads (Swanton 1973; 1974); and shields (Dickinson and Härke 1992). Information on textiles, beads, combs and on organic material preserved in metalwork is taken from the relevant specialist reports, including information from English Heritage Centre for Archaeology conservation reports.

Grave plans and objects are fully illustrated, the objects presented as grave groups. Scales are as follows:

1:1   beads, brooches, toilet sets, rings, buckles, combs and shield studs
1:2   spears, pots, knives, steels, latch-lifters, Frankish buckle, hanging bowl
1:3   seax, bronze tripod bowls, bucket

The Frankish buckle in Grave 48 is an exception, being shown at 1:2, while the schematic drawing from X-ray is at 1:1

Abbreviations: BB = Birte Brugmann; PWR = Penelope Walton Rogers; IR = Ian Riddler; SA = Sue Anderson; JW = Jacqui Watson; VF = Val Fryer; SCC = Suffolk County Council; SRO = Suffolk Record Office; L = left, R = right

Grave 1 *(157)*
(Plates 1–3; Figs 5, 58, 87–90)
Dimensions: Length *c.*2.0m; Width 1.25m; Depth 0.32m. The grave lay on the edge of the excavation and the western end of the grave had been quarried away.
Fill: dark grey/black sandy silt and organic light brown clayey sand.

Grave 1 lay within ring-ditch (*182*), 0.90m wide, 0.30m deep with steep sides. Fill of ring-ditch: mid-brown sandy clay, cobbles; single Iron Age sherd.

The western part of Grave 1 was lost to the quarry face, the remaining portion surviving to a depth of 0.32m below the excavated natural surface. Around the southern, eastern and part of the northern sides was a slot or channel 50mm wide at the base of the grave cut. This indicates a chamber with a near-vertical retaining wall, recorded to the depth of the excavated profile (0.32m) and about 1m wide.

Three iron objects (SF 1035a–c) were found above the waist. Objects 1035a and b had been mounted onto boards of ash and may have been fittings attached to a cover (discussed below, Chapter 4.I). 1035c, an iron rod or nail shaft, is recorded here as a grave-good (11).

Skeleton (*198*): adult. Leg bones only remain, but indicate a body with head turned to the north, *i.e.* to its left.

Grave-goods: various objects lay in the grave or chamber, some singly, others in groups. A complex of objects and material lay by the R side, all associated with the seax (1) and shield (2). Mounts from the shield board were found, but possibly moved in relation to the shield board. The position of the shield boss (2a) and the location of the five shield board mounts (2c–g) suggests some movement within the 'chamber'. A large bronze bowl (3a, b) was found at the R side, and a spearhead (6) by the L side. By the L foot lay a bucket (7), iron ring (9) and bronze sheet clips (8a–c), possibly the remains of a drinking horn.

A dark grey-black organic material and light brown silty sand (*185*) underlay the shield and sword, possibly staining from the shield and its leather covering.

A sample of the fill (*184*) of the bowl (3) produced charcoal, mineral-replaced wood, a black 'corky' material, bone and a burnt stone. A sample of the fill (*208*) of the bucket (7) produced charcoal, mineral-replaced wood and bone (VF).

Seax
1a   Iron **seax** (1026), 475mm+. Horn hilt, remains of leather sheath. Böhner 1958 'broad' type.
1b   Horn **fragments** (1036), part of seax? (and leather fragment (not illustrated)).
1c   Bronze **sheath mount** (1029), stud with disc-head (triskele) decoration, 16mm diameter.
1d   Bronze **buckle** (1034), oval frame, three rivets. Plate 16mm x 16mm, frame 24mm wide. Leather strap.

Shield (Plates 1–3)
2ai   Iron **shield boss** (1010), conical, with silvered hemispherical apex: silver and garnet ornament; 80mm diameter, 78mm high. The shield boss was fixed to the board by six iron domed rivets, silver-plated, with wire circlets (one of the rivets, 2b (1010), is a cabochon garnet dome in a beaded silver wire circlet, 18mm diameter; others are 14mm diameter). Remains of textile and other organic material, possibly animal skin or leather. Dickinson and Härke Group 7.
Textile: on the outer face of the cone, in a single patch, 60mm x 50mm, in the middle of one side (Plate 1).
(i) In single layer flat against the metal, tabby weave, 12/Z x 12/Z per cm; fibre not identified, but grey appearance in contrast with ginger of other textile, suggests linen.
(ii) Outside (i) a coarse twill, probably 2/2, 7/Z x 7/Z per cm; fibre wool.
(iii) A third organic material in association with (i) and (ii), but closer to apex of cone, is possibly animal skin or leather (PWR).
2aii   Iron **shield grip** (1010b), 164mm long. Dickinson and Härke type 1a.
Textile: on opposite face from wood of shield board, traces of a crumpled medium-weight textile: no technical details possible (PWR).
2b   Iron/silver **shield boss rivet** (1010). Cabochon garnet dome in a beaded silver wire circlet; dome 18mm diameter
2c   Iron/silver **shield board mount** (1028). Solid domed stud, beaded wire circlet, square shaft; dome 25mm diameter.
2d   Iron/silver **shield board mount** (1027), below (1010). Solid domed stud, beaded wire circlet, square shaft; dome 25mm diameter.
2e   Iron/silver **shield board mount** (1023), Solid domed stud, beaded wire circlet, square shaft; dome 25mm diameter.
2f   Iron/silver **shield board mount** (1024), Solid domed stud, beaded wire circlet, square shaft; dome 25mm diameter.
2g   Iron/silver **shield board mount** (1044), Solid domed stud, beaded wire circlet, square shaft; dome 25mm diameter.
(The disposition of the five board mounts (2c–2g) would suggest a board at least 600mm in diameter, with mounts 2c–2e close together, and mounts 2f and 2g on the other side of the board, about 350mm apart).

Plate 1 Grave 1: shield boss, side view, showing textile

Plate 3 Grave 1: shield boss, apex

Plate 2 Grave 1: shield boss, garnet stud

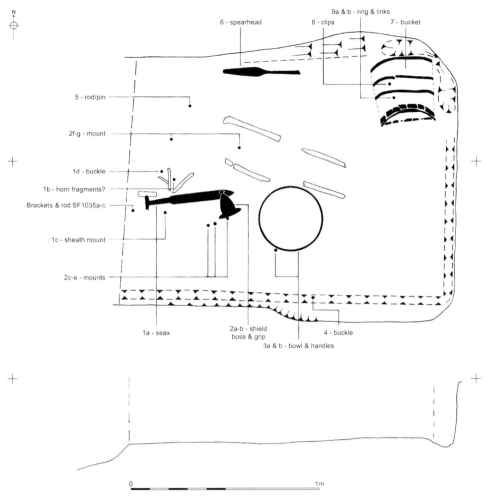

Figure 5 Grave 1, plan and section. Scale 1:20

Bronze bowl

3a Bronze sheet **bowl** (1003), with tripod footring, 340mm diameter. At left side (with two handles (1022)).

3b Two cast bronze **drop-handles** (1022), flat-sectioned.

4 Iron **buckle** (1033), oval frame, three bronze rivets, with flat sheet silver heads. Plate *c*. 20mm x *c*. 35mm, frame 30mm wide. Remains of leather strap. Traces of textile.
Textile: traces of poorly preserved textile running from back of buckle over edge of buckle loop: no technical details possible.

5 Iron **rod/pin** (1045).

6 Iron **spearhead** (1011), at right side. Over 410mm long. Alder or hazel shaft. Traces of textile. Swanton type E3?.
Textile: detached fragments, largest 15 x 8mm, of 2/2 chevron or diamond twill, 16/Z x 14/Z per cm; fibre fully processed flax or hemp. Traces on the socket of the spearhead may be of the same textile (PWR).

Bucket

7 Iron-bound **bucket**, with traces of oak staves (JW).

7a Iron bucket **handle** and attachments (1008), twisted at either end, U-section in centre, attached by a hooked plate riveted to the staves by two rivets to top band.

7b Three iron bucket **hoops** (1009, 1031–2).
[Probable diameter, top *c*.250mm, base *c*.260mm; top band 23mm wide, middle band 10mm wide].

Possible drinking horn

8a–c Three bronze sheet **clips** (1042), fragments, possibly vessel clips.

8a, b Two strips of bronze sheet, about 4mm wide, with lip on one edge. Bent as if fitted around two small bars. 8a is 35mm long, 8b is 38mm long.

8c Clip, 8mm wide, 9mm deep, decorated in two bands, with incised crossing lines and a hatched chevron. Rivet hole. Would fit a vessel rim about 4mm thick. Associated with fragments of horn (JW). Remains of a drinking horn?

9 Iron **ring and links** (1041).

9a Iron ring, fragment, about 90mm diameter.

9b Parts of two small iron links, about 8mm diameter, corroded together, possibly part of a chain. One is *c*.12mm diameter, the other *c*.7mm diameter.

10 Iron **knife**, fragment of blade (1005), traces of leather on blade, *c*.70mm long.

11 Iron **rod**, possibly the shaft of a **nail** (1035c), found with 1035a and b (above). 76mm long, shaft 5mm diameter.

Grave 2 *(171)*
(Figs 6, 90)
Dimensions: Length 1.90m; Width 1.10m (0.75m to 'shelf'); Depth 0.4m.
Narrow cut with rounded ends and 'shelf' on the southern side.
Fill: mid-brown sandy loam.
Grave 2 lay within a ring-ditch (147). Fill of ring-ditch: mid-brown silty sand.
Skeleton (173): male, *c*.16–18. The burial was extended, with legs straight and arms crossed at the waist. The head had fallen to one side.
Grave-goods: the grave-goods were together at the left side of the body.

9

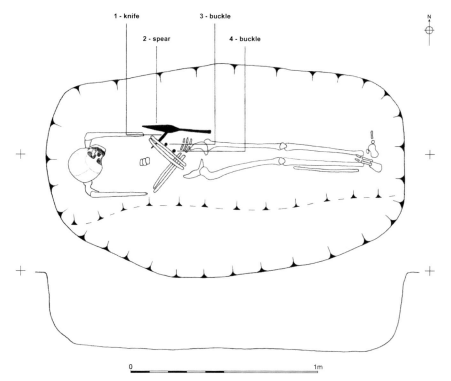

Figure 6 Grave 2, plan and section. Scale 1:20

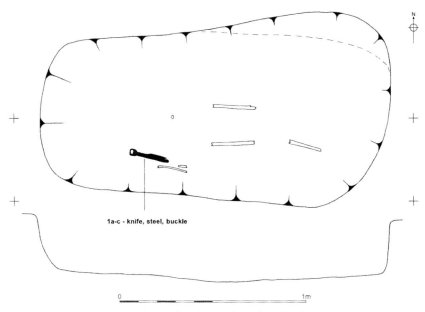

Figure 7 Grave 3, plan and section. Scale 1:20

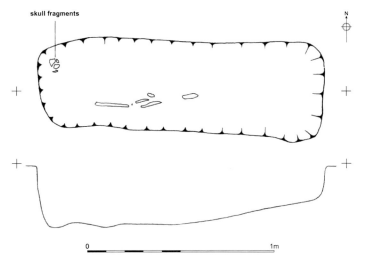

Figure 8 Grave 4, plan and section. Scale 1:20

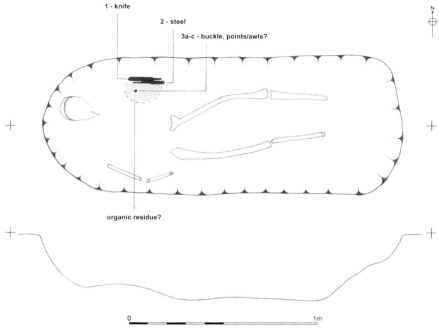

Figure 9 Grave 5, plan and section. Scale 1:20

1   Iron **knife** (1013), 128mm+. Traces of textile; leather(?), possibly sheath. Traces of horn on tang. Evison Type 1?
Textile: on one face, on blade close to tang, 15 x 10mm of organic remains in four layers, from the top down:
(i) top two layers, tabby weave, 16/Z x 10/?Z per cm; fibre not identified;
(ii) a finer tabby, *c*. 28 x 24 per cm; no further details possible;
(iii) leather, presumed to be a sheath.
On opposite face, in loose folds running across the knife, tabby repp 28 x ? per cm, possibly the same as (ii) on the other face; the close-set system of the tabby repp weave runs along the length of the blade (PWR).

2   Iron **spear** (1012), shaft of ash. 370mm long. Swanton type F2?

3   Bronze **buckle** (1014), small, oval frame. Iron rivets. Plate 16mm x 10mm, frame 24mm wide. Leather strap. Traces of textile.
Textile: on ?front at edge of plate, outside the leather of the strap, a curling fragment, 8 x 7mm, of tabby repp, 28/Z x 24/Z per cm, as on knife 1013; fibre not identified (PWR).

4   Bronze **buckle** (1015), small, oval frame, three rivets, incised decoration. Plate 32mm x 24mm; frame 32mm wide. Leather strap.

Grave 3 *(213)*
(Figs 7, 90)
Dimensions: Length 1.85m; Width 0.90m; Depth 0.30m.
Fill: mid-brown sandy silt.
Skeleton (215): ?male, adult. Head to W? Supine, legs extended.
Grave-goods: at upper right side, close to arm, possibly a set of tools in a textile container.

1a   Iron **knife** (1043a). Horn handle, leather on blade; textile. 170mm long. Evison Type 1?

1b   Iron **steel** (1043b), bone or antler handle. Textile. 144mm long.

1c   Iron **buckle** (1043c), double-tongued. Slightly tapered plate 25mm x 30mm, frame *c*.35mm wide. Traces of leather.
Textile: on one side of ?buckle and lapping on to opposite face, 30 x 25mm of tabby weave, 12-14/Z x 12/Z per cm; fibre fully processed flax or hemp. (PWR)

Grave 4 *(189)*
(Fig. 8)
Dimensions: Length 1.55m; Width 0.95m; Depth 0.50m; Square end at east, rounded at west.
Fill (171): mid-brown sandy loam.

Skeleton (191): adult, female. Burial lying on side. Head to west.
Grave-goods: no remains.

Grave 5 *(177)*
(Figs 9, 91)
Dimensions: Length 1.90m; Width 0.70m; Depth 0.30m.
Fill: mid-brown sandy silt.
Skeleton (179): adult male? mature. Extended, head to west, supine, with splayed legs.
Grave-goods: tools (1) and (2) were found corroded together at the head end (?left side), in a small organic stain, possibly a leather bag. Three further objects (3a–c) were found together nearby, possibly part of the same bag or contents.

1   Iron **knife** (1019), 192mm+. Horn handle, with organic residue, leather? Evison Type 1?

2   Iron **steel** (1020), 178mm. With organic residue, leather?

3a–c   Group of iron objects (1021)

3a   Iron **buckle**, oval frame, semi-oval plate. Plate 15mm x 10mm, frame 15mm wide. This was possibly part of a bag.

3b   iron **point/awl**, (hazel handle). Over 30mm long. (Drawn from X-ray).

3c   iron **point/awl**, (willow/poplar/alder/hazel handle). 37mm long. (Drawn from X-ray). With a plyed thread wrapped or tied around the point just below the handle.
Textile on awl (3c): (i) Detached fragment, 15 x 10mm, attached to wood presumably from the awl handle: tabby weave, 18/Z x 16/Z per cm; fibre coarse plant-stem fibre, possibly hemp.
(ii) At the edge of the handle, running across the awl, several parallel threads, probably binding the handle: Z-spun, 0.7mm diameter; fibre partially processed flax/hemp.(PWR)

Grave 6 *(174)*
(Figs 10, 91)
Dimensions: Length 1.80m; Width 0.70m; Depth 0.40m.
Fill: mid-orange-brown clayey silty sand.
Skeleton (176, 192): two individuals, 6a (north) and 6b (south). 6a (176), young; 6b (192), young, possibly female? Heads to west.
Grave-goods: two glass beads at the right shoulder of 6b.

11

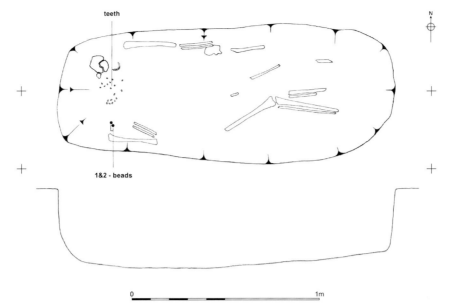

Figure 10 Grave 6, plan and section. Scale 1:20

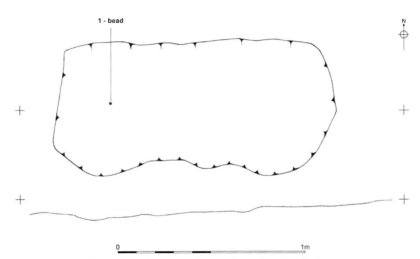

Figure 11 Grave 7, plan and section. Scale 1:20

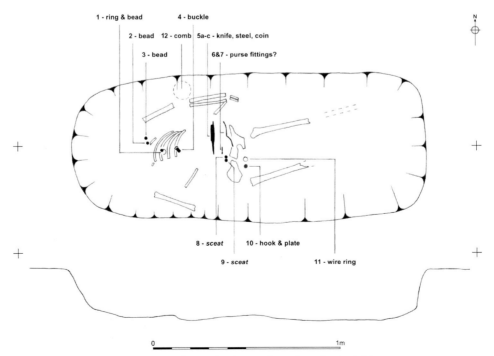

Figure 12 Grave 8, plan and section. Scale 1:20

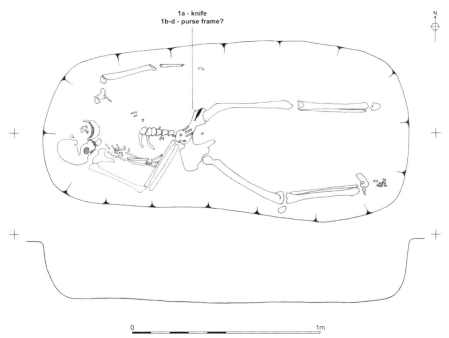

1a - knife
1b-d - purse frame?

N

0 _____ 1m

Figure 13 Grave 9, plan and section. Scale 1:20

1   Glass **bead** (1016–7), two fragments of translucent turquoise, cylinder, wound.
2   Glass **bead** (1018), wound, opaque yellow, biconical.

Grave 7 *(217)*
(Figs 11, 91)
Dimensions: Length 1.50m; Width 0.70m; Depth 0.10m.
Very shallow grave; no more than 0.10m deep (possibly partly machined away).
Fill: mid-orange brown clay/silt. Chalk and charcoal flecks.
Skeleton: no remains.
Grave-goods: found towards west end of grave.

1   Glass **bead** (1046), opaque green, cylinder, wound.

Grave 8 *(543)*
(Figs 12, 91)
Dimensions: Length 1.90m; Width 0.80m; Depth 0.20–0.25m.
Neatly cut regular grave, but quite shallow. Square end at east, rounded at west.
Fill: mid-brown silty sand, occasional flints.
Skeleton (554): adult, ?female. Burial extended, with straight legs and arms splayed.
Grave-goods: several objects were found around the upper part of body. At chest were beads, ring and buckle (1–4). At waist, left side, the remains of a probable leather bag with contents (5a–c, 6). Also at the waist were two coins (8) and (9) and iron object (7), possibly part of the bag (6). Objects (10) and (11) were nearby in the pelvic area. Fragments of comb (12) were found by the L arm.

1   Silver **wire ring, fragment** (1207), with glass *bead* (1206), opaque turquoise faience, globular, wound.
2   Glass **bead** (1208), opaque red, barrel, wound.
3   Glass **bead** (1209), semi-translucent, wound, biconical.
4   Bronze **buckle** (1196), most of pin missing three rivets.
5a   Iron **knife** (1210). Horn handle, traces of textile, leather. Plate 19mm x 10mm, frame 14mm wide. Evison type ?2. 230mm long.
5b   Iron **steel** (1210b). Traces of textile, leather. 254mm long. Across steel, especially over tip, cabled cords, over 1.0mm

Plate 4 Grave 9: skeleton, during excavation

thick, Z2S2S, possibly binding steel and knife together; fibre not identified (PWR).

5c   Silver **sceat** (1210c) (drawn from X-ray). Weight 1.27gm.

13

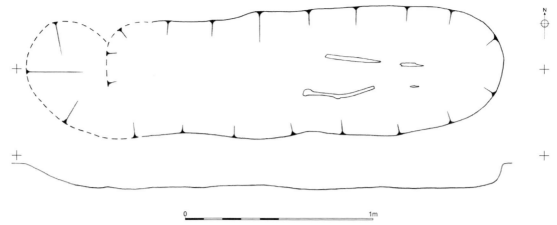

Figure 14 Grave 10, plan and section. Scale 1:20

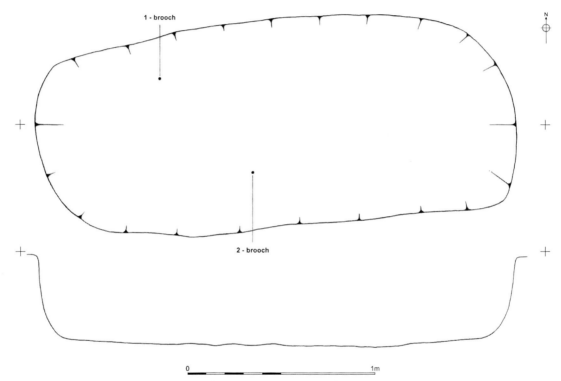

1 - brooch

2 - brooch

Figure 15 Grave 11, plan and section. Scale 1:20

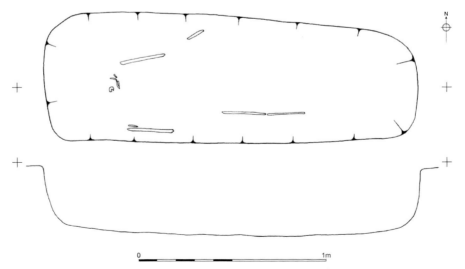

Figure 16 Grave 12, plan and section. Scale 1:20

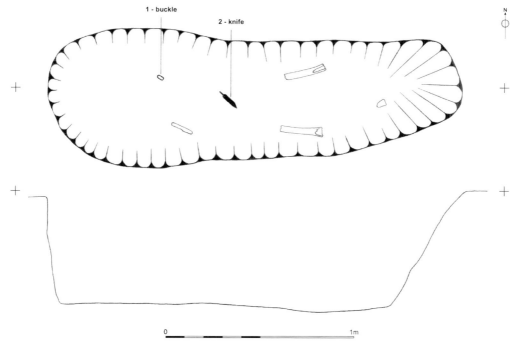

Figure 17 Grave 13, plan and section. Scale 1:20

6 Iron **'pins'** (1211), possibly a purse frame?. Traces of textile, leather?. Textile: covering object in folds, tabby weave, 16/Z x 12–14/Z per cm; fibre flax/hemp (PWR).

7 Iron **'pin'** (1203), crushed threads.

8 Silver **sceat** (1201), cross-and-bird type. Weight 0.67gm.

9 Silver **sceat** (1202), cross-and-bird type. Weight 1.21gm.

10 Bronze suspension **hook and plate** (1205), 19mm overall length.

11 Bronze wire slip-knot **ring** (1204), knotted ends, thicker in the middle (2mm) than at ends. Diameter of ring 15mm.

12 Fragments of bone/antler **comb** (1251). (Not planned). A fragmentary single-sided composite comb, for which only the middle section now survives. The comb consists of two fragmentary connecting plates of antler, pierced by four iron rivets. Four antler tooth segments survive, most of which retain the area enclosed by the connecting plates. There are no surviving teeth, however. There were originally six teeth per centimetre, based on saw-marks on the lower edge of the connecting plate, and the traces on the lower edges of the tooth segments.

The decoration of the comb can only be reconstructed with some difficulty, given the poor survival of the connecting plates. It is possible to see several single ring-and-dot patterns, as well as traces of paired diagonal crossing lines. The single ring-and-dot patterns appear to have been set in a single line. Their relationship with the paired diagonal lines is unclear. Double bounding lines are present on both sides, and the decoration of the comb appears to be the same on both sides. Length: over 64mm (IR).

Grave 9 *(193)*

(Plate 4; Figs 13, 92)

Dimensions: Length 1.95m; Width 0.90m; Depth 0.30m.

Fill: mid-brown sandy clay.

Skeleton (199): male, young-middle-aged. The burial lay extended, with right leg splayed and left arm out to one side, away from the body (Plate 4).

Grave-goods: at the left hip, by the hand, remains of possible bag (1b–1d) and contents (1a).

1a Iron **knife** (1025a), 117mm+. Horn handle, leather sheath. Evison Type 3.

1b Bronze **fitting** (1025b), small tube, with rivet. 6mm long.

1c Iron **buckle** (1025c), oval frame. 10mm wide.

1d Two iron **bars** (1025d)

Grave 10 *(225)*

(Fig. 14)

Dimensions: Length 2.1m; Width 0.65m; Depth 0.10m.

Fill: mid-brown sandy silt.

Skeleton (227): male, adult. Lower long bones only. Bone in poor condition.

Grave-goods: no remains.

Grave 11 *(195)*

(Figs 15, 92)

Dimensions: Length 2.50m; Width 1.1m; Depth 0.40m.

Neatly cut grave; square end at west.

Fill: mid-brown grey clay sandy silt.

Skeleton: no skeletal remains.

Grave-goods: two brooches were found, one at the head end (1), the other at the centre, south side (2).

1 Silver metal 'safety pin' **brooch** (1030). Broken but at least 30mm long. Pecked zig-zag decoration across face of brooch.

2 Silver metal 'safety pin' **brooch** (1037). Decorated as (1), but eroded.

Grave 12 *(197)*

(Fig. 16)

Dimensions: Length 2.0m; Width 0.65m; Depth 0.30m.

Neatly cut grave, narrow.

Fill: mid-brown loamy sandy silt.

Skeleton (207): adult? Extended, with head to west.

Grave-goods: no remains.

Grave 13 *(221)*

(Figs 17, 92)

Dimensions: Length 2.1m; Width 0.7m; Depth 0.55m.

The grave had a tapering shape, width 0.75m at the west end, 0.60m towards the east.

Fill: soft brown silty clay loam.

The site record states: 'around both legs was an iron staining', which could suggest some vanished iron object.

15

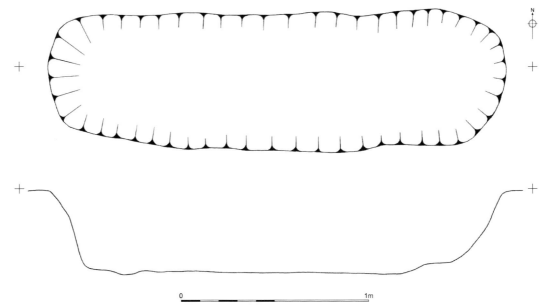

Figure 18 Grave 14, plan and section. Scale 1:20

Skeleton (221): adult, possibly male. Some fragments of bone survived, all were very fragile.

Grave-goods: knife (1) found in probable waist area, buckle (2) at upper left.

1   Iron **knife** (1048), horn handle, traces of textile. Evison Type 3. 110mm long. Textile: on tip of knife traces of a medium-weight textile with yarn 0.7mm diameter: no further details possible (PWR).

2   Bronze **buckle frame** (1047), D-shaped. 25mm wide.

Grave 14 *(200)*
(Figs 18, 92)
Dimensions: Length 2.40m; Width 0.70m; Depth 0.4m.
Fill: dark brown sandy clay; occasional chalk lumps and frequent large flints.
Skeleton: no remains.
Grave-goods: not planned.

1   Iron **awl/point** (1038). 40mm long overall. Bent or L-shaped. Square section.

Grave 15 *(609)*
(Fig. 19)
Dimensions: Length 1.55m; Width 0.80m; Depth 0.25m.
Neat and regular grave.
Fill: mid-orange-brown sand; patches of mid-brown clay.
Skeleton (611): female, young adult? Head to west. The disposition of the bones, with pelvis 'face down', suggests an unusual burial position, perhaps crouched.
Grave-goods: no remains.

Grave 16 *(585)*
(Figs 20, 92)
Dimensions: Length 1.2m; Width 0.65m; Depth 0.20m.
Very neat grave, rounded ends.
Fill: Mid-brown sandy silt and clay; small lumps of chalk.
Skeleton: No remains.
Grave-goods: A bead and ring were recorded, found centrally in the grave.

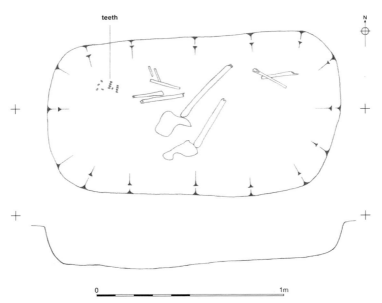

Figure 19 Grave 15, plan and section. Scale 1:20

1   Silver wire **ring**, twisted (1213). Plain silver wire thicker in the middle (2mm) than at ends. Terminals wound back on ring. Max. diam. of ring 25mm (BB).
2   Glass **bead** (1212), wound, globular, petrol-blue with red-on-white spots.

Grave 17 *(202)*

(Fig. 21)
Dimensions: Length 1.25m; Width 0.65m; Depth 0.30m.
The grave had a 'waisted' shape.
Fill: mid-orange-brown clayey sand.
Grave 17 lay inside a penannular ring-ditch (239), 4.25m diameter; 0.5m wide; 0.15m–0.20m deep. Fill of ring-ditch: mid-brown sand.
Skeleton: no remains.
Grave-goods: none.

Grave 18 *(230)*

(Fig. 22)
Dimensions: Length 1.90m; Width 0.75m; Depth 0.40m (sloping).
Fill: mid-dark brown clayey sand and mid-brown sand. Roman sherd in fill.
Skeleton (232): adult male, middle-aged. Head to west. Extended, with arms close to sides. Right arm under body.
Grave-goods: none.

Grave 19 *(204)*

(Figs 23, 92)
Dimensions: Length 2.15m; Width 0.80m; Depth 0.40m.
Fill: mid-brown sandy silty soil; specks of chalk and large flints.
Skeleton (206): adult male, old. Head to west, extended, with arms close to body, lower right arm flexed across body.
Grave-goods: a buckle and knife were at the pelvis, left side.

1   Iron **knife** (1039), 146mm. Horn handle, remains of leather? Evison Type 5? 150mm long.
2   Bronze **buckle** (1040), oval frame, 22mm wide, pin decorated with double incised lines. Rectangular plate 20mm x 14mm, with two dome-headed bronze rivets.

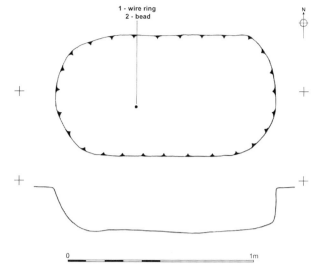

Figure 20 Grave 16, plan and section. Scale 1:20

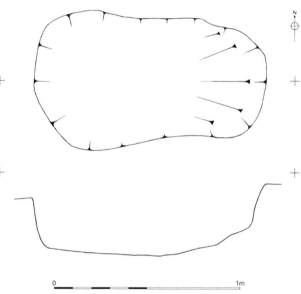

Figure 21 Grave 17, plan and section. Scale 1:20

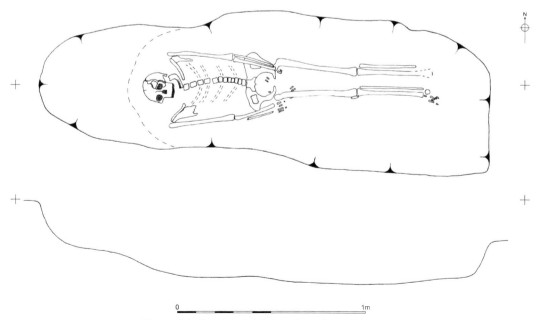

Figure 22 Grave 18, plan and section. Scale 1:20

17

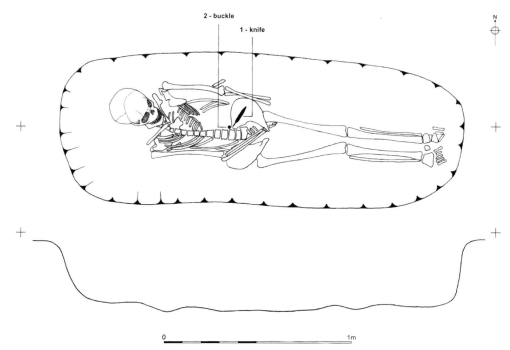

Figure 23 Grave 19, plan and section. Scale 1:20

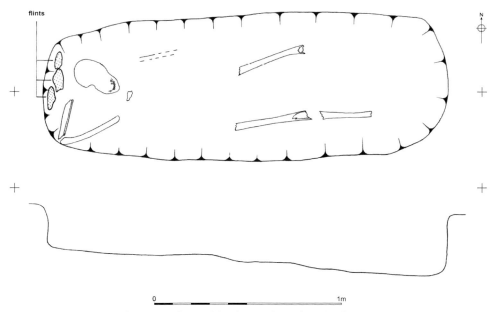

Figure 24 Grave 20, plan and section. Scale 1:20

Grave 20 *(660)*
(Fig. 24)
Dimensions: Length 2.15m; Width 0.80m; Depth 0.30m.
Neat and regular grave with three large flints at the west end of the grave, behind the skull, possibly a setting for the head.
Fill: mid-brown clayey sand with clay and chalk.
Skeleton (660): male, young. Burial with head to west. The position of the arm bones indicates some movement after burial.
Grave-goods: no remains.

Grave 21 *(211)*
(Fig. 25)
Dimensions: Length 1.85m; Width 0.80m; Depth 0.15–0.20m.

Shallow grave, square ends.
Fill: dark clay and silt, chalk flecks.
Skeleton: no remains.
Grave-goods: none.

Grave 22 *(235)*
(Fig. 26)
Dimensions: Length 1.9m; Width 0.6m; Depth 0.30m.
Irregularly shaped grave with 'stepped' profile, some 0.20m deep at the east end, sloping up at the west end.
Fill: brown/grey silty clay, with small sherds of abraded pottery.
Skeleton: no remains.
Grave-goods: none.

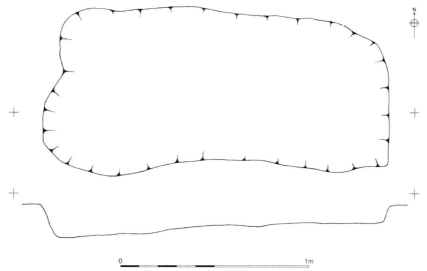

Figure 25 Grave 21, plan and section. Scale 1:20

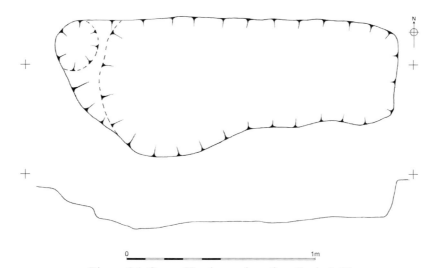

Figure 26 Grave 22, plan and section. Scale 1:20

Grave 23 *(581)*
(Fig. 27)
Dimensions: Length 1.15m; Width 0.5m; Depth 0.15m
Very shallow grave.
Fill: light brown silty sand, with clay and chalk.
Skeleton: no remains.
Grave-goods: no remains.

Grave 24 *(141)*
(Plates 5–7; Figs 28, 92–3)
Dimensions: Length 2.95m; Width 1.4m; Depth 0.30–0.40m.
Rectangular, with straight sides.
Fill: upper fill; mid-orange-brown silty sand. Lower fill; mid-orange-brown silty sand.
Skeleton: no remains.
Grave-goods: the remains of a shield were found at the west (head?) end of the grave, a pot at the east (?foot) end and a spearhead at the south side. A soil block was lifted and then excavated in the laboratory with a full record of the process (Graham 2001b). The soil block comprised above all a large bronze bowl (2), and when excavated, a section of a bone/antler comb (3) was found inside the bowl, near its base. X-rays revealed the comb to be fragmentary.

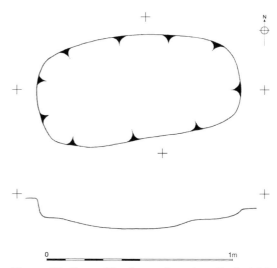

Figure 27 Grave 23, plan and section. Scale 1:20

19

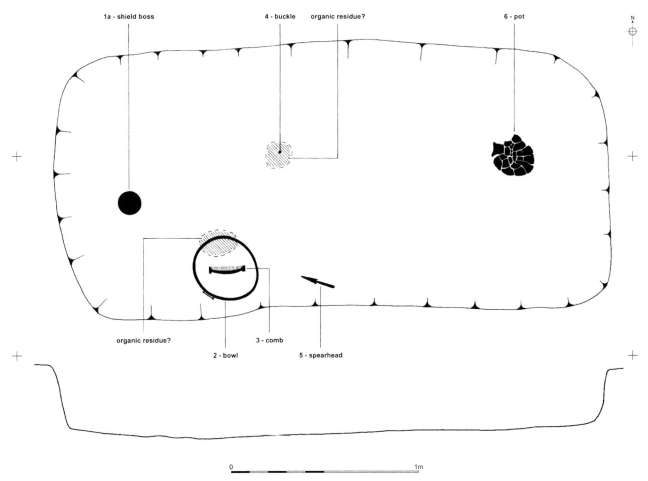

Figure 28 Grave 24, plan and section. Scale 1:20

1a   Iron **shield boss** (1001), 128mm diameter, 128mm high, conical with narrow flange. Board of ash, covered in leather on both sides. Textile imprints. Dickinson and Härke Group 7? Textile: on the outer face of the cone, on one side, from apex to flange, imprints of textile in loose folds: (i) possibly a tabby repp, approximately 12/S x 6/?; fibre not identifiable from imprint; (ii) a second textile seems to be interfolded with the first, possibly an ordinary tabby Z x ?; fibre not identif-iable(PWR).

1b   Iron **grip** (1001), over 55mm long.

1c   Three iron **rivets** (1001), mushroom-shaped, 15mm long (drawn from X-ray).

2   Sheet bronze **bowl** (1002), spun, with simple out-turned rolled rim, tetrapod footring and two rectangular drop handles with triple central moulding and 'pads' at corners of handles. Soldered lugs. 340mm diameter, 105mm deep. Textile imprints and traces. (Associated staining (162); included fragments of plant material, possibly some form of woven matting (JW). Textile and other organic material under bowl (Conservation Report: Graham 2001b). Textile: when the bowl was first examined by the conservator (JW), it was described as 'wrapped in fine tabby weave'. This textile now survives as (i) a separately packaged area from beneath the bowl, (ii) well-preserved pieces adhering to 'Base 1', outside the area of the foot-ring, and (iii) poorly preserved imprints on the outer face of other fragments: these last reach from the base to the rim and dip inside the rim to a depth of about 15mm. There are further remains (iv) in association with organic residue from inside the pot.
(i) From beneath the bowl, largest area 30 x 20mm, tabby weave, 18/Z x 22–24/Z per cm; fibre too decayed to identify (Plate 5).
(ii) On fragments 'Base 1', (a) 10 x 8mm of tabby weave, 16/Z x 16/?; fibre fully processed flax or hemp. Some coarser threads dipping into the weave may represent needlework. (b) inside

area of foot-ring, matted twists of Z-spun yarn, probably a fringe from (a); fibre fully processed flax or hemp (Plate 6).
(iii) Scattered imprints of a tabby weave with thread-counts of 14–16 threads per cm; spin not clear; fibre not identified.
(iv) A green (copper-alloy) imprint on the organic material from inside the bowl, tabby weave of approximately 18 x 18 threads per cm (PWR).

3   Antler/bone **comb** (1250), fragmentary and partially preserved. The surviving sections comprise: decorated side-plate, with incised decoration, fragment of tooth-plate. Length: *c.* 210mm.
A fragmentary single-sided composite comb, now stained green from proximity to its container, which was a copper alloy bowl. The comb consists of a fragmentary connecting plate of antler, now in eight pieces, perforated by seven iron rivets. A part of one tooth segment survives in reasonable condition, and there are also small pieces of five further tooth segments. There were originally five teeth per centimetre, based on saw-marks on the lower edge of the connecting plate.
The surviving connecting plate is decorated by a sequence of paired crossing diagonal lines, each of which is set under an iron rivet. Between these lie groups of four double ring-and-dot motifs, with single ring-and-dot motifs above and below each rivet. The patterns are bounded by paired edging lines and the top of the connecting plate has a pattern of diagonal hatching along its entire length. The end segment is decorated by double ring-and-dot motifs across the available space. Its precise shape is not clear (IR).

4   Bronze **buckle** (1006), small oval frame, 36mm wide. (Associated black staining (0170)).

5   Iron **spearhead** (1004). 180mm overall. Swanton Type J? Fragments of stems, grass? Shaft of alder or hazel sapling (JW) (Plate 7).

6   **Pot** (168), at E end of grave. Bottle, narrow-necked jar, with rouletted cable decoration. 250mm high, 200mm diameter. Found whole, but crushed.

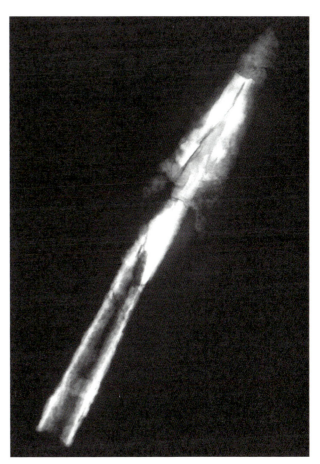

Plate 7 Grave 24: spearhead/arrowhead from X-ray

Plate 6 Grave 24: Textile on base of bronze bowl

Plate 5 Grave 24: Textile beneath the bronze bowl

21

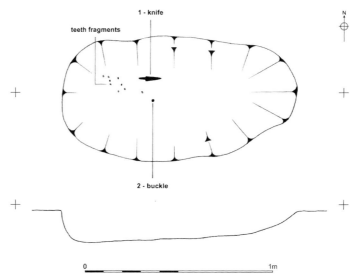

Figure 29 Grave 25, plan and section. Scale 1:20

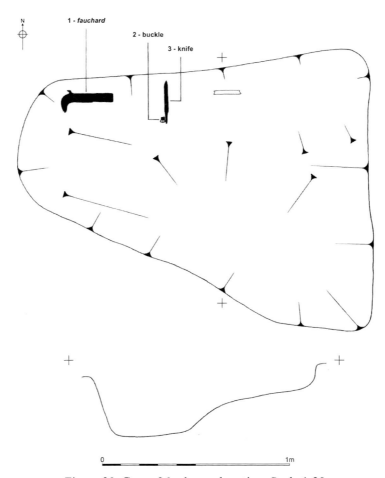

Figure 30 Grave 26, plan and section. Scale 1:20

Grave 25 *(545)*
(Figs 29, 93)
Dimensions: Length 1.2m; Width 0.65m; Depth 0.15m.
Irregular grave.
Fill: mid-orange-brown clayey sand.
Skeleton (547): sex unknown, child *c*.6 years old. Only
teeth survived, at west end of grave.

Grave-goods: both close together, in central (possibly
waist) area.

1   Iron **knife** (1199), Evison Type 1. 120mm long.
2   Bronze **buckle** (1200), (no plate) D-shaped loop, 38mm wide;
     under a dark stain.

22

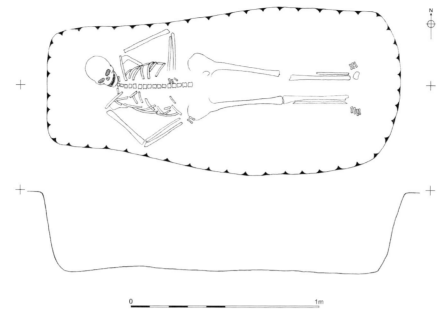

Figure 31 Grave 27, plan and section. Scale 1:20

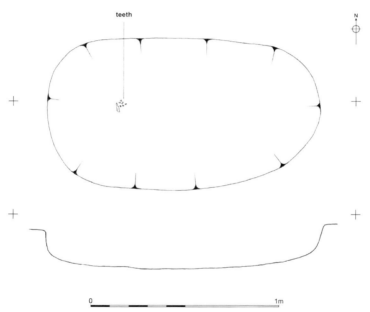

teeth

Figure 32 Grave 28, plan and section. Scale 1:20

Grave 26 *(540)*
(Figs 30, 94)
Dimensions: Length 1.3m; Width 0.6m; Depth 0.3m.
Very irregular grave, possibly two graves (one aligned west–east, the other north-west–south-east). Some disturbance is likely.
Fill: mid-grey-brown sandy silt.
Skeleton (542): sex unknown, ?adult.
Grave-goods: fauchard (1) at head end, buckle (2) and knife (3) together, by north edge.

1   Iron **fauchard** (1195), 280mm long traces of textile. Textile: On one face of blade, 85 x 70mm 2/2 diamond twill, 10/Z x 9/S per cm; fibre wool, possibly pigmented (dark brown or black). Pattern in S-spun system reverses after 10,10,13 threads (Fig. 81) (PWR).

2   Bronze **buckle** (1197), oval frame, 30mm wide, square plate 21mm square, with three rivets. Traces of textile, leather. Textile: on back of inner belt plate (*i.e.* probably against body),

10 x 7mm of textile woven in tabby weave, 14/Z x 12/Z per cm; open weave. Fibre well-preserved, fully processed, plant fibre, either hemp or low-grade flax; includes naturally brown as well as off-white fibres (PWR).

3   Iron **knife** (1198), 230mm long, with horn handle, pelt scabbard. Evison Type 1.

Grave 27 *(340)*
(Fig. 31)
Dimensions: Length 1.85m; Width 0.90m at east to 0.65m at west. Depth 0.40–0.45m.
Neatly-cut grave. Grave tapers east–west.
Fill: mid-brown clay, silty sand. Chalk and flint.
Skeleton (342): female, young. Burial extended, legs straight, arms partly splayed, with lower arms drawn in, head tilted.
Grave-goods: no remains.

23

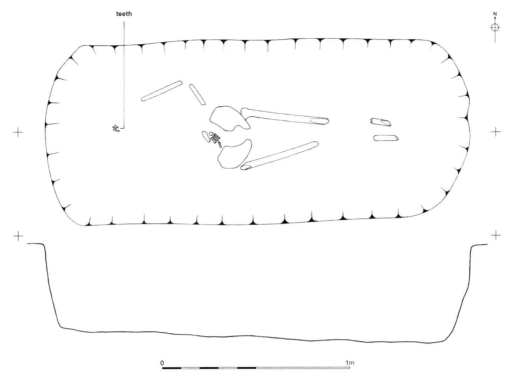

teeth

0   1m

Figure 33 Grave 29, plan and section. Scale 1:20

Grave 28 *(330)*
(Fig. 32)
Dimensions: Length 1.45m; Width 0.80m; Depth 0.25m.
Fill: mid-brown sandy silt.
Skeleton (332): sex unknown, child, *c*.3 years old.
Fragments of skull and teeth towards the west end of the grave.
Grave-goods: no remains.

Grave 29 *(551)*
(Fig. 33)
Dimensions: Length 2.25m; Width 0.95m; Depth 0.40m–0.45m.
Neat and regular grave, sharply cut.
Fill: mid-brown silty sand with clay.
Skeleton (553): male, young? Burial extended, with head to west. Left arm bent and hand at the waist.
Grave-goods: no remains.

Grave 30 *(308)*
(Plates 8–11; Figs 34–7, 59–77, 95–8)
Dimensions: Length 2.60m; Width 1.55m; Depth 0.50–0.60m.
Large rectangular grave. The profile of the base suggests a lining once existed, with three depressions in the base, at west, centre and east.

Around the north-west, west, south and south-east edges of the base of the grave ran a 'channel', at its narrowest about 90mm wide, expanding in the south-east part of the grave. This is likely to have been for a wooden structure or chamber, lining the grave, containing the burial.

A large number of iron strips and fittings, some with traces of wood grain, were found around the burial, indicating a bed. At the head, a complex of concentric strips and rivets represent a decorated headboard. Two twisted stays connected this complex with the main frame

of the bed, represented by long wooden bars, two each side, associated with iron strips, rivets and eyelets.

The eyelets (three with traces of leather) were ranged along the wooden bars and are interpreted as fixings for mattress supports.

Two iron objects SF 1107/1138 and SF 1137 were found in the centre of the grave, one above each lower arm, and are interpreted as fixings for a cover or canopy. Two lines of large rivets at head and foot are possibly part of this cover. These rivets may be identified as maritime clench nails but identification of the cover as part of a small boat remains uncertain (see Chapter 4.IV below).

Fragments of an iron rivet (1176), with head about 20mm diameter, were found in the central depression below the burial, close to twisted wire bar (5) and chain link (6), the latter identified as grave-goods. Rivet 1176 may be from the bed (see Chapter 4.III below).

Fill (309): mid-brown silty clay, scattered flints and charcoal flecks. A sample from the fill produced charcoal, mineral-replaced wood, 'cokey' material and small fragments of possible cremated bone (VF). *NB*: intruder disturbance in area of bowl, but with no evidence for loss of any object (J. Newman, pers. comm.).

Skeleton (337): adult, female, mature. Burial was extended with head to the west. The legs were straight, the left arm was at the side, the right arm slightly flexed across the body. The skull was flattened and the lower legs and feet apparently displaced, possibly as the bed or chamber collapsed (Plate 8).

Soil blocks 0345, 1104 and 1140 were taken from the burial and excavated in the laboratory (Cox 2001; Graham 2001a; Graham and Cox 2001).

Grave-goods: besides the objects associated with the 'bed', the grave contained a number of objects, recorded singly and in three main groups in Soil Blocks: 0345, 1104 and 1140.

24

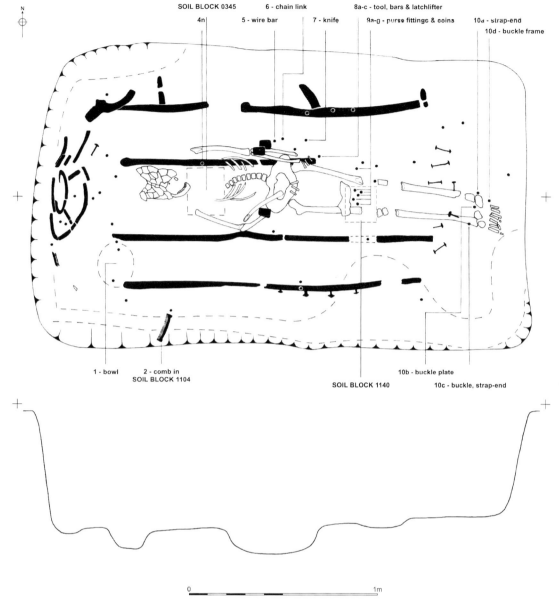

Figure 34 Grave 30, plan. Scale 1:20

A bronze bowl (1) was found at the upper R of the body, next to remains of the bed. A comb (2) lay at the edge of the grave, overlying the groove for the wall of the chamber; this was excavated as Soil Block 1104. At the upper chest, Soil Block 0345 contained a number of objects: coin pendant (3a), beads (4) and toilet sets (3b and c). A wire bar (5), and chain link (6), lay close by the L hand. A knife (7), tools and a latch-lifter (8a–c), also lay in this area. Straps and buckles were found at the feet: strap-end (10a) at the L ankle, strap-end and buckle (10b, c) at the R ankle. Close to the knees, Soil Block 1140 contained the remains of a possible bag (9a–d and 9g) and its contents (9e–f).

Soil Block 0345
Soil block 0345 was lifted and excavated in the laboratory (Cox 2001) and found to contain a number of silver objects in its upper layer. Its 'layers' were:

A (top layer)   A thin soil covering organic material. The top layer contained possible wood, highly fragmented and cracked, with grain apparently parallel to the N–S alignment of the long fittings from the iron bed.

B (middle layer)   A thin layer of organic material. Ivory/bone bead (4f) might be associated with wire bead 3k (1226); ivory bead 3m might be associated with wire bead 3l (1230).

C (bottom layer)   A 'layer' of artefacts, recorded as toilet sets (3) and beads (4). A thin strip of ?wood overlay a small pebble (1247)
Beads 3n and 3o found in Soil Block 0345 are currently missing. 3n is a crystal bead, 3o is of glass.

Soil Block 1104
Soil block 1104 was excavated in the laboratory (Graham and Cox 2001). The block was ochre-brown in colour, and contained the remains of a comb (2).

Soil Block 1140
Soil block 1140 was approximately rectangular and constituted two distinct layers: a dark top layer; probably organic material, with several bronze objects, possibly the remains of a bag and its contents (9a–g); an ochre-brown bottom layer (like blocks 0345 and 1104: Graham 2001a)).

Grave-goods
1   Fragments of bronze **hanging-bowl** (1090). *c.*170–210mm diameter. Hammered-down T-section rim, concave neck with slight carination. Traces of textile. Detached fragment of probable cast mount; no clear trace of solder. Textile: detached

25

Plate 8 Grave 30: skeleton and remains of bed, during excavation

Plate 9a, b Grave 30: Coin pendant 3a

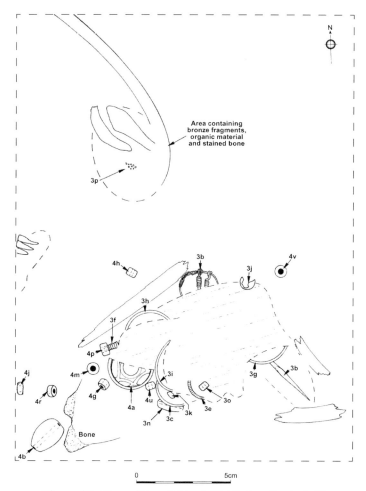

Figure 35 Grave 30, soil block 0345 plan. Scale 1:20

fragment, 9 x 8mm, fully mineral-replaced (mineralised) remains, consisting of:

(i) seven or eight parallel cords or threads, 0.8mm diameter, arching over

(ii) the folds of a fine textile. No further details possible (PWR). A sample of soil from the bowl produced charcoal and mineral-replaced wood (VF).

2   Bone/antler **comb** (1104), single-sided, with curved decorated back-plates. The comb is virtually complete. It is a single-sided composite with two end segments and ten tooth segments secured to two connecting plates by nine iron rivets. The connecting plates are decorated by a continuous sequence of single ring-and-dot motifs running in a medial line. The connecting plates also have doubled framing lines and a fine diagonal patterning along the top edge, which is continued across the tops of the tooth segments. The end segments also include decoration, with single ring-and-dot motifs spread across the available space. The decoration of the comb is the same on both sides. Both connecting plates and tooth segments are made of antler and there is no evidence for the use of bone. A number of the comb teeth survive, indicating that there were originally five per centimetre. They show some traces of wear. Estimated original length: 175mm (IR).

Bag and contents (Plates 9 and 10)

3a   Gold **coin pendant** (1225), coin of Dagobert I (AD 629–639), Mint of Arles, with corrugated gold sheet suspension loop, with strip of beaded wire on loop (Plate 9). Weight 4.08gm (including loop).

3b   Silver **toilet set** (1118, 1120, 1126); three implements on a silver wire ring. Two picks, spoon or ear scoop, and green bead 4x (1249) on shaft of pick (Plate 10).
Ring made of wire not thicker in the middle than at ends, fragmented and incomplete (20mm long); ends set in loops (two remain), their terminals wound back on ring. Pick (SF 1120) decorated with groups of incisions along handle; handle end set

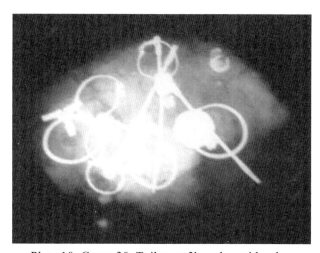

Plate 10 Grave 30, Toilet set 3b and c, with other objects, in soil block 0345

in double loop for suspension and wound back on shaft. L. 84mm. Second pick (SF 1126) decorated and suspended as first, L. 81mm. Ear scoop (SF 1118) decorated and suspended as picks, L. 76mm Suspension loops of tools worn where touching (BB).

3c   Silver **toilet set** (1125, 1231–3); three implements on a silver wire ring ('hand'/nail cleaner, knife and pick or spearhead). Ring made of wire thicker in the middle (1mm) than at ends; terminals wound back on ring. Diam. 18mm. Toothpick (SF 1231) with beaded handle; terminal folded into suspension loop. L. 29mm. ?Knife (SF 1233) with beaded handle;

27

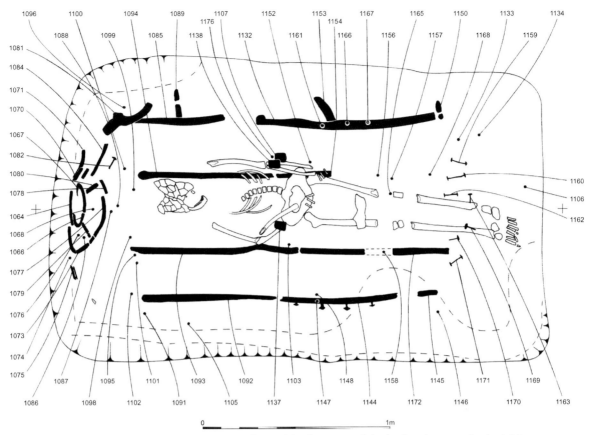

Figure 36 Grave 30, plan and section, with elements of the bed and cover. Scale 1:20

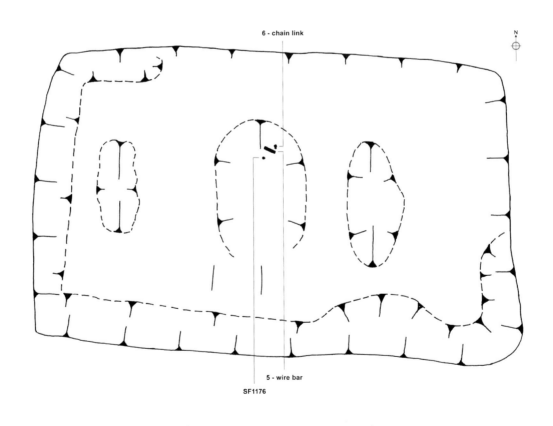

Figure 37 Grave 30, base of grave. Scale 1:20

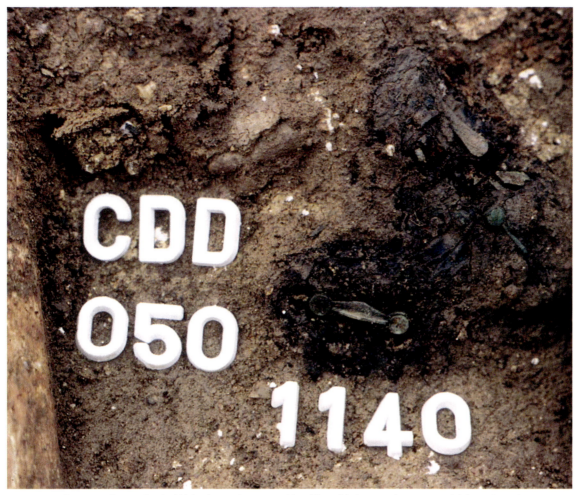

Plate 11 Grave 30 Soil block 1140 *in situ* (detail), with bag and contents (objects 9a–g)

suspension ring ?punched or ?cast; L. 28mm. ?Nail cleaner (SF 1232) with plain handle, terminal folded into suspension loop. Fork formed by punches. L. 28mm (BB).

3d Silver **wire ring** with **spangle** and **scutiform pendant** (1227–9), each lozengiform with raised central boss, stamped borders. Ring (SF 1229) made of wire thicker in the middle (1mm) than at ends; terminals wound back on ring. Diam. 12mm. Scutiform pendant SF 1227 has pyramid-shaped central boss and is decorated with triangular punch-marks comprised of smaller triangles; loop ribbed and soldered on, appears slightly worn. Diam. of sheet 11mm, height of boss 3mm. Spangle SF 1228 has dome-shaped boss and is decorated with lines of punched dots. One corner of sheet is perforated for suspension. Diam. of sheet 10mm, height of boss 1.5mm (BB).

3e Silver **ring**, twisted wire (1124). Wire beaded in the middle and plain at ends; in the middle thicker (2mm) than at ends. Bezel made of plain coiled ends, their terminals wound back on ring. Diam. of ring 24mm; inside 19mm (BB).

3f Silver **suspension ring** (1127), knotted terminal. Bead 4a was attached.

3g Silver **suspension ring** (1121), knotted terminal. Plain silver wire, thicker in the middle (2mm) than at ends. Ends form two halves of a coil, their terminals wound back on ring. Diam. of ring 28mm (BB).

3h Silver **suspension ring** (1122), knotted terminal. Silver wire with beaded sections, appears worn; wire thicker in the middle (2mm) than at ends. Ends set in loops, their terminals wound back on ring. Diam. of ring 23mm (BB).

3i Silver **suspension ring** (1123), knotted terminal. Plain wire, thicker in the middle (1mm) than at ends. Ends set in loops, their terminals wound back on ring. Diam. of ring 23mm (BB).

3j Two silver hemispheres **bead/pendant** (1128), possibly fragments of bulla pendant.

3k Copper-alloy wire **bead**, biconical (1226), traces of textile. Through the middle a suspension cord 1.5–2.0mm wide, structure not clear, but fibre is flax or hemp (PWR). Ivory/bone bead 4f could have been associated.

3l Copper-alloy wire **bead**, biconical (1230), traces of textile. Ivory bead 3m could be associated.

3m Ivory **bead** (1241), possibly associated with 3l.

3n Crystal **bead** (1108). Missing.

3o Glass **bead** (1117). Missing.

3p Copper-alloy **sheet** fragments (1131), associated with bone and organic material.

4a Glass **bead** (1119), blue-green, with annular twist trail, found attached to silver suspension ring 3f (1127). Running through wire mount is a multi-strand cord, 1.5–2.0mm thick, structure not clear, but fibre partially processed plant fibre, almost certainly flax (PWR). Plain silver wire thicker in the middle (2mm) than at ends. Ends form two halves of a coil, their terminals wound back on ring. Diam. of ring 26mm.

4b Amethyst **bead** (1110), pale, almond shaped.

4c Amethyst **bead** (1243), pale, almond shaped.

4d Amethyst **bead** (1245), pale, almond shaped.

4e Ivory/bone **bead** (1246), fragment.

4f Ivory/bone **bead** (1235), possibly associated with 3k.

4g Glass **bead** (1112), opaque orange, wound, barrel shaped.

4h Glass **bead** (1115), opaque, orange, wound, barrel shaped.

4i Glass **bead** (1236), opaque orange, barrel shaped, wound or folded.

4j Glass **bead** (1109), opaque red, drawn, globular.

4k Glass **bead** (1242), opaque red, [**drawn**], globular, crimped.

4l Glass **bead** (1244), opaque red, barrel shaped, folded.

4m Glass **bead** (1113), opaque red, barrel shaped, [**drawn**].

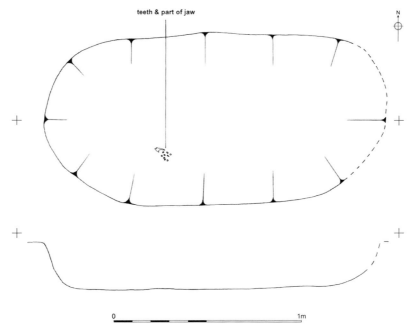

teeth & part of jaw

Figure 38 Grave 31, plan and section. Scale 1:20

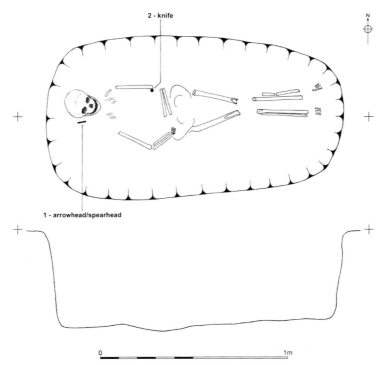

2 - knife

1 - arrowhead/spearhead

Figure 39 Grave 32, plan and section. Scale 1:20

4n	Glass **bead** (1129), opaque red, globular, folded.
4o	Glass **bead** (1240), opaque red, polyhedral, drawn or folded.
4p	Glass **bead** (1114), opaque red, barrel-shaped, wound.
4q	Glass **bead** (1239), semi-translucent light green, globular, drawn.
4r	Glass **bead** (1111), semi-translucent green, globular, wound.
4s	Glass **bead** (1237), semi-translucent green, barrel shaped, drawn.
4t	Glass **bead** (1238), semi-translucent light green, barrel shaped, wound.
4u	Glass **bead** (1130), semi-translucent green, barrel shaped, wound.
4v	Glass **bead** (1116), semi-translucent white, globular, drawn.
4w	Glass **bead** (1248), semi-translucent white, cylinder, wound or folded.
4x	Glass **bead** (1249), green, globular, drawn. Attached to 3b.

5	Iron **twisted wire bar** (1177), in central depression.
6	Bronze **chain link** (1178), in central depression.
7	Iron **knife** (1151), 53mm+. Leather sheath. Evison Type 4.
8a–c	Three iron objects, possibly the remains of a **chatelaine**
8a	Iron **tool** (1155), flat section, over 65mm long.
8b	Iron **latch-lifter** (1155a), over 70mm long.
8c	Three iron **bars** (1155b), one on loop.

Bag and contents (Plate 11)

9a	Bronze **bag fitting** (1139), 29mm long.
9b–c	Two bronze **bag fittings** (1140 a and b), attached to leather
9d	Bronze **strap-end** (1140c)
9e	Bronze **coin** (1140d), Roman, House of Valentinian (nummus). Obverse […] diademed bust R. Reverse SECVRITAS

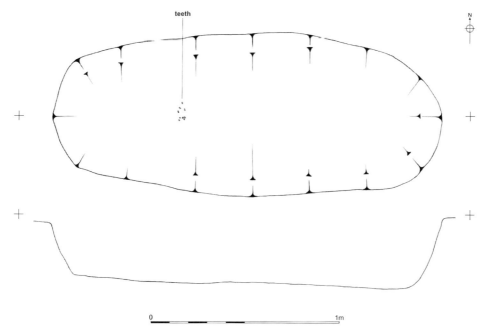

teeth

0   1m

Figure 40 Grave 33, plan and section. Scale 1:20

REIPVBLICAE Victory advancing L. Mint mark: OF\?\\?. Mint of Arles or Lyons AD 367–375. Weight 2.08gm.

9f   Silver **sceat** or base metal replica (1142). Weight 0.39gm.

9g   Bronze **suspension ring and attachment** (1136), 35mm long overall, 18mm diameter. Possibly part of chatelaine (8). Textile: on outer surface of one of plates, lapping over edge, 9 x 5mm, off- white textile woven in tabby weave, 20/Z x 18/Z per cm. Fibre fully processed, fine plant fibre, almost certainly flax (PWR).

10a   Iron **strap-end** for shoe buckle (1173), 36mm long, 7mm wide.

10bi–iii Iron **shoe buckle, plate** (1174) possibly fragments of triangular buckle 16mm x 12mm.

10ci   Iron **shoe buckle** (1175); 14mm x 14mm, frame 38mm wide. Two rivets.

10cii   Iron **strap-end** (1175), 29mm long.

10d   Iron **shoe buckle, frame and pin** (1164), oval, frame 18mm x 11mm. Drawn from x-ray.

Grave 31 *(320)*
(Fig. 38)
Dimensions: Length 1.80m; Width 0.90m; Depth 0.30m.
Neatly cut grave.
Fill: mid-brown grey sandy silt.
Skeleton (325): child, *c.*7 years old. Teeth and part of jaw surviving.
Grave-goods: no remains.

Grave 32 *(346)*
(Figs 39, 99)
Dimensions: Length 1.60m; Width 0.85m; Depth 0.50m.
Neatly cut grave.
Skeleton (348): ?male, *c.*11–12 years old. Burial with head to west, with straight legs, hands together at waist.
Grave-goods: arrowhead or spearhead (1) at R side of head; knife (2) at L elbow.

1   Iron **arrowhead** or **spearhead** (1141), 100mm long, at right side of head. Traces of textile. Textile: diagonally across blade, 10 x 2mm, medium-weight ZS textile, weave unclear; fibre not identified (PWR).

2   Iron **knife** (1143), over 104mm. Horn handle, traces of textile, leather? Textile: traces of textile across blade; no details possible (PWR).

Grave 33 *(328)*
(Fig. 40)
Dimensions: Length 2.05m; Width 0.85m; Depth 0.30m.
Fill: mid-brown silty clay.
Skeleton (343): child, *c.*4 years old. Teeth only survive, towards west end of grave.
Grave-goods: no remains.

Grave 34 *(481)*
(Fig. 41)
Remnant of east end of grave on edge of quarry, at least 1.2m wide.
Fill: mid-brown sandy clay.
Skeleton (483): sex unknown, adult. Bones of right foot only, rest quarried away.
Grave-goods: no remains.

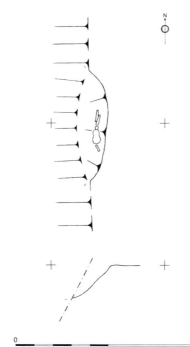

0   1m

Figure 41 Grave 34, plan and section. Scale 1:20

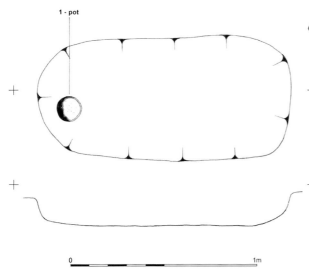

Grave 35 *(335)*
(Figs 42, 99)
Dimensions: Length 1.35m; Width 0.65m; Depth 0.15m.
Fill: mid-brown sandy silt.
Skeleton: no remains.
Grave-goods: to the west end of the grave.

1   **Pot** (338). Baggy jar, handmade, near complete, burnt residue
       internally. 150mm diameter.

Grave 36 *(326)*
(Fig. 43)
Dimensions: Length 1.85m; Width 0.75m; Depth 0.30m.
Grave with 'shelf' on north side.
Fill: mid-brown silty loam.
Skeleton: no remains.
Grave-goods: no remains.

Figure 42 Grave 35, plan and section. Scale 1:20

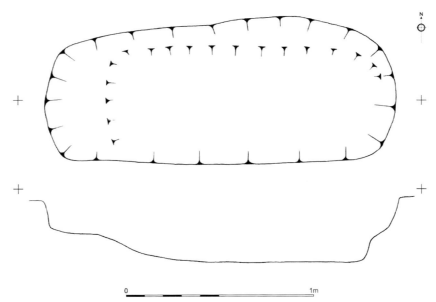

Figure 43 Grave 36, plan and section. Scale 1:20

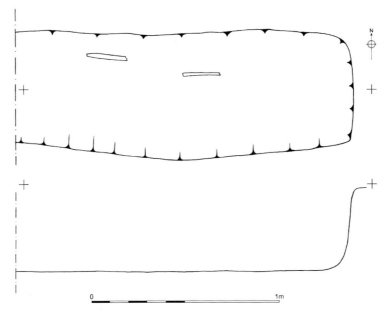

Figure 44 Grave 37, plan and section. Scale 1:20

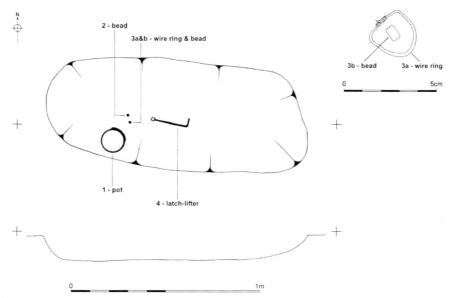

Figure 45 Grave 38, plan and section, scale 1:20. Detail from field drawing, scale 1:2

Grave 37 *(315)*
(Fig. 44)
Length 1.80m or more; Width 0.65m; Depth 0.40m.
Grave runs out of excavated area.
Fill: mid-brown silty sand, with some clay and chalk.
Skeleton (317): adult.
Grave-goods: no remains.

Grave 38 *(513)*
(Figs 45, 99)
Dimensions: Length 1.4m; Width 0.6m; Depth 0.15m.
Very shallow grave. Close to pit (151).
Fill: mid-brown clay silt.
Skeleton. no remains.
Grave-goods: pot (1) lay by the probable upper right side of the body, with beads and wire ring (2, 3a and b) over the body, and the latch-lifter (4) in the likely waist area.

1	**Pot** (515). Near complete. Baggy, wide-mouthed jar. 100mm diameter.
2	Glass **bead** (1191), opaque red, barrel shaped, wound.
3a	Silver wire **ring** (1192), knotted ends. Plain silver wire, thicker in the middle (2mm) than at ends. One terminal wound back on ring, other not preserved. Max. diam. of ring 24mm (BB).
3b	Glass **bead** (1190), opaque green, cylinder, wound.
4	Iron **latch-lifter** (1193), possibly two, corroded together. 170mm long.

Grave 39 *(306)*
(Fig. 46)
Dimensions: Length 2.40m; Width 1.1m; Depth 0.15m.
Fill: mid-brown silty clay with occasional large flints and charcoal flecks.
Skeleton: no remains.
Grave-goods: no remains.

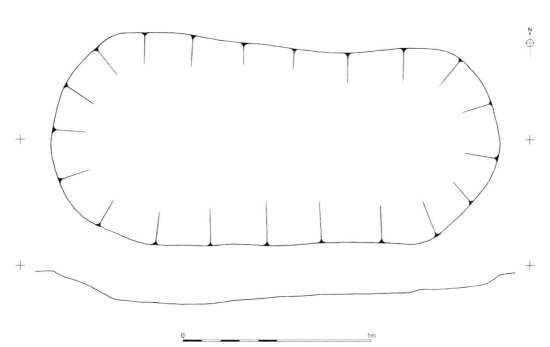

Figure 46 Grave 39, plan and section. Scale 1:20

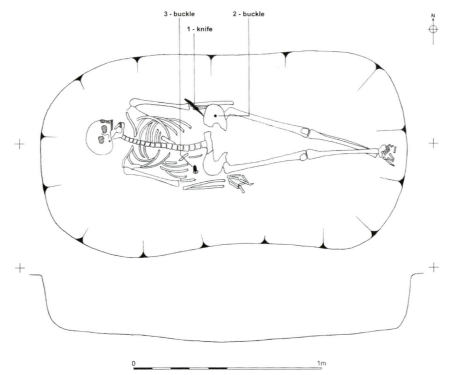

Figure 47 Grave 40, plan and section. Scale 1:20

Grave 40 *(297)*
(Plate 12; Figs 47, 99)
Dimensions: Length 1.95m; Width 1.0m; Depth 0.30m–0.35m.
Fill: mid-brown sandy silt and chalky clay.
Skeleton (301): adult, ?male, old. Head to west. Extended with arms at sides, feet crossed at ankles and head turned to left. Bones in good condition, especially where resting on chalky clay. Position of the extremities suggests little movement after burial.

Grave-goods: knife (1) and buckle (2) were found at the L side, buckle (3) at the R side.

1   Iron **knife** (1062), 136mm+. Traces of horn handle, leather? sheath. Evison Type 5.

2   Bronze **buckle** (1065), oval frame, square plate, three rivets. Plate 26mm x 22mm, frame 16mm wide.

3   Bronze **buckle** (1063), oval frame, tongue-shaped plate. Plate 33mm x 19mm, frame 25mm wide.

Plate 12 Grave 40: Skeleton during excavation

Plate 13 Grave 42: Skeleton during excavation

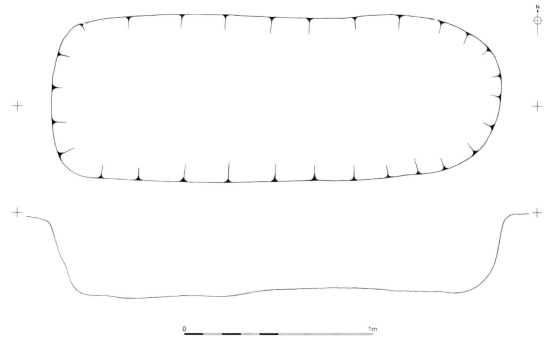

Figure 48 Grave 41, plan and section. Scale 1:20

Grave 41 *(304)*
(Fig. 48)
Dimensions: Length 2.40m; Width 0.90m; Depth 0.40m.
Fill: mid-brown silty sand.
Skeleton: no remains.

Grave 42 *(286)*
(Plate 13; Fig. 49)
Dimensions: Length 2.2m; Width 0.95m; Depth 0.20m.
Fill: mid-brown sandy silt.
Skeleton (288): adult, female, middle-aged or older. Extended; head to west and fallen to left. Arms at side, but with hands over pelvis.
Grave-goods: no remains.

Grave 43 *(322)*
(Fig. 50)
Dimensions: Length 1.90m; Width 0.75m; Depth 0.30m.
Neatly cut grave.
Fill: mid-brown silty clay; occasional charcoal flecks and clay lumps.
Skeleton (324): adult, middle-aged? Head to west, extended. Preservation varied: legs nearly complete.
Grave-goods: no remains.

Grave 44 *(275)*
(Figs 51, 100)
Dimensions: Length 1.90m; Width 0.85m; Depth 0.10m.
Fill: sandy silty loam.
Skeleton (293): age and sex unknown.

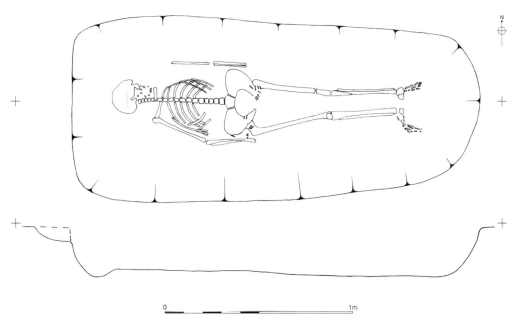

Figure 49 Grave 42, plan and section. Scale 1:20

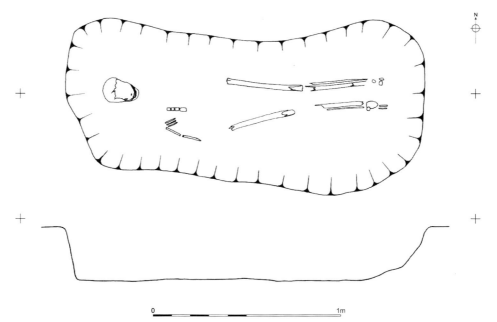

Figure 50 Grave 43, plan and section. Scale 1:20

Grave-goods: wire ring (1) and beads (2) were found at the west (head) end. Knife (3) at was at the right side, knife (4) and latch-lifter (5) were found together at the left side, in the probable waist area. Two objects (6) and (7) were sieved out, with location in the grave unknown.

1   Silver wire **ring** (1052), with wound-back terminals. Plain silver wire thicker in the middle (2mm) than at ends. Terminals wound back on ring. Diam. of ring 22mm (BB).

2   Three **beads** (1049–1051):
     2a Glass **bead** (1049), opaque red, biconical, wound.
     2b Glass **bead** (1050) semi-translucent green, globular, wound?
     2c Amethyst **bead** (1051), pale, almond shaped.

3   Iron **knife** (1053, 1056), 87mm+. Horn handle, leather on blade. Traces of textile. Evison Type 3(?). Found at right side. Textile: a single thread, S-spun, 0.8mm diameter, wool

(partially pigmented) forms a spiral path along the sharp edge of the blade. Probably sewing thread from leather sheath (PWR).

4a   Iron **knife** (1054), horn handle, leather sheath. 100mm long. Textile.

4b   Bronze **ring** (1054b), possibly finger ring, 36mm diameter. At left side, with (1055).

5   Iron **latch-lifter** (1055). 240mm long. Traces of textile. Textile: poorly preserved traces all over object: (i) probably tabby weave; no further details possible; (ii) S-plied cords, either a fringe or a tablet weave (PWR).

6   Iron **object** (1057), possibly a terminal, traces of textile (drawn from X-ray). Possibly part of a ring or penannular brooch c.25mm diameter.

7   Amethyst **bead** (1058), pale, almond shaped.

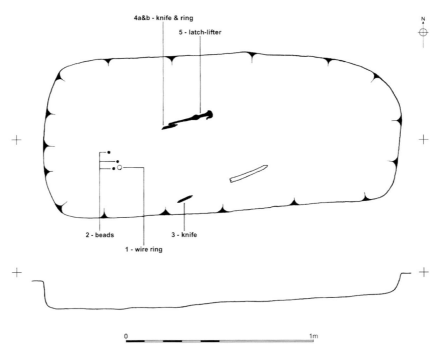

Figure 51 Grave 44, plan and section. Scale 1:20

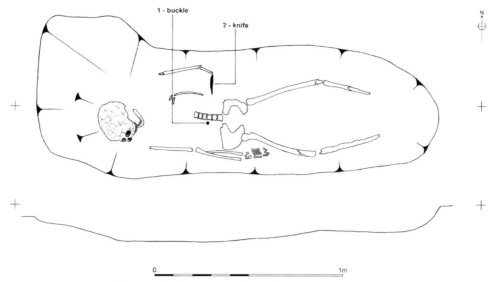

Figure 52 Grave 45, plan and section. Scale 1:20

Grave 45 *(312)*

(Figs 52, 100)
Dimensions: Length 2.25m; Width *c.*0.7m; Depth 0.15m.
Cut by pit (289).
Fill: mid-grey/brown silty clay/sand.
Skeleton (314): male, young-middle-age. Burial extended with splayed legs and head to right. Arms at side. Bone condition poor, except right hand.
Grave-goods: knife (1) and buckle (2) lay in the waist area, presumably on a belt. The buckle was found 'almost vertical with buckle end down'.

1	Bronze **buckle** (1069), oval frame 28mm wide, rectangular plate, 29mm x 19mm, two rivets.
2	Iron **knife** (1072), 108mm+. Horn on tang, traces of leather sheath? Evison Type 1.

Grave 46 *(426)*

(Figs 53, 100)
Dimensions: Length 1.50m; Width 0.55m; Depth 0.20m.
Expanded at east end. Shallow grave.
Fill: mid-brown sandy silt, mottled, with yellow clay.
Skeleton (428): sex unknown, *c.*15–16 years old. The arrangement of the body is unusual, with upper leg bones splayed or fallen outwards and head fallen to the left. Arms by side.
Grave-goods: object (1) was at the chest, buckle (2) was at the waist.

1	Bronze sheet **object** (1180), fragment, tapered, 10mm long, rivet at wide end; possible lace-end.
2	Bronze **buckle** (1179), oval frame 15mm wide, tongue-shaped plate 14mm x 10mm.

Grave 47 *(453)*

(Figs 54, 101)
Dimensions: Length 1.45m+; Width 0.90m; Depth 0.20m.
Grave truncated at the west by pit (295); slopes down from the east.
Fill: mid-brown clayey sand.
Skeleton (455): sex unknown, adult. Leg bones survive. Head to west?
Grave-goods: two iron objects (1a, b), associated with leather, found towards the head end.

1a	Iron **knife**, (1182) horn handle, leather sheath? 112mm long.
1b	Iron **tool** (1182), fragments. With looped end, tapering rectangular section, with a 'nibbed' end, over 92mm long. Traces of leather.

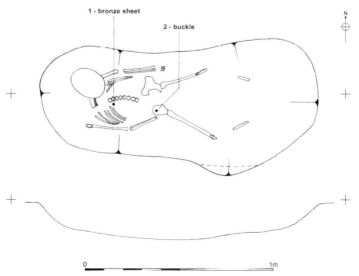

Figure 53 Grave 46, plan and section. Scale 1:20

37

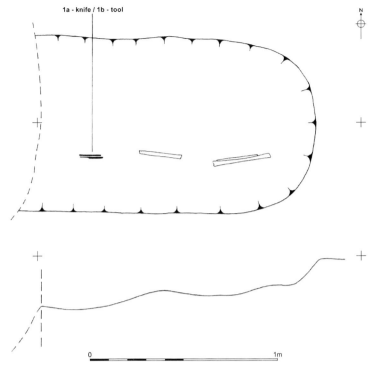

Figure 54 Grave 47, plan and section. Scale 1:20

Grave 48 *(446)*

(Figs 55, 101)

Dimensions: Length 2.25m; Width 0.85m; Depth 0.30m. Rounded ends.

Fill: light brown sandy silt and yellow clay. Bones in good condition; feet missing.

Skeleton (448): ?male, young–middle-aged. Burial extended, with head to the west; legs straight and hands crossed at the waist. The head had fallen to one side.

Grave-goods: the seax (1) was found at the left side. The objects were found together and not separately planned.

1   Iron **seax** (1181), 395mm. Horn handle. Böhner 1958 'broad' type.

2a, b   Iron **buckle** and tongue (1215, 1217), triangular, three rivets, oval frame, tapered plate with silver inlaid decoration in a hatched pattern.

The design respects and emphasizes the three rivets (now lost), and suggests two former studs. This creates curved fields enclosing a central panel whose decoration is now lost. The curved fields are hatched, to create a skewed ladder effect, with rows of small dots at each end. These emphasize the terminal rivet and the pin base. 70mm x 40mm, frame 47mm wide. Length 105mm overall. The decoration on the pin base consists of a single outline, enclosing a triangular panel, with hatching.

3a, b   Two iron **fittings/mounts**, (1216, 1218), traces of horn, possibly bag or box fittings; (a) about 42mm long, (b) about 30mm long.

4   Iron **steel** (1219), leather on blade, 132mm long (drawn from X-ray).

5   Iron **knife** (1220). Horn handle, leather sheath? Evison Type 1? 124mm long.

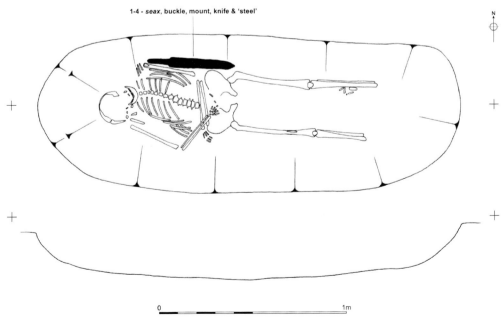

Figure 55 Grave 48, plan and section. Scale 1:20

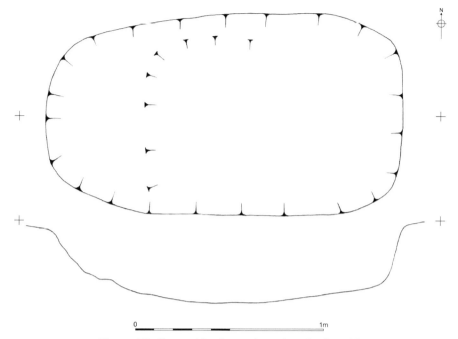

Figure 56 Grave 49, plan and section. Scale 1:20

Grave 49 (479)
(Fig. 56)
Dimensions: Length 1.90m; Width 1.10m; Depth 0.30–0.40m.
Square ends. Grave had a 'shelf' at the west end.
Fill: light-mid-brown silty sand. Pottery in fill.
Skeleton: no remains.
Grave-goods: no remains.

Grave 50 (299)
(Figs 57, 102)
Dimensions: Length 2.15; Width 0.75m; Depth 0.15m.
Neatly cut and regular grave.
Fill: mid-orange-brown sand.
Skeleton: no remains.
Grave-goods: iron tools (1) and (2) were found close together near the centre of the grave, with rivet (3) nearby.

1   Iron **tool** (1060), rectangular section, 50mm long.
2   Iron objects, possibly **knife** and **steel** (1059), 114mm long. In remains of a bag or sheath.
3   Iron **rivet** (1061), 17mm long.

Other objects
(Fig. 102)

Bronze rolled sheet **tube**, fragment (1007). Long tube, possibly waste from manufacture of aglets (lace ends). Metal-detector find (Context 677).
Iron **tool** (1222), possibly a curry comb. ?Roman. Found on spoilheap.
Iron **object** (1224), encrusted in mineral-replaced organic material. Found in small pit (565). Textile: (i) on one face and on part of opposite face, 30 x 30mm, medium-fine textile; no further details possible; (ii) on opposite face only, 15 x 15mm, coarser textile, possibly a piled weave, 6/Z x ? per cm; fibre hair/wool; swirls of fibre on one face probably represent a pile (PWR).
Iron **ferrule** (1194). 75mm long, 16mm diameter. Found in ditch (187).

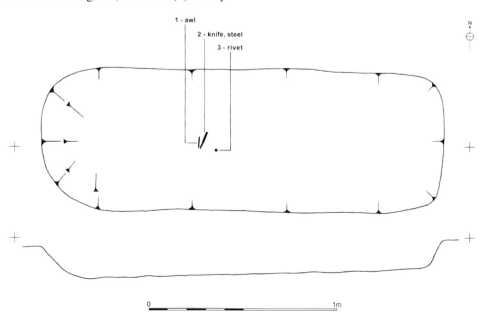

1 - awl
2 - knife, steel
3 - rivet

Figure 57 Grave 50, plan and section. Scale 1:20

Chapter 4. Evidence for Chambers, Covers and Bed in Graves 1 and 30

I. Grave 1: evidence for chamber and cover

Chamber

The western part of Grave 1 was lost to the quarry face, the remaining portion, about 2m, surviving to a depth of 0.32m below the excavated natural surface. Around the south, east and part of the north side of the grave was a slot or channel 50mm wide at the base of the grave cut. Its closeness to the side of the grave cut suggests a near-vertical retaining wall, for a chamber about 1m wide. In excavation, this slot was seen as a vertical 'soil shadow', distinct from the main fill of the grave, and presumably the trace of the wooden chamber. In the north to south profile, this slot was recorded on both north and south sides, with soil shadow being recorded to the top of the excavated profile (0.32m).

A bucket lay in the corner of the chamber, at the foot end, and a spear lay along the north edge. The other grave-goods lay to the south of the body, although the positions of the shield mounts suggest that it lay in part over the body; the relative positions of the mounts and the boss may suggest some movement within the grave.

Cover

Two iron objects (SF 1035a and b) were found together in the waist area, and apparently were both mounted onto boards of ash, possibly part of a cover (Fig. 58). They were found next to iron rod (11) SF 1035c.

1035a *c*. 130mm long and 60mm wide, bent to form a U-shape, with unequal arms, with nails 30mm long; the internal gap is between 8–12mm.

1035b *c*. 110mm long and 50mm wide, bent to form a U-shape about 100mm high with unequal arms. The internal gap is about 14mm wide.

These two objects (1035 a and b) represent a pair of brackets, the unequal lengths of the arms of which may indicate fixing to a shaped structure, rather than a flat surface. They did not appear to be part of any bed structure (like that in Grave 30) and it is possible that they belonged to a curved cover above the body. These objects may be compared with the two brackets found with the bed burial at Lapwing Hill, Derbyshire (illustrated by Speake 1989, fig. 87).

At the Street House cemetery, Yorkshire, the bed burial had two iron 'staples', fixed to the top of the bed

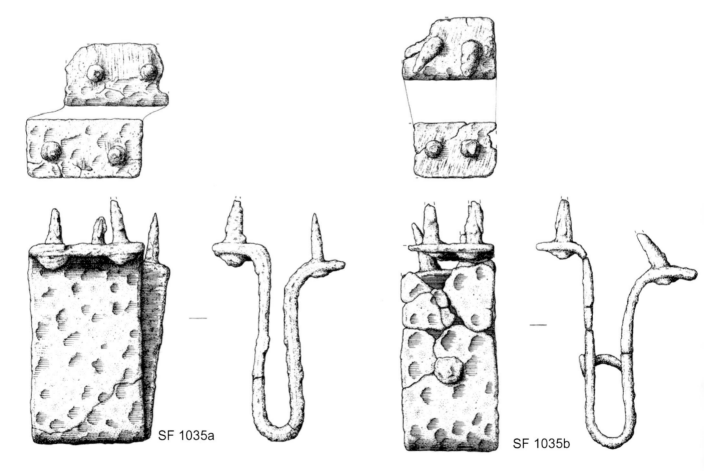

SF 1035a

SF 1035b

Figure 58 Grave 1, brackets. Scale 1:2

40

sides, towards the foot end. Each was 60mm long and 40mm wide, with an 'eye' or opening about 40mm by 37mm, thought to be intended to hold something, but too thin and insecure for a carrying pole (Simmons forthcoming).

In Grave 1, the two brackets were found close together, in the waist area, with iron rod (11), and all recorded as a single object (1035).They were the sole metal objects, apart from the grave-goods. As noted below, in Grave 30 the two brackets were found a little distance apart, either side of the waist, and are thought to have been associated with two lines of large rivets, at either end of the grave. If the brackets in Grave 1 were for carrying poles for some sort of cover, then any other fixings were of wood. Whilst the form and locations of these objects are clear, whether Grave 1 had a cover over the burial is not certain.

II. Grave 30: evidence for chamber, bed and cover

Chamber
Around the north-west, west, south and south-east edges of the base of the grave ran a 'channel', at its narrowest about 90mm wide in the south-west corner, expanding in the south-east part of the grave to 200mm. This channel is best interpreted as the setting for a wooden wall around the grave, its curving shape on plan suggesting vertical boards. The implied structure was c.1.30m x 2.40m. Besides the channel, the base contained three 'scoops' and in the largest, central, scoop, three objects were recorded: twisted wire bar (5) and chain link (6), both probably grave-goods, and scraps of iron rivet (1176), more probably part of the 'bed' (see below). The scoops were irregular and with no clear purpose.

The evidence for a bed and another structure, possibly a cover (below) lies in the remains of a wooden structure and associated fittings such as eyelets and cleats found above, below and to the side of the body, the remains of a wooden board decorated with iron strips at the head end of the grave, and stays that once connected it to the sides of the bed. The stays, cleats, eyelets and other items can be

paralleled in other bed burials, where the eyelets usually held straps to support a mattress or similar.

The evidence for a cover comes from the two iron brackets on either side of the body, in the waist area, and two lines of large rivets, at the head and foot ends of the burial, and these are interpreted as fixings for a wooden structure placed above the burial.

Bed
Within the possible chamber, four parallel lengths of wood were recorded, with many associated fittings such as cleats or rivets. Some of these bore traces of fabric/textile, and some form of central support. At the head (west) end, a complex of metal strips and rivets is interpreted as a decorated headboard, with a design of two concentric circles. In the field, it was noted that:

'Rivets were fitted to the lower side sections and the end of the 'bed' at intervals of c.14cm. The positions of the rivets in the upper side sections is less clear, but eyelets/cleats were fitted to the frame in at least three places.

The head of the bed may have been decorated with two concentric iron rings, secured by rivets and brackets, or an iron-bound circular shield of the same design was located at the head (west) end of the grave.'

Cover
As in Grave 1, two sets of iron objects, probably brackets or large 'staples', were found at the centre of the grave, above the lower arms, 300mm apart and c.500mm from the sides of the chamber (Fig. 59).

1137	Above the right arm, 1137 is a folded iron sheet, pierced by a long nail or rivet. 1137 is c. 90mm long overall, and c. 40mm wide, with an internal gap 80mm x 15mm.
1107 and 1138	Above the left arm, 1107 and 1138 were pieces of a single object, like 1137. 1107/1138 is c. 130mm long and 45mm wide, with an internal gap of 120mm x 17mm.

Large rivets or clench nails were found in two lines across the burial at the foot and the head ends, about 1.8m apart. They imply a board 60–70mm thick, and are interpreted as fixings for a curved structure running the length of the burial, the curvature being implied by the angles of the rivet heads.

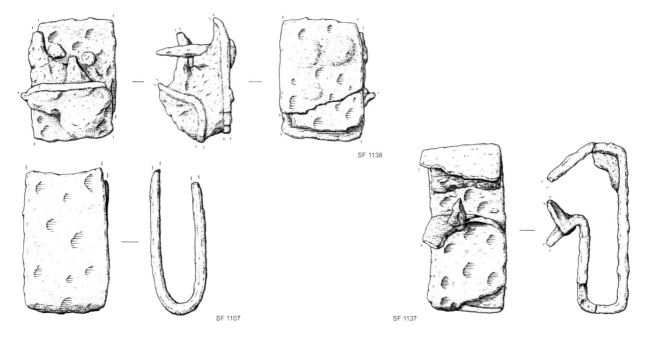

SF 1138

SF 1107

SF 1137

Figure 59 Grave 30, brackets. Scale 1:2

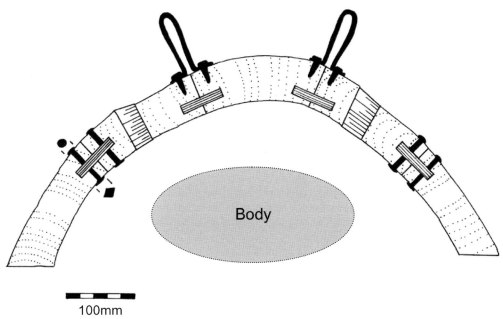

Body

100mm

Figure 60 Grave 30, possible reconstruction of cover (*Centre for Archaeology*)

It is suggested that the brackets were attached to this 'cover' (Fig. 60) allowing it to be carried or manoeuvred into position (see below). Above the body, soil block 0345 had a top layer of a 'woody' organic material (Fig. 35), which may have been part of a collapsed cover. The possibility that this structure may have been part of a boat is discussed below (see Chapter 4.IV).

III. The examination and reconstruction of the bed burial
by Jacqui Watson
(Figs 61–77)

(Abbreviations: TLS transverse longitudinal section; RLS radial transverse section)

Introduction
During excavation, Grave 30 was recognised as a bed burial within a chamber, but due to the conditions on site the metalwork was recovered as large fragments or in groups. Two soil blocks containing metalwork and organic materials were removed, one at neck/chest area (Soil Block 0345) containing jewellery, and the other a possible bag and its contents placed on the right thigh (Soil Block 1140). A third soil block (Soil Block 1104) contained a comb (2). These personal items are catalogued in Chapter 3 Catalogue of Graves.

The soil on the iron bed furniture appeared to be a loamy clay, which had dried as a hard heavy deposit onto the metalwork. Its removal revealed little organic material for study. Where possible the iron fragments were repaired with adhesive, but much of the iron remained in fragments whose relative positions were known only from the alignment of wood grain preserved on them.

There are well over 100 fragments of ironwork associated with this grave, and not all are necessarily part of the bed itself. The bed fittings include the headboard stays and the decorative metalwork on the headboard and sides. The eyelets and large rivets appear, on close examination, to be related to the chamber which contained the burial, although this is not certain.

Based on the grave plan (Fig. 34), the bed in Grave 30 seems to be about 1.9m long, but the width remains uncertain as the positions of the sides and the eyelets suggest the bed had probably been dismantled before being placed in the grave, although it must have been at least 0.6m wide to accommodate the headboard. The depth of the sides is not obvious, but is presumed to be around 0.3m like the bed from Edix Hill, Barrington (Malim and Hines 1998). The headboard must have been over 0.5m in both height and width to incorporate the decorative ironwork.

Two lines of large rivets at the head and feet of the skeleton indicate the presence of a large wooden structure that ran the length of the grave. It seems to have been made up of five or six boards joined together, with a curved or barrel-shaped section. This may have been a cover for the whole grave or just the burial.

The bed, chamber lining and cover were all of ash (*Fraxinus* sp.). This species is commonly found in the wood and charcoal remains from nearby sites in Suffolk, where it had been used for structures and fuel (Murphy 2001). Ash was also used for the construction of other bed burials, for example Swallowcliffe Down, Wiltshire (Speake 1989) and Barrington, Cambridgeshire, where the natural springiness of ash timber was thought to be one of the reasons it was chosen (Malim and Hines 1998, 264).

1. Headboard stays
(Figs 61–3)
The iron headboard stays attached the sides of the bed to the headboard. Only one of the two headboard stays remains intact (1081a, Figs 61–3), the other is broken into pieces (1075, 1101) found some distance from each other. This adds to the impression that the bed was dismantled, or even broken, to go in the grave.

The central part of each stay is twisted, with one terminal shaped to fit over the side of the bed and the other flat to be attached to the headboard. The shaped terminals show that the bar stood at an angle. The wood grain preserved on headboard stay 1081a indicates that the headboard itself was originally reclining at an angle of 100° in relation to the sides of the bed. Possibly the main function of the headboard stay was to support the headboard at this angle. The upper end of these stays indicates that the headboard was originally 25mm thick.

1081   Three objects a–c found together.
        a. The north-side headboard stay, complete with attachments for side rail and headboard. This piece is heavily encrusted with clay and stones and is still linked with a cleat 1081b that attached two sections of the headboard.
        b. The cleat 1081b has a twisted section that would have been on the outside of the headboard, and the distance between the two plates is c.5mm.
        c. Large rivet 1081c aligned at approx 90° and across the cleat (1081b), possibly belonged with the 'cover' and is discussed and illustrated with the other large rivets in section 5 (below).

1075   Cleat. Fragment of iron plate that attached the headboard stay to the headboard on the south side. The distance between the two plates is 23.8mm. One side is a twisted bar and the other a flat plate, making this the opposite pair to 1081b positioned near the

Figure 61 Grave 30, position of headboard stay in grave

headboard stay, on north side. Associated with a fragment of the headboard stay.

1101   Fragment of south headboard stay, the N-shaped bracket that was attached to the side of the bed. The distance between the bracket sides is approx. 25mm — the thickness of the headboard.

2. Headboard
(Figs 64–67)
The headboard was originally a wooden panel on which iron strips were probably mounted as two concentric circles with bars between them. The iron circles appear to have been made from a flat piece of iron just over 1mm thick: the outer circle is approx. 0.5m in diameter.

The ironwork from the west (head) area of the grave has suffered a great deal of damage, some of it at the post-excavation stage, but it is also clear from the edges covered in re-deposited clay and calcite (calcium carbonate) that a number of the breakages must have happened at the time of burial or soon after. As a result most of the strips were not in their original positions at the time of excavation (Figs 64–5), and their interpretation as being arranged simply in two concentric circles is by no means certain. On the inner circle there is clear evidence that it was not a complete circle, as there are two nailed terminals which appear to be intentional (Fig. 66).

Wood grain was recorded where it remained on the ironwork, which was apparently attached to a large board made up of at least three pieces of wood. The ironwork that could be pieced together using the site drawings and aligning the wood grain is illustrated in Figure 67. This

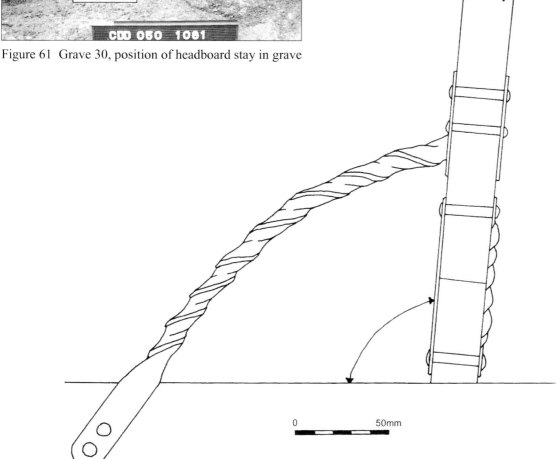

0   50mm

Figure 62 Grave 30, headboard stay (SF1081a); side view

43

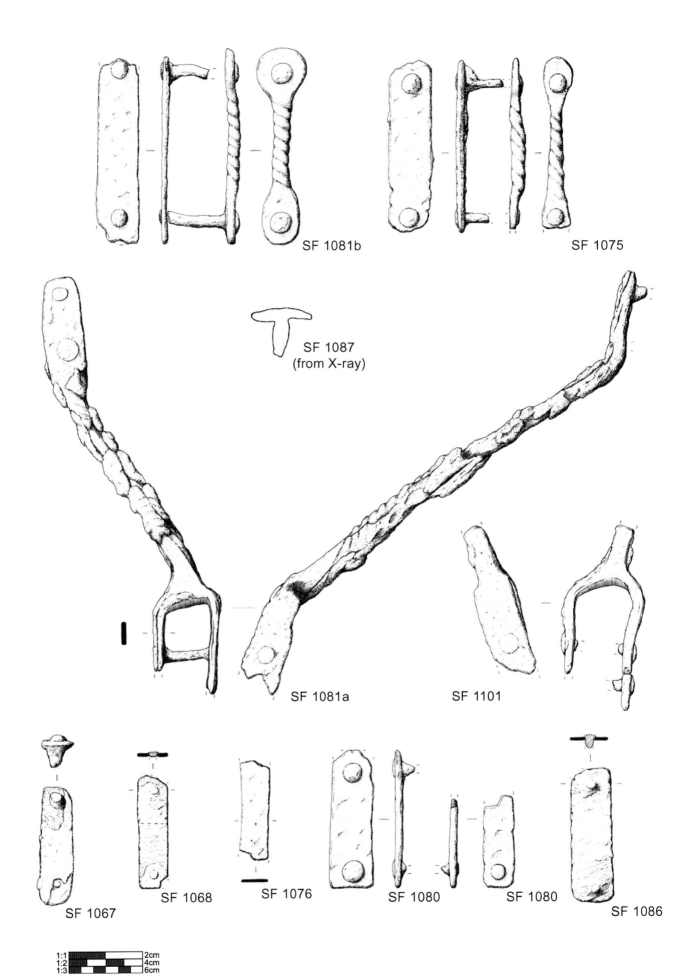

SF 1081b

SF 1075

SF 1087
(from X-ray)

SF 1081a

SF 1101

SF 1067

SF 1068

SF 1076

SF 1080

SF 1080

SF 1086

1:1
1:2
1:3

2cm
4cm
6cm

Figure 63 Grave 30, headboard stays and associated fittings. Scale 1:2

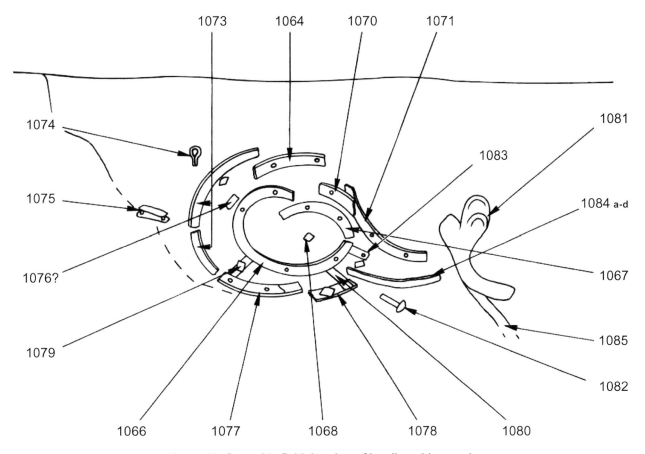

Figure 64 Grave 30, field drawing of headboard ironwork

gives a very basic and simplified view of how the headboard might have appeared. The ironwork on the headboard is undecorated, with a flat surface, whereas in the case of the cleats 1081b and 1075 attaching the stays the twisted parts are intended to be visible from the back. Very little of this metalwork was used to hold the sections of the headboard together, and must have been decorative. Fragments of the inner circle may have had leather between the ironwork and the wood.

1066	Fragments of the inner circle: an inner diameter of 220mm: the strip is about 16mm wide. One section may have leather

between the wood and iron.
Broken nails on the inner ring are 10.5mm and 10.8mm long.

1064, 1073, 1077, 1070	Sections of the outer ring. The internal diameter of this ring is 392mm and it is about 16mm wide. On this ring are three nails with shanks 10.9mm, 13.9mm, and 15.0mm long. This gives the minimum thickness of the headboard at this point.
1067	One plate of small cleat with TLS preserved near broken rivet, length of shank 12.4mm (Fig. 68).
1068	Two halves of a broken cleat with a minimum depth between the two plates of 19mm. Originally attached to TLS, changing to RLS (possibly the same piece of wood). Broken side attached to oblique TLS. Small fragment of a diamond-shaped stud (Fig. 68).

Figure 65 Grave 30, headboard metalwork in grave

45

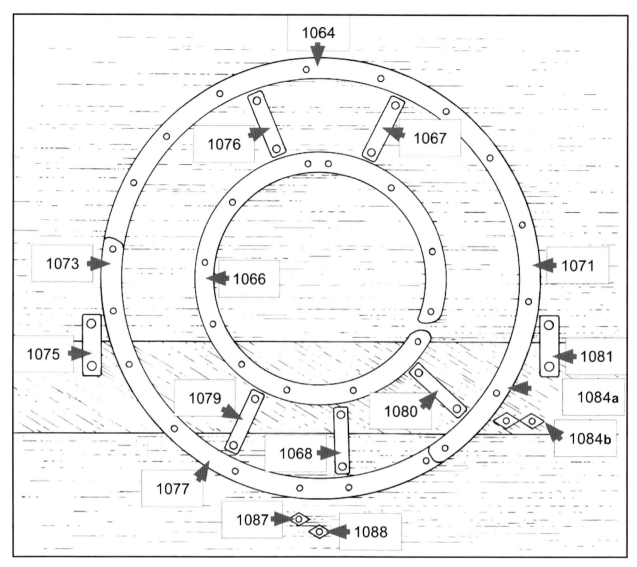

Figure 66 Grave 30, reconstruction of headboard, not to scale

1071   Iron strip, curved, with traces of rivets.

1076   Possible small cleat from between the rings. One fragment was originally attached to TLS ash, with the grain across the width of the strip.

1078   Iron strip, curved, fragmentary, about 40mm long.

1079   Iron strip, about 95–100mm long.

1080   Fragments of cleat, shown on field drawing to be positioned between the inner and outer rings. Attached to RLS. Its likely position indicated by the preserved wood grain is shown on headboard drawing (Figs 64–66).

1084a   Fragment of strip from the outer circle, about 170mm long and 16mm wide. Associated with studs 1084b, an eyelet 1084c and large rivet 1084d (see below).

1084b   Two diamond-shaped studs in different sizes, with broken shanks. The larger stud was attached to TLS.

1086   One plate of a possible cleat, shown on the field drawing to be positioned between the two circles. Attached to TLS at one end, and the wood at the other end is RLS with the grain in a different alignment. Although no join is visible, it seems likely that this cleat was positioned over the join between two boards that formed the headboard (Fig. 68).

1087   Four diamond-shaped studs, two shanks, c.21mm long, probably represents two rivets. Two of the heads were attached to TLS, one to a RLS, and one was uncertain. One of the nail shanks had wood with an oblique TLS, and could have joined either pair.

1088   Possible diamond-headed stud.

3. Side Rails
(Figs 69–72)

There are four side rails, A–D, two on each side, which appear to run the length of the bed and are presumed to be an upper and a lower rail. The iron strips were 20mm wide and attached to the wooden sides by rivets about 35mm long, the rails being about 28mm wide. There seem to be eighteen rivets on each side, possibly nine rivets associated with each rail and spaced at approximately 200mm intervals.

Right side rail A
With eight possible rivets used to attach the iron rail to the side of the bed.

1092a   Iron strip with wood preserved on one side and textile on the other. Associated with two rivets (and an eyelet 1092b, see below).

1144   Long iron strip with five rivets. Originally attached to TLS ash. Textile on other side (two rivets, c.28mm long).

1145   Lower part of rail with rivet. Rivet with circular head c.20mm diameter, and c.35mm overall. Fragments (not illustrated).

Right side rail B
With ten possible rivets used to attach the iron rail to the side of the bed.

1093   Long iron strip associated with eight rivets. One has a tapering shank 26–28mm long. Wood is preserved on one side with textile on the other. Strip originally attached to TLS. Also, what appears to be a piece of iron strip fused onto a large piece of flint

46

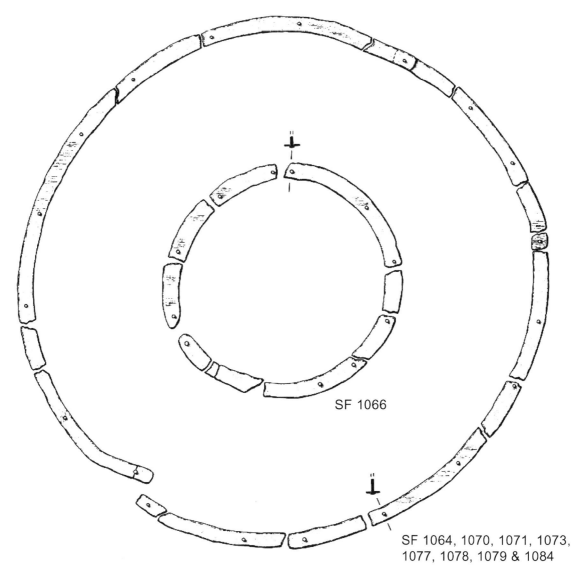

SF 1066

SF 1064, 1070, 1071, 1073,
1077, 1078, 1079 & 1084

Figure 67 Grave 30, headboard ironwork. Scale 1:4

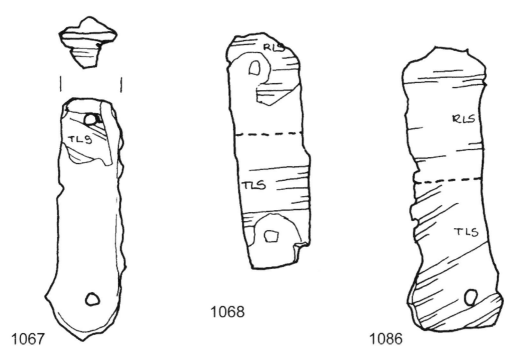

1067

1068

1086

Figure 68 Grave 30, grain detail on small brackets

with textile. Wood is crushed between the flint and iron, and textile is preserved on top.

1158 Fragment of iron strip, probably part of the rail, with degraded textile on one side and powdery corrosion on other.

1172 Fragments of rail and two/three broken rivets with small patches of mineral preserved wood (originally attached to TLS ash). On the other side are some fragments of mineral preserved textile, but too damaged to identify weave. Rivets give a minimum depth of wood as *c*.28mm. On one of the rivet-heads are the remains of a few mineral preserved threads.

1095 Iron stud, fragment, head *c*. 20mm diameter.

1103 Iron nail, fragment, *c*. 15mm long.

Left side rail C
With six rivets used to attach the rail to the side of the bed

1094 Iron strip with three rivets. Mineral preserved wood on one side indicates that the strip was originally attached to RLS. The rivets show that this edge was tapered and 19–22mm thick. Associated with a small fitting which appears to have some type of plaited cord wrapped round it.

1152 Iron strip, two fragments, 40mm long, 20mm wide.

1154 Fragments of iron rail (and a rivet). Wood is preserved on one side and textile on the other. (The rail was originally attached to RLS). There appear to be several layers of textile, possibly a 2/2 twill, overlain in some places by lines of 'plied' thread across the width of the rail — maybe a fringe.

1156 Fragment of rail with mineral preserved wood on one side and textile on the other.

1157 Rivet in fragments, probably from the side rail. The head was originally mounted on RLS.

1165 Iron rivet or nail, fragmentary, head diameter *c*. 25mm.

1176 Iron stud, *c*. 20mm long, head *c*. 20mm diameter. Found close to bracket 1107/1138.

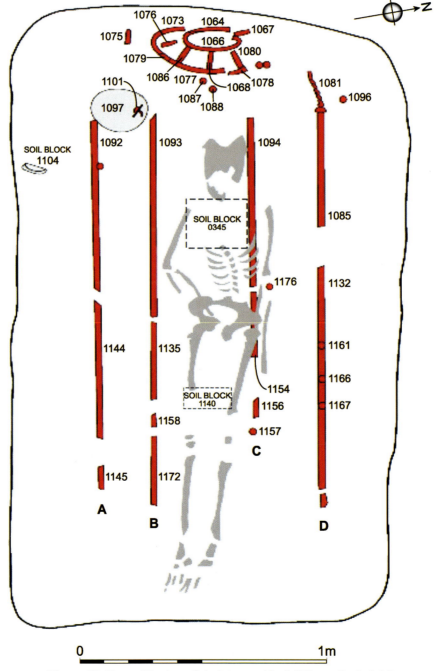

Figure 69 Grave 30, plan of skeleton and bed fittings. Scale 1:15

48

Left side rail D
Possibly twelve rivets used to attach the rail to the side of the bed.

1085a Wood preserved on one side and textile preserved on the other. There are three large rivets that attach the strap to the wooden side of the bed. The head is tapered so that the depth of wood is 23mm on one side and 30mm on the other. Associated with eyelet 1085b.

1096 Small group of fragments that could originally have been part of either upper or lower strip.

1132 Iron strip associated with a rivet. The rivet is badly damaged, but shank is c.20–26mm long. Strip originally attached to RLS.

(Three rivets: one at least is 34.6mm long and smallest 27mm). Fragments (not illustrated).

1150c Small fragment of iron rail with a complete rivet, shank c.24mm. long; the rail was originally attached to an oblique TLS (with two, possibly three, eyelets 1150a and b, in fragments).

1161 Diamond-headed stud with fragments of mineral preserved textile on head, but in a very poor condition. Rail originally attached to oblique TLS (not illustrated).

1166 Domed-headed rivet head, probably from the side rail (not illustrated).

1167 Broken rivet from side rail (not illustrated).

Right Side-rail A

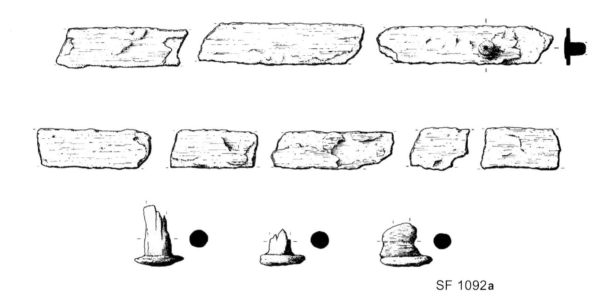

SF 1092**a**

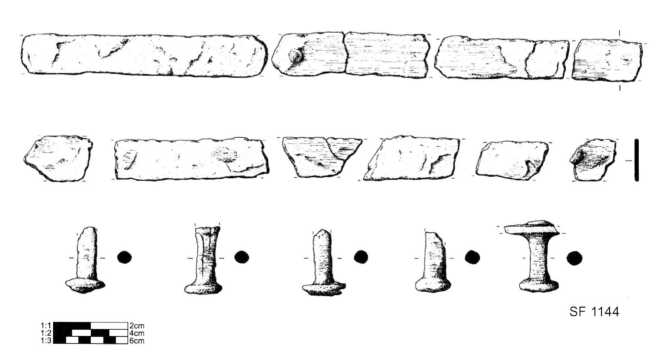

SF 1144

1:1 2cm
1:2 4cm
1:3 6cm

Figure 70 Grave 30, bedrail (RHS) outer. Scale 1:2

4. Eyelets or loop-headed spikes
(Figs 72–4)

Several eyelets, or loop-headed spikes, were originally mounted on wood that was initially presumed to be the sides of the bed, but they are in fact located around the bed (Fig. 73). There are around sixteen eyelets amongst the fragments of ironwork, but the positions of only twelve are recorded on the field drawing. On the south side, at least, they appear to be arranged in three pairs, with two pairs of eyelets at the head end and one pair below the feet. It has been assumed that the remaining eyelets mirror those *in situ*, to give three pairs on each side and two eyelets at each end.

All the eyelets appear to have been hammered into wood without the ends being turned over. They appear to have been fixed onto boards with a tangential surface

Right Side-rail B

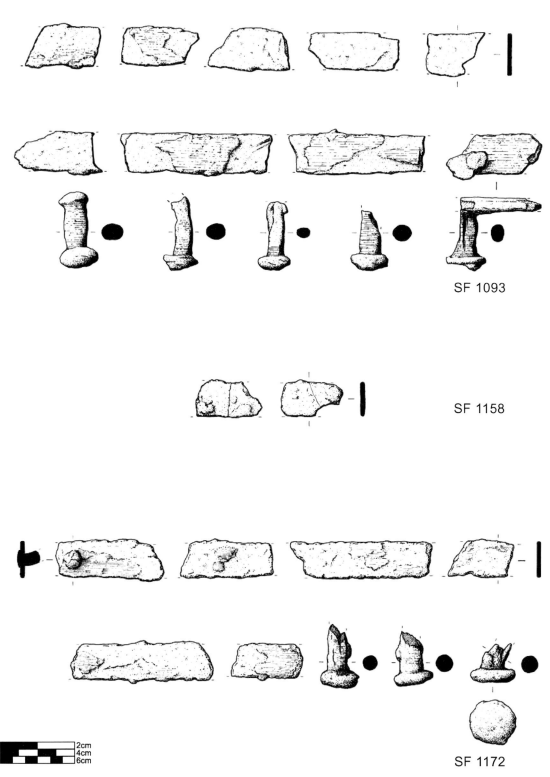

SF 1093

SF 1158

SF 1172

Figure 71 Grave 30, bedrail (RHS) inner, 1093 and 1172. Scale 1:2

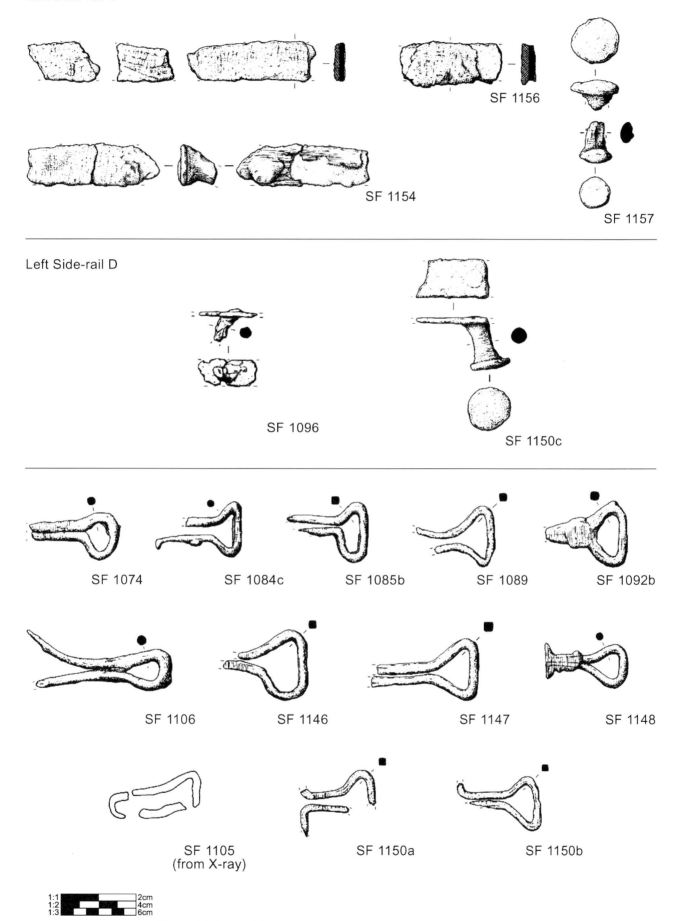

Left Side-rail C

SF 1156

SF 1154

SF 1157

Left Side-rail D

SF 1096

SF 1150c

SF 1074

SF 1084c

SF 1085b

SF 1089

SF 1092b

SF 1106

SF 1146

SF 1147

SF 1148

SF 1105
(from X-ray)

SF 1150a

SF 1150b

1:1   2cm
1:2   4cm
1:3   6cm

Figure 72 Grave 30, bedrail (LHS) inner, outer and eyelets Scale 1:2

(TLS), with the loops aligned with the grain — this means that if the loops were placed in a horizontal position, the planks they were attached to would have been placed horizontally within the grave, not vertically.

Only three of the loops have any organic remains preserved on them, probably strips of leather. The triangular loops also make them more appropriate for use with leather strapping, approximately 15–20mm wide, rather than cords or ropes.

The function of these eyelets is not clear, especially since the bed would appear to have been dismantled or collapsed, although a role to support a feather mattress has been suggested in other bed burials. The bed from Swallowcliffe Down, Wilts, had fourteen eyelets fixed in the sides of the bed and most of these have the remains of cords in the loops. In that case the eyelets were thought to have been used to suspend a wooden lattice-work panel from the sides of the bed and hold a mattress. One of the

beds from Barrington (grave 18), had eleven eyelets attached to the bed structure, positioned with the eyes upright on the sides and on the headboard. The remains of leather straps were found in the loops and these may have been used either to support a mattress or, less likely, to hold the body firmly in place while lowering into the grave.

At Coddenham the original alignments of the eyelets is not certain, but their positions allow them to be part of the bed, and this is the preferred interpretation [KJP]. However, the eyelets are not certainly part of the main bed structure, and could have been used to lower the bed sections into the grave.

1074   Eyelet found among the metalwork at headboard. Some mineral preserved organic material is preserved, wood with TLS on spike and possible traces of leather on inside of loop (Fig. 74).

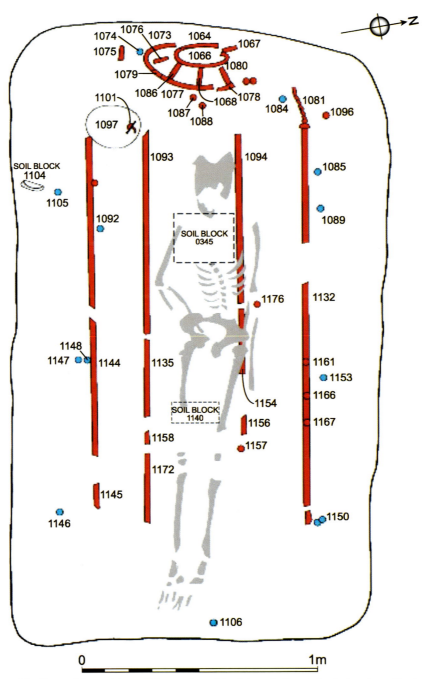

Figure 73 Grave 30, position of the eyelets (blue) in relation to bed structure. Scale 1:15

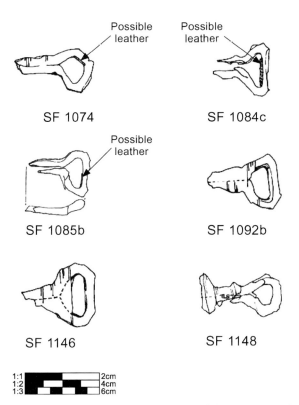

SF 1074 Possible leather

SF 1084c Possible leather

SF 1085b Possible leather

SF 1092b

SF 1146

SF 1148

1:1 | 2cm
1:2 | 4cm
1:3 | 6cm

Figure 74 Grave 30, organic material and traces of wood grain (TLS) present on the eyelets. Scale 1:2

1084c   Small eyelet associated with small studs 1084a, b and large rivet 1084d. Possible strip of leather c.17mm wide and c.1.5mm thick, in the flattened top of the loop (Fig. 74).

1085b   Eyelet found with pieces of side rail 1085a. Possible traces of leather in loop, but very indistinct. No wood remains on the spikes (Fig. 74).

1089   Eyelet.

1092b   Put into TLS, of a diffuse porous wood, and the depth of wood preserved is 28mm (Fig. 74). Part of side rail 1092a.

1105   Small eyelet with triangular loop, possibly even two broken ones.

1106   Large eyelet from centre bottom of grave. No organic material preserved on the loop or shank (Fig. 74).

1146   Eyelet put through TLS, probably ash. Terminals are broken, but it had been put in a piece of wood at least 32mm thick. No other organic material was preserved on the loop (Fig. 74).

1147   Eyelet on upper right side rail (1144) and next to 1148. No preserved organic material, but has long spikes so could have been mounted in a piece of wood over 30mm thick.

1148   Eyelet with a possible min. depth of wood as 25mm (Fig. 74). A smaller eyelet than 1147, but with folded over terminals. Wood on shank TLS.

1150a, b   Two/three eyelets in fragments. The most complete has no organic material preserved. The bottom of the spike is turned over indicating that this eyelet could have been put through a piece of wood c.30mm. Found with side rail 1150c.

1153   Small triangular-headed eyelet associated with a broken rivet with diamond-shaped head (not illustrated).

1189   One eyelet and a possible second. No organic material is preserved on either, but the most complete could have been attached to a piece of wood c.23mm in depth (not illustrated). Recovered from spoil (not planned).

5. Lines of large rivets across the grave
(Figs 75–6)

Large rivets were found in two lines at either end of the grave across its width. They appear to have been used to secure loose wooden tongues joining shaped boards together. There are eight rivets at the head end and eight at the foot (Fig. 76).The angles of the heads of these rivets

suggest that they held a curved structure, which overlay the burial. If a pair of rivets indicates the join between two boards, eight rivets would suggest that this structure was made from five boards running along the grave and held together with loose tenons. This structure was possibly associated with the two brackets 1107/1138 and 1137 found in the centre of the grave (see 6. Structural metalwork).

The apparent internal curvature is probably exaggerated because of the corrosion of the rivet-head. It would seem reasonable to assume that both sets of rivets are the two ends of the same structure, possibly representing either a curved grave cover or a canopy to the bed. The carpentry represented here resembles that identified on a group of silver-headed rivets preserving chunks of wood from the royal grave at Taplow, Bucks (British Museum display, Room 41).

Most of these rivets have one diamond-shaped head, the other circular, and where evident, it would appear that diamond heads were arranged on the concave, presumably inner surface of the 'cover'. These rivets may be identified as clench nails. For further discussion of these rivets as evidence of a boat, see Chapter 4.IV below. The grain alignment of the tenons indicates that small pieces of wood were used rather than pieces of wood the whole length of the cover.

Rivets from west end of grave

1081c   Large rivet (recorded with the headboard stay 1081a and the decorated cleat 1081b on the headboard). One terminal has a diamond-shaped head and the other is circular. The length of the shank is 61mm.

1082   Shank is 65mm long, with traces of mineral preserved wood with the grain across the shank.

1084d   The rivet is in many fragments, but has both diamond-shaped and circular heads and a shank of c.60mm. Under the circular head is a sliver of wood with TS next to the head, while the rest of the preserved wood has a TLS — probably this represents a small wedge of wood used to fill the space in a pre-drilled hole. Both pieces of wood are possibly ash. Associated with fragments of curved iron strip, two diamond-headed studs and a loop-headed eyelet 1084a–c.

1091   Several nail or rivet shanks with mineral preserved wood — the group probably represents two large rivets. Two of the shanks have evidence for loose tenons c.13–15mm thick. Bar with three spurs, broken.

1098   Circular-headed stud with a broken shank; it is unclear if this belongs with bottom side rail or is part of large rivet from roof/canopy. Head attached to RLS (not illustrated).

1099   Rivet with shank 56–60mm long, with traces of mineral preserved wood.

1102   Rivet with shank 59–62mm long and circular head. Associated with a fragment of tapering iron strip, oblique TLS ash on one side and a few threads of textile on the other. The strip is narrower than either the side rails or decorative ironwork on the headboard. Group found in copper alloy bowl (1).

Rivets from east end of grave

1133   Length of shank 65mm, but not enough wood preserved to know if it originally had a loose tenon (not illustrated).

1134   Complete rivet with both circular and diamond-shaped heads. The length of the shank is between 58–63mm, and the preserved wood has a TLS. There may be evidence for the remains of a loose tenon preserved on the shank.

1149   Complete rivet with circular and diamond-shaped heads, and the length of shank c.61mm. Originally attached to RLS. Possible evidence for loose tenon. Found in spoil, not planned.

1159   Round-headed rivet with broken shank, 22mm long. Originally attached to a piece of wood with RLS. Little wood preserved on shank.

1160   Diamond-headed rivet. The length of the shank is 70mm.

1162   Length of shank is 65mm.

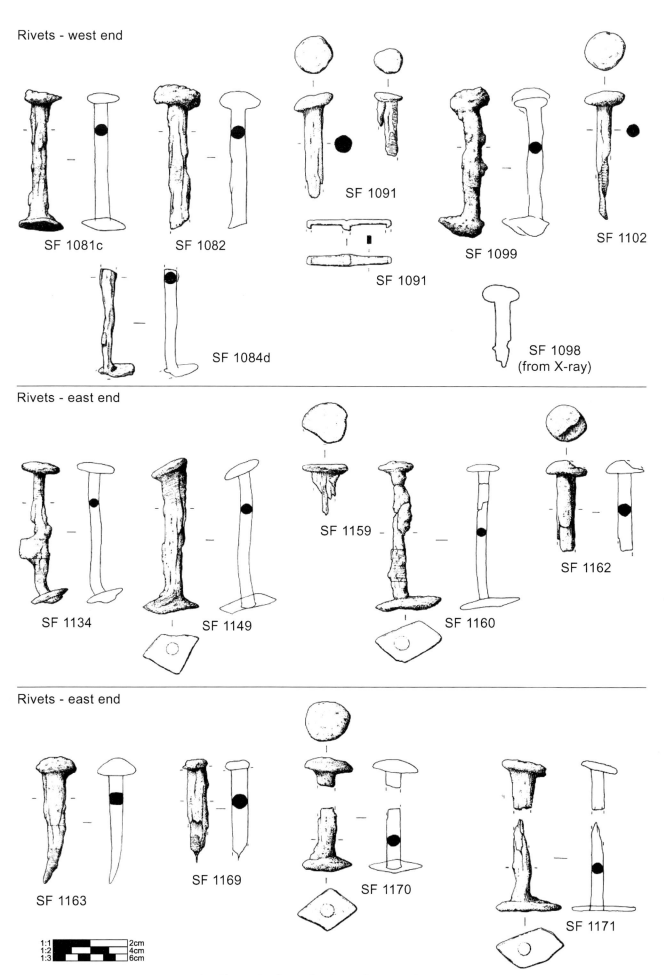

Rivets - west end

SF 1081c   SF 1082

SF 1091

SF 1091

SF 1099

SF 1102

SF 1084d

SF 1098
(from X-ray)

Rivets - east end

SF 1159

SF 1162

SF 1134   SF 1149   SF 1160

Rivets - east end

SF 1163   SF 1169   SF 1170   SF 1171

1:1
1:2
1:3
2cm
4cm
6cm

Figure 75 Grave 30, large rivets. Scale 1:2

1163 Nail with circular head and possible remains of loose tenon c.12.5mm.

1168 Circular end of large rivet (not illustrated).

1169? Broken rivet, only circular head and part of shank remains, c.51mm long. Possible trace of loose tenon at the lower end, with an oblique TLS visible.

1170 Fragmentary rivet, with two diamond-shaped heads. One of the heads has mineral preserved textile, but little more than a few threads. The same head was attached to TLS, and the wood was probably ash.

1171 Rivet, length of shank possibly 60mm. One side has a diamond-shaped head and the other is circular.

6. Structural metalwork
(Fig. 76)
Two large brackets, 1137 and 1107/1138, were positioned on top of the skeleton at the waist (see Fig. 76) and are not part of the bed structure, but are suggested to be brackets for carrying the cover. Two similar brackets were found in Grave 1 and were possibly used to attach pieces of wood to a grave cover to carry and manoeuvre it into position, either across the whole grave or just covering the body. Figure 60 illustrates the potential shape of this cover in Grave 30, with the associated fittings and how it might have related to the body.

1137 Large folded piece of iron sheet of uncertain use. The grave plan indicates that it was found on top of the skeleton's right arm, so it may have been attached to the a cover.

1107/ Large folded piece of iron sheet of uncertain use. The grave plan
1138 indicates that it was found on top of the skeleton's left arm, so it may have been attached to a grave cover (1138 is part of 1107).

These brackets and their measurements are discussed above in 4.II.

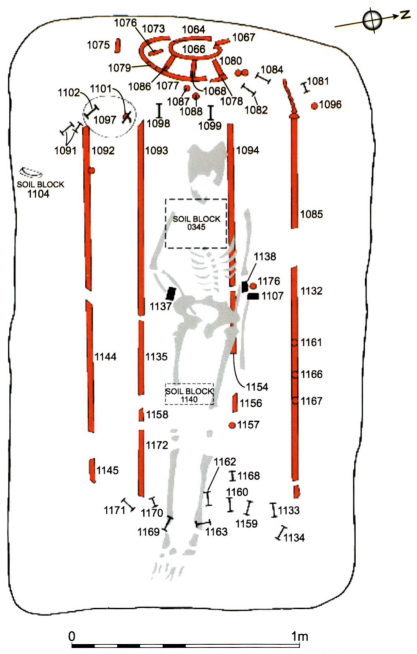

Figure 76 Grave 30, large rivets and brackets (black) in relation to bed structure. Scale 1:15

Discussion

(Fig. 77)

After examining all the iron fragments for organic remains and checking their relative depth within the grave cut it has become clear that the only way the sides of the bed could have reached their positions was if the bed had been dismantled for the burial, as suggested by Richard Darrah (pers. comm.). In this way the sides of the bed would be on display with the body placed centrally on top. The bed might have used tusked-tenon joints for the sides, as these can easily be dismantled and re-assembled when required (as used on Viking furniture including beds; Anon. 2005).

There was no direct evidence for a mattress, but textile remains were found on the iron rails near the skeleton, which suggests some sort of textile covering, found on all the side rails, square to the iron strips. The body was simply dressed, with the only metal dress fastenings being the buckles and strap-ends present on the shoes. Personal items, including an antler comb, copper-alloy bowl, jewellery and a purse, were arranged on and around the body. The two lines of large rivets/clench nails show that the burial was then covered with a curved wooden structure that might have extended the full width of the chamber or just been restricted to the bed, or even just the body. The levels of the large brackets, 1137 and 1107/1138, seem to suggest that they were mounted on top of this structure, possibly to carry poles that could be used to manoeuvre the cover into position.

The limited amount of wood preserved on the ironwork of the bed means that only the simplest reconstruction can be made, and one has to bear in mind that the original may have been highly decorated with intricate carving or even painted. The evidence is slight, but could suggest a leather covering to the headboard, with the ironwork above. In manuscripts of a later date (Hoffman 1983), beds are depicted with carved sides and drapery. There were also textile remains on the headboard and footboard studs.

The construction of beds with the headboard fixed at an angle of 100° to the horizontal plane of the bed appears to be a common feature of the Anglo-Saxon beds found in England, for example those from Barrington, Cambs (Malim and Hines 1998), and Swallowcliffe Down, Wiltshire (Speake 1989). Speake notes that Scandinavian examples have headboards in the same position, but without the support of an iron headboard stay. The construction of the English beds is unlike the construction of the cot-like furnishings in the Merovingian graves from Oberflact, South Germany (Paulsen 1992), where the sides have been made from lathe-turned spindles with no associated metalwork.

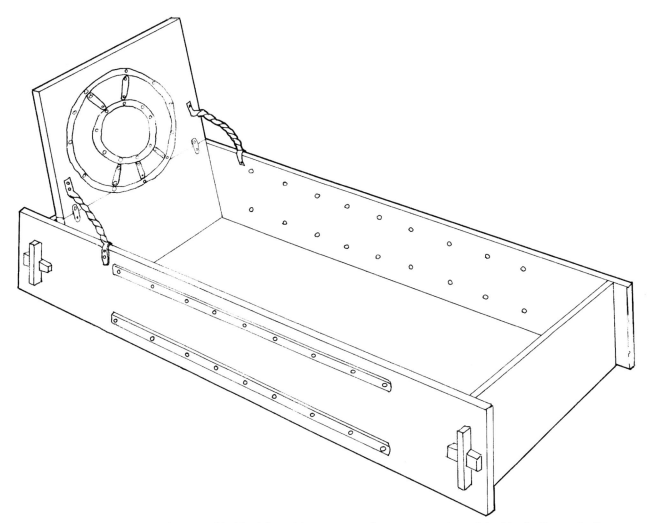

Figure 77 Grave 30, the assembled bed (based in part upon the reconstruction of the Shudy Camps bed)

IV. The grave structures: a discussion
by Kenneth Penn

Reconstructions of the grave structures in Graves 1 and 30 have already been published in *English Heritage Research News* (Watson 2005–6) and featured on BBC TV's *Hidden Treasures* series. The corroded and confused nature of the remains allows some differences in interpretation, especially with regard to the eyelets, which are considered here (KJP) to have been part of the bed's structure, as observed in bed burials elsewhere, rather than attached to the chamber walls.

Both Graves 1 and 30 appear to have been burials in a wooden chamber, and both were probably originally roofed, although no evidence survived and the existence of a putative cover could be argued to indicate the lack of a roof (see below). Chamber graves are rare, usually associated with high-status burials, for example, the 'princely burial' at Prittlewell, Essex (Blair *et al.* 2004), and often with barrows, as in Grave 1 at Coddenham. At Prittlewell, the burial chamber or grave lining was very large, 4m by 4m, in a pit 1.4m deep, and contained the burial in a coffin (or perhaps on a bed) but with no roof (Blair *et al.* 2004). In Grave 1 at Coddenham a shallow slot along the south and east sides (and along part of the north side) may have been for the 'walls' of a wooden structure like that found at Prittlewell, about 1m or more wide, but with no sign of a coffin. Instead, the positions of the shield boss and board mounts suggest some movement within a void, and may also point to the shield being placed against a wooden side wall.

Both Graves 1 and 30 had pairs of large iron brackets near their centres, possibly associated with a canopy or roof, perhaps to secure or locate carrying poles. The discovery of brackets in both Grave 1 (no bed) and Grave 30 (bed) points to these being connected to the chamber or some other structure, perhaps a canopy above the burial, rather than a bed. In Grave 1, the two iron brackets (SF 1035) should be compared with the brackets from Lapwing Hill, Derbyshire, which were part of a bed burial found in the early 19th century (Speake 1989, 104, fig. 87). The record is imperfect, and the schematic grave plan shows nine eyelets spaced around the body. The positions of the two (or possibly four) brackets are not known since they were drawn later, but Speake has suggested they were either corner fixings or fixtures to contain carrying poles, 'with openings *c.* 40mm tapering to *c.* 24mm (Speake 1989, 104–5). In Grave 30, wood remains found in Soil Block 0345, above the chest, were parallel with the bed and must be from a cover or roof.

At Spong Hill, Norfolk, neither of the two chamber graves had metal fixings. Grave 31 was very large, about 3m by 2m and 1.2m deep, containing a wooden chamber 2.1m by 1.1m, clearly retained by the grave filling. Grave 31 had been robbed in antiquity and the chamber collapsed. In grave 40, the chamber was larger, 2.4m by 1.3m, and neatly fitted the grave. The grave appeared to have planks on the floor, and a roof or other framework with turf above (Hills *et al.* 1984, 80, 93, figs 40, 49).

Hills, in discussion of graves 31 and 40 at Spong Hill, Norfolk, noted a lack of clear records of chambers in English graves, although the evidence from several rich graves suggested that chambers may have existed: Taplow, Bucks, Broomfield, Essex and Asthall, Oxon (Hills *et al.* 1984, 172–3). She noted that on the continent, chamber graves were widespread in the 6th and early 7th century, and as with Spong Hill graves 31 and 40, most recorded structures had no iron fixings, but were presumably pegged or jointed.

Since 1984, O'Brien (1999) has added a little to this list, and included some possible examples, her certain examples being a short list of mostly high-status sites which include Benty Grange, Derbyshire, Boss Hall grave 74 and Buttermarket, Ipswich. Another possible example is the large box or coffin that housed a double burial in grave 19 at Harford Farm, Norfolk, although this was smaller than the grave itself and therefore could be described as a double coffin (Penn 2000). Like the two Spong Hill graves, Boss Hall grave 74 and a possible example at Bergh Apton (grave 71) (Green and Rogerson 1978) belong to the 6th century, whilst others are 7th century.

Boss Hall grave 74 is a true chamber grave, in that it was a large grave 1.5m by 1.8m with timber planking around the edge of the grave on two sides, enclosing one or more burials, at least one a weapon burial, but also with no floor or roof/lid (Scull 2009, 13–15, fig. 2.5). Boss Hall grave 51 was similar, with a wooden lining but no floor, roof or lid. At Buttermarket, Ipswich, although forty-five of seventy-one graves had evidence for a wooden lining or container, only two were large enough to be called chambers rather than coffins. These were grave 2203, a chamber 1.0m by 1.90m (containing a coffin) and grave 2339, a chamber 0.60m by 1.10m (Scull 2009, figs 3.10 and 3.12).

A chamber grave was also found in Mound 14 at Sutton Hoo, with a bed burial in a wooden chamber or timber-lined grave, formed of individual upright planks. The grave had been robbed, but was presumed to be that of a high-status woman on a bed or coffin (Carver 2005, 107, fig. 46). Burial 16 was of a possible female in a 'box bed' or coffin with a lid rather than a chamber (Carver 2005, 143).

In the Merovingian area on the continent, chamber graves are concentrated along the valleys of the Meuse and Moselle, and in great numbers; they date from the 6th century and on into the 7th century, and the later burials are often less well-furnished than the earlier ones. The coincidence of barrows and chambered graves is striking, and they were possibly a single phenomenon. An example is the cemetery at Basel-Bernerring, where, of some forty graves, ten were large wooden chambers and three were under barrows (James 1988, 115–6).

Bed burials
In his review of the 'bed-burial phenomenon' in England, Speake identified seven certain examples of bed burial (Speake 1989), but recent years have added several others, including Barrington graves 18B and 60, and Coddenham Grave 30.

According to Speake (1989, 98), 'the custom of bed burial was a phenomenon in the 7th century that has not been given due recognition in archaeological literature'. There are now over a dozen examples of Anglo-Saxon bed burials known in England. These have been excavated at various times and identification of the remains as beds is not always certain: for example, the possibility that the body in the Sutton Hoo ship burial was on a bed has been much aired, but it may be that the remains are those of the 'planked framework of a cart or wagon', rather than a bed (Speake 1989, 111).

The Coddenham bed burial appears quite elaborate, with not only headboard and reinforced sides, but possibly a canopy, evidenced by two brackets (Fig. 77). The metalwork that forms beds is often quite distinctive and includes constructional elements such as eyelets (for leather straps?), cleats, and headboard struts (often twisted), as well as decorative elements such as the complex headboard found in Coddenham Grave 30 (Malim and Hines 1998, 267).

In the discussion of Barrington grave 18B, it was noted that headboard stays were then only paralleled in beds in the Cambridge area: Barrington grave 18B; Cherry Hinton; Shudy Camps; Burwell (Malim and Hines 1998, 267). Coddenham Grave 30 could perhaps be seen as an outlier of this distribution, but recent finds also include Collingbourne Ducis, Wilts and Loftus, N. Yorks (below), and this feature now has a very wide distribution.

Like Speake, Malim and Hines also saw a contrast with continental bed burials, where Merovingian-period beds were of turned wood, and suggested instead that the English examples were related to Scandinavian tradition, although this rested upon the single example of the rich burial at Högom, Sweden (Malim and Hines 1998, 267). As to date, Malim and Hines note that the English bed burials all appear to be 7th-century and the practice 'a rare one', used primarily, perhaps solely, for female burials (Malim and Hines 1998, 67).

In Wiltshire, at Collingbourne Ducis, further excavations on the site of the known cemetery recovered burials of 6th/7th-century date. Amongst these was a bed burial, thought to be 7th-century, of an adult woman aged 45 or more, whose sole surviving accompaniment was a pot. The fittings on the bed allow it to be reconstructed, with a pair of twisted headboard stays, cleats along the sides of the bed, to hold two boards together and perhaps eyelets within the sides (http://www.wessexarch.co.uk; accessed 06/02/2009).

The most recent discovery is that at Street House Farm, Loftus, North Yorkshire, where a remarkable cemetery of 109 graves contained an unusual arrangement of paired burials in a square around a bed burial (grave 42). This burial was that of a woman and was richly furnished. Of the 109 burials, five had gold and silver objects of 7th-century date. The bed in grave 42 was c.1.8m by 0.80m with an inclined headboard attached by two twisted iron stays. The two sides were each made from two boards, held together by decorative cleats. At the foot end, each corner appeared to have large U-shaped fixings or staples, like those in Coddenham Grave 1, but considered too flimsy for a carrying pole (Sherlock 2008; Simmons forthcoming).

Bed burial appears a widespread practice, found in South/East Anglia, Wilts/Dorset, with outliers in Derbyshire and the north, but with no example yet found in Kent (Speake 1989, 110). Bed burials seem to be a 7th-century phenomenon, mostly associated with 'rich' burials, often under a barrow, but without a barrow in the case of Grave 30 at Coddenham. Adults, possibly all females, and children could be accorded bed-burial, but the evidence points to a high status for almost all of them.

A 'pseudo-boat-burial'?

If the putative cover of the bed burial in Grave 30 was fixed with unused clench nails, the choice of such rivets may have been a practical choice of what was available, and no 'maritime' signal may have been intended, although the availability of these nails itself may raise questions about boat building locally. It should be noted that clench nails have been used for furniture, especially doors, although they would not normally be curved structures (R. Darrah pers.comm.).

It has been suggested that what is identified as a curved cover may be the remains of a boat and that the use of clench nails helps lead to this identification, especially since they are usually used to bring together two pieces of wood very tightly and they are long enough (c. 65mm shanks) to join two quite thick boards, a measurement that would indicate a sea-going craft (Stuart Brookes pers. comm.).

	Certain/ uncertain	Sex/age	Associated objects
Coddenham, Suffolk, Grave 30	C	F	Coins, bowl, comb, purse, pendant, toilet sets
Swallowcliffe Down, Wilts	C	F	Satchel, comb, silver brooches
Collingbourne Ducis, Wilts	C	F 45+	Pot
War Ditches, Cherry Hinton, Cambs, Grave 4	C	10–12	Unfurnished
Ixworth, Suffolk (West 1998, fig. 127 sub Stanton Misc.)	C	F	Gold/garnet pendant cross, disc brooch
Shudy Camps, Cambs Grave 29	C	?M	-
Lapwing Hill, Brushfield, Derbyshire	C	?	Weapons (?)
Winklebury Hill, Wilts, Grave 9	?	?	Disturbed. Satchel?
Woodyates, Pentridge, Wilts	?	F	Beads
Roundway Down, Wilts	?	F	Gold chain, pin, beads
Shudy Camps, Cambs Grave 24	?	?F, young	Gold and glass bead pendant
Barrington, Cambs, Grave 18B	C	F17–25 and C. 3	Weaving batten, comb, knives, key, 2 silver necklace rings, spindlewhorl, wooden vessel/box?
Barrington, Cambs, Grave 60	?	F25–32	Brooches, knife, silver ring, stud, chain links, pin
Sutton Hoo, Suffolk, Mound 14	?	?F	Robbed (purse, chatelaine, iron-bound tub)
Sutton Hoo, Suffolk, Burial 16	?	?F	Knife, chatelaine, pin, bead, bag?
Galley Low, Derbyshire	?		(Geake 1997, 149)
Street House, Loftus, N Yorks	C	F	Beads, gold/garnet jewellery, pendants

Table 1 Bed burials in England

Identification of this curved structure as part or parts of a clinker-built boat is attractive, especially given the form of the rivets, with round heads and lozengiform roves (as found at Sutton Hoo). At the head end, the line of eight rivets was *c*. 1.1m long, at the foot, a line of eight rivets *c*. 0.70m long, with the two brackets about midway between the lines. On the Sutton Hoo ship the strakes between the frames were held together by clench nails, found every 100–150mm apart, and in Grave 30 they were a similar distance apart. At Sutton Hoo, however, the ship was of oak, whereas the Grave 30 structure was of ash.

Nonetheless, it is worth recalling the variety of 'pseudo-boat-burials' recorded at Caister-on-Sea, Norfolk, where thirteen graves of 8th-century date each contained between two and thirty-seven clench nails, mostly placed above the body in rows, which were thought to represent recycled boat timbers used as coffin covers, or even as 'grave-goods' rather than as lids (Brookes 2007, 3–5, 7; Darling with Gurney 1993). At Caister, the clench nails were mostly 30–40mm long, with square shanks (Darling with Gurney 1993, 52–3). It should be noted that in wooden structures, clench nails become distorted in fixing and would break upon removal, so the nails themselves could not be recycled.

Against the idea of a boat being recycled is the fact that the wood here is ash, whereas boats are generally of oak. Also, there is no evidence of caulking or other form of waterproofing, such as hair. There is evidence for loose tongues or tenons fixing the boards together, which are more appropriate for furniture than boats. The clench nails appear to be organised in pairs either side of a join, whereas in clinker construction the nails are usually arranged in single lines and would be found more frequently spaced along the length of the grave rather than a group clustered at each end (J.Watson and R.Darrah pers. comm).

However, if part of a boat was used to cover the grave, as suggested by Stuart Brookes (pers. comm.), then some deliberate signal may have been intended. In the case of the Kentish 6th and early 7th-century examples of 'pseudo-boat-burials', these are argued to have indicated a link to maritime heritage 'imbued with... spiritual significance', and more widely, a resistance to Frankish overlordship and Christian culture, later becoming part of Christian iconography (Brookes 2007, 15).

It may be noted that one of the Kentish examples (or an adjacent grave), at Thorne Farm, Minster, probably contained a looped pendant of an imitation Frankish solidus (Perkins 1985).

If Grave 30 can be dated to around the 660s, then it was a generation or so later than the ship burials at Sutton Hoo in Mounds 1 and 2. At this date in the mid or later 7th century, a Nordic anti-Christian alignment may be unlikely.

	1	2	3	5	6	7	8	9	11	13	14	16	19	24	25	26	30	32	35	38	40	44	45	46	47	48	50
Roman coin																	1										
Anglo-Saxon coin							3										1										
Coin/pendant																	1									1	
Seax	1																										
Seax sheath mount	1																										
Shield boss	1													1													
Shield grip	1													1													
Shield mount	4													3													
?Arrowhead																		1									
Fauchard																1											
Bead					2		3					1					32			2		4					
Brooch									2								2										
Pendant																											
Necklace ring							1					1					6			1		1					
Finger ring							?										1										
Pot														1			1		1	1							
Bowl	1													1			1										
Bucket	1																										
Drinking horn? (repair)	1																										
Knife	1		1	1		1	1	1		1		1	1	1	1	1	1	1			1		1	1	1	1	1
Buckle	2	2	1	1			1	1		1			1	1	1	1	2			2	2		1	1		2	
Latch-lifter																	1			1		1			1		
Sharpening steel	1		1	1			1							1			?								1		
Point/awl				2							1											1					1
Tool																	3										
Box fitting?																	1										
Purse fitting?							1	1									1										
Comb							1							1			1										
Toilet set																	2										
Ring and links	1																1										
strap-end																	2										
?							1	1									2										1
Bed fittings																	1										
Bracket (canopy?)	2																3										

Table 2 Grave-goods

Chapter 5. The Grave-goods

I. Coins and coin pendant

Graves 8 and 30 each produced three coins; all appear to have been amongst the contents of bags or purses.

Grave 8
5c (SF1210c) Anglo-Saxon coin
8 (SF 1201) Anglo-Saxon coin
9 (SF 1202) Anglo-Saxon coin

Grave 30
3a (SF1225) Solidus of Dagobert I (629–639), mounted on a loop
9e (SF 1140d) Roman coin
9f (SF 1142) Anglo-Saxon coin

Roman coin in Grave 30

In Grave 30, soil block 1140 contained a collection of objects, possibly in a bag, including a sceat and a Roman coin (9e; SF 1140d). This has been identified by Dr Adrian Marsden of Norfolk Museums and Archaeology Service as a coin of Valens, possibly Valentinian I.

Roman coins are common objects in Anglo-Saxon graves of the 6th and 7th centuries, mostly in graves of women, and are found in most cases as single examples. They may have been ornamental or had an amuletic use (White 1988, 163). Meaney (1981, 216) noted an increase in unperforated Roman coins in Christian-period graves, and these included Roman coins at Burwell grave 24 (two at the neck), grave 7 (at the hip), and Shudy Camps grave 11 (with glass fragment by the knees). Other examples, probably with other objects in bags or other containers, were possibly kept as a curiosity or charm (Meaney 1981, 216). Such objects may represent chance finds, especially with a Roman site near to hand, and became part of female bag collections rather than hung on the body.

Coin pendant in Grave 30

Besides the Roman coin, Grave 30 contained a coin pendant (3a; SF 1225), with a solidus of Dagobert I (629–639), from the mint of Arles, on a suspension loop of corrugated gold sheet, which was decorated with a strip of beaded wire, soldered on. This was found as part of a group of objects at the chest, along with a necklace and two toilet sets.

In Geake's sample of twenty-three graves with coins, fourteen contained twenty Roman coins altogether, four of which were pierced or mounted, whilst the other nine graves had twenty-seven coins altogether of 7th- to 9th-century date, six of which were pierced or mounted (Geake 1997, 32).

Gold coins, nearly all found mounted for suspension, are familiar objects in Kentish graves, and are sometimes seen as evidence of strong Frankish influence at the Kentish court. Amongst these objects may be counted the looped imitation solidus from Thorne Farm, Minster, Kent, possibly from a 'pseudo-boat-burial' (Perkins 1985), the four Merovingian gold coins of late 6th-century date, mounted on loops, contained in the Canterbury St Martin's 'hoard' and six coin pendants from Faversham, Kent (Webster and Backhouse 1991, 24). Archibald

(1995) points to other coin pendants from Kent (a looped solidus of Sigebert III (634–56) in Finglesham grave 7, and another at St Peter's, Broadstairs), and Buckland, Dover grave 110 had two looped Pada thrymsas.

Outside Kent, examples come from Rainham, Essex, Boar's Hill, Oxford, and Balderton, Notts (Perkins 1985), whilst a pierced bronze imitation of a Vanimundus tremissis comes from Lechlade, Glos (grave 179) (Boyle *et al.* 1998, 130).

The potential importance of continental coins as dating evidence in graves has been stressed by Evison (1987, 63), who highlighted three other instances from Kent: Gilton grave 41 with a coin of AD 585; Sarre with 'Coptic' bowl and four coin pendants, the latest of Chlotar II *c.*AD 620; and Sibertswold grave 172 with coins of the later 7th century.

However, these coins often appear to have already been old when converted into a pendant and then buried, and can be no true guide to date of burial. Instead, the use of Frankish coins as pendants may be part of the later 7th-century accessory suite, and may be part of a more deliberate 'Romanising' effort, rather than Frankish influence, and also reflect access to these items across England.

East Anglian grave-finds are few: at Buttermarket, Ipswich, grave 4275 contained two counterfeit coins, each a late tremissis mounted as a pendant, and the late 7th-century grave at Boss Hall, besides four looped scutiform gold pendants, contained a gold coin of Sigebert III, once mounted for suspension as a pendant (loop now missing) and a Series B sceat (Scull 2009).

Several other coin pendants are known from East Anglia, all of them stray finds: a garnet-framed copy of a solidus of Emperor Maurice (AD 582–602) from Bacton, Norfolk (Speake 1970); the Wilton cross from south-west Norfolk, where an early 7th-century solidus of the Emperor Heraclius (AD 611–641) is fixed in a gold and garnet cruciform frame (Webster and Backhouse 1991, 27–8); a pendant with coin of Emperor Honorius (AD 393–423) from Bromeswell, Suffolk (BML 009); a Gallic tremissis from Bloodmoor Hill, Gisleham, Suffolk (Newman 1996); and a tremissis of Bishop Aditus II (AD 674–689) mounted as a pendant, from Bawdsey, Suffolk (BAW 053; Plunkett 2001, 73), which evidences coins being mounted late in the 7th century. An unmounted Merovingian 7th-century gold tremissis has been recorded from Sudbourne, Suffolk (PAS Annual Report 2004, 54: PAS SF-F8EA61), whilst two Merovingian gold tremisses (both unmounted) have been found with the Prittlewell 'princely burial' in Essex (Blair *et al.* 2004).

It is not impossible that these coins advertise some Frankish connection, real or desired, although this may have been weaker in the later 7th century. It has been noted, however, that in many cases the cross in the design is often prominently displayed, rather than the head side, and Meaney argued that these coins were worn as 'specifically Christian amulets' (Meaney 1981, 201). Like the solidus from Boss Hall, the Coddenham coin had a cross in its design and a loop placed so that the cross was visible to the wearer as an upright cross, perhaps a visible sign of the wearer's religious allegiance.

The Anglo-Saxon sceattas in Graves 8 and 30
by Michael Metcalf

Two graves of females produced coins: Grave 8 with three Anglo-Saxon coins in a bag or purse, the burial with knife, buckle, comb and beads; Grave 30, the bed burial, with two bronze vessels, beads, Roman coin and coin pendant, silver toilet sets, and a single Anglo-Saxon coin.

Grave 8

8 (SF 1201)	Primary sceatta, Series B, and of the scarce variety BI,G; *c*.AD 700x710; 1.00gm. This coin, which shows the bird laterally reversed, is from the same dies as a coin in the King's Lynn grave find. The obverse is certainly from the same hand as the three specimens known to Rigold, of which one was in the Broadstairs grave find (Rigold 1960). Another specimen of BI,G has since come to light at Clacton (Coin Register 1990, no. 169, 1.20g), and a die-duplicate of the same at Ely (Coin Register 1999, no. 52, 1.03g).
5c (SF 1210c)	Primary sceatta, Series A, very sharply struck and in fresh condition. Die Rigold, A2, 5; weight 1.28g. Possibly early in Series A, perhaps even in the 680s.
9 (SF 1202)	Primary sceatta, Series B, variety BIB (*i.e.* with bust rather than head); *c*.AD 685–70. The reverse has an annulet near the left and right hand limbs of the cross, and also pellets in the two lower angles, cf. BIB, 7–9, but different dies. The reverse legend, beginning from 6 o'clock, is clear because of the off-centre striking, and reads ·· ËVNVM (as on BIA, 10 and BIC, 1–2, but not recorded by Rigold in BIB; Rigold 1960; 1966). There is another specimen of BIB, 7–8 from Coddenham, site CDD 022.

The Broadstairs grave find (and that from Finglesham) are among the earliest in the sequence published by Rigold (1960; 1966). The dating effectively rules out the possibility that BI,G is from the tail-end of the issues of the (East Saxon?) mint which produced Series B. The crude and distinctive style of the bust points to BI,G being imitative. Its place of origin, in so far as one can guess at it from the five provenances now on record, would seem to be English, and probably not too far from Essex or Suffolk. The probable date of BI,G is a few years earlier than the Aston Rowant hoard, say *c*.AD 700 x 710 (Archibald 1975, 87, no. 347; Rigold and Metcalf 1984, 246).

Graves with three coins are very rare, Ozengell, Kent being one of few known examples (over which there is some uncertainty) (Rigold 1960; Metcalf 1984). This example comprised two sceattas in a purse, possibly of Series B (an antiquarian find, not described) with a Byzantine gold coin of Justinian I or II (Metcalf 1984).

Grave finds with just two coins are known from Buckland, Dover grave 110 (two pale gold thrymsas of Pada), Buttermarket, Ipswich grave 1356 (two sceattas of Pada), and grave 4275 (two sceattas of Pada), and Sarre (two sceattas of Pada). From Boss Hall, Ipswich grave 93, came a gold solidus of Sigebert III and a sceat of Series B. The slightly later practice of including eight sceattas with a burial may possibly reflect the valuation of four pennies to a shilling.

Grave 30

9f (SF 1142)	Anglo-Saxon sceat. The coin is so indistinct that it is not even obvious to what series of sceattas it might belong. The metal is very coppery, whereas early 8th-century sceattas ought to be of good silver. One would guess that (like the Lechlade Vanimundus grave-find from grave 179

(7th-century date, female) (Metcalf 1993, 84; Boyle *et al.* 1998, 130) it is a base-metal replica, good enough for funerary use — rather than a regular coin from a period when general debasement had gone to the extreme, *e.g.* from the 740s or 750s. One can make out a crosslet in the outer circle of legend, at the 12 o'clock position, above what looks like the top half of a facing head.

A base-metal copy may be of essentially the same date as its prototype, with current ideas placing the beginnings of Series A and B some way after AD 660, but the radio-carbon date of AD 600–660 (95% confidence) for Grave 30 is very early, there being a gap between the two ranges.

II. Weapons

Coddenham produced what may be weapons from Graves 1, 2, 24, 32, 48 and possibly 26. Some of these objects may have been 'display pieces' or tools rather than functional weapons (especially given the silver mounts on the shield in Grave 1), and the two seaxes were possibly hunting knives (Gale 1989, 80).

	1	2	24	26	32	48
Seax	*					*
Shield	*		*			
Spear/arrow	*	*	*		*	
fauchard				*		

Table 3 Weapons in graves

Seaxes in Graves 1 and 48

Coddenham produced two seaxes, from Graves 1 and 48; both weapons are typical of Böhner's 'broad type', and both have short tangs, for a single-handed grip (Böhner 1958; Geake 1997, table 4.14).

The seax is a Frankish weapon, found in 6th- and 7th-century graves on the continent but only in 7th-century graves in England, and it may be significant that both Coddenham seaxes were associated with other possible continental objects. Seaxes in English graves are usually light weapons and may be hunting knives, rather than offensive weapons (Evison 1961, 278; Gale 1989, 80). The seax in Grave 1 has a sheath stud, of continental type, besides a spear and shield, iron-bound tub and bronze bowl. The weapon in Grave 48 was buried with a large Frankish belt buckle, knife and steel.

Grave 1
The seax in Grave 1 was 475mm long overall (blade 340mm) and 50mm broad, with traces of a grip of horn and a sheath (and a sheath stud). Its shape, straight edges converging to the point, is consistent with Evison's knife Type 4, of 7th-century date (Evison 1987, 113). The sheath was of leather, probably sealed at the blade edge with decorated studs, of which one survives.

Besides the seax itself, Grave 1 contained a single seax stud, that is, a circular stud used to hold together the edges of, and decorate, the leather sheath. These were usually in sets of five or six, running down one edge of the sheath. The Coddenham example was a single find and is 'flat' in section. Sheaths or studs of this kind are usually associated with larger weapons, commonly with 'broad' forms between 40mm and 60mm wide (Coddenham 50mm).

The Coddenham stud, with a simple triskele design, may be compared with the four more elaborate studs from the Tattershall Thorpe grave, dated to *c*.AD 640–670 (Hinton 2000, 58). In Hinton (2000), Scull discusses such studs and notes that they are found in England at Tattershall Thorpe and at Buttermarket, Ipswich (grave 1306). The Buttermarket examples are circular 'boxes' in section, and bear a bipartite design in Style I.

Scull noted that leather seax sheaths with decorative studs are quite widely found on the continent, but very rare in England; the example from Buttermarket grave 1306 forms part of an assemblage more at home on the Continent than in England: 'the weight of the evidence strongly suggests that the seax and sheath…are from the Continent' (Scull 2009, 252).

On the continent, the chronology of such studs has been studied by Nieveler and Siegmund; the Coddenham stud appears to be a simpler version of their type 4.2 which came into use in Niederrhein Phase 8B to 9, which together span the period 610 to 670 (Nieveler and Siegmund 1999). Continental examples are also figured by MacGregor, who shows an example from Andernach (undated): a discoid head cast with a triskele incised with three lines (MacGregor 1997, 98, no. 48.7).

At Southampton, six seaxes were found in the recently-excavated cemetery, including two broad seaxes. Graves 3520 and 5352 also contained seax studs. These bear triskele 'knots' like Coddenham and are also argued to be of continental origin and late 7th to early 8th century in date (Birbeck *et al.* 2005, 59–60, figs 13–4).

The studs at Southampton and Ipswich are from essentially coastal sites, whilst Tattershall Thorpe lies on the River Witham between Boston and Lincoln, and may have been an inland port. Coddenham too, may be regarded as the Ipswich hinterland. The decorated shield boss in Grave 1 may be a display piece, and the same may be true of this elaborate seax.

Grave 48

The seax in Grave 48 was shorter, 390mm overall (blade 270mm) and 45mm broad, with traces of a horn grip and leather sheath. It may also fall into Evison's knife Type 4. This was buried with a large Frankish inlaid buckle for a sword belt (?), a knife and a steel, and two small iron mounts, associated with horn.

In England the seax belongs to the 7th century, many in the later half, at a time when there was a reduction in other weapons (Evison 1987, 31; Meaney and Hawkes 1970, 43), and some cemeteries seem to have little other than seaxes; broader seaxes date to the turn of the 7th and 8th centuries. In her study of conversion-period burials, Geake noted thirty-six examples, always found singly; of these nine were of the 'broad' variety, seven were associated with a vessel and fourteen with other weapons (Geake 1997, 14).

Spears in Graves 1, 2, 24 and 32

As one might expect of a late 7th- to early 8th-century cemetery, there were few weapons, and just four graves contained spears, two of which were small enough to count as arrowheads (Graves 24 and 32). A recent analysis of spearheads from 6th-century graves (mostly) in East Anglia, based on shape, suggests that there were no distinct 'types', but a continuum of shapes, although certain shapes and sizes had greater currency at different periods and therefore have a chronological significance (Penn and Brugmann 2007, fig. 4.3). Types with greatest currency in the 6th century are those absent in the 7th century (Geake 1997, 69–70).

According to Swanton's classification of shapes (Swanton 1973; 1974), the four Coddenham spearheads may be:

The spear in Grave 1 had a shaft of ash sapling (1–2 years old) and may have therefore been a ceremonial object. This is made more likely by the elaborate character of the shield, more evidently a display object with its silver and garnet fittings.

The objects in Graves 24 and 32 may be arrowheads rather than spears. Grave 24 has a short barbed head with a long shank (narrow cleft); Grave 32 has a short leaf-shaped blade and long shank (narrow cleft). Surviving

examples show that right through the Anglo-Saxon period the most common type of arrowhead was a leaf-shaped blade on a cleft socket, like the example in Grave 32.

Arrows are not a common feature of Anglo-Saxon graves, being essentially a continental type and possibly a hunting weapon: they are thought to be mostly early (Böhme 1974, 110–111; Welch 1983, 135). Arrowheads from Anglo-Saxon graves were listed by Manley (1985). These included four from Spong Hill, Norfolk (6th century), but of his sample, barbed examples (like that in Grave 24) were exceedingly rare. One of the graves excavated at Eriswell, Suffolk, contained a group of arrowheads, found together, points downwards, rather than singly (Carver 2005, 249), but the Sutton Hoo grave 12 example was a single find, like Coddenham Grave 24.

Grave 24

Swanton classified spearheads with barbed heads as his series A, but his examples had long shanks (some 180mm overall) and long barbs and were usually early, for example, a spearhead from Bifrons, Kent, at *c*.250mm long, barbed with a shortish shank and split socket (Swanton 1973, fig. 4e). His A1 is Roman in date, A2 very long at over 1m. The two arrowheads from Sutton Hoo have long curved barbs and are therefore unlike the Coddenham weapons (Bruce-Mitford 1975, fig. 56).

The object had grass over the open end of the socket, suggesting that it was broken to fit the grave (JW).

Grave 32

A short spearhead or arrowhead (100mm) with a narrow leaf-shaped blade, the same length as the shank. This may be a short Swanton C1, but that is an early type, whilst Swanton's C5 is longer (160–260mm) with a narrow cleft with a straight profile and no strickening. The object in Grave 32 is probably an arrowhead rather than a spearhead.

Shields in Graves 1 and 24

Shields were found in two well-furnished graves, and were both remarkable types. Both shield bosses are tall 'sugarloaf' forms as defined by Evison in her discussion of the later types of shield boss, including tall cones (Evison 1963). Dickinson and Härke have since analysed all shield types and their fixings, distinguishing eight shield boss forms (Groups 1–8), with their Groups 3, 6, 7 and 8 being later forms (Dickinson and Härke 1992).

Both the Coddenham examples fall into Dickinson and Härke's Group 7, found quite widely, but especially in Kent and the eastern counties, in later 7th-century burials (Dickinson and Härke 1992, 21). Geake saw them continuing into the 8th century, a little later than argued by Dickinson and Härke (Geake 1997, 67–8). Compared with the 6th century, there are few shield burials in the 7th century (Dickinson and Härke 1992, 63), but those were increasingly significant, to judge from the associated objects. More recent analysis suggests that the sugar-loaf forms first came into use in the two decades before AD 650 (Scull 2009, 254).

Both shields were made of ash (*Fraxinus*), covered in leather on both sides. In the case of the shield in Grave 1, a thicker skin was used on the reverse than the front. This arrangement has been noted on many shield groups, but the reason is unknown (Watson 1995), although treating

Grave	Shaft	Type/date	Other grave-goods	Skeletal remains
1	Alder or hazel	E3; 6th/7th	Seax, shield, bronze bowl, tub	Adult
2	Ash	F2; 6th/7th (Geake 1997, 69)	Knife, buckle	Male, 16–18
24	Alder or hazel	[Barbed arrowhead?]	Shield, bronze bowl, pot, comb	-
32	Beech	[Spear or arrowhead?]	Knife	? male, *c*.11–12

Table 4 Spearheads: types and dating

Grave		Depth of flange	Depth of stud
1	Wood of grip is probably ash. Leather on front *c.* 1.5mm thick, on the back, 4mm thick.	-	14.4mm
24	Narrow flange on boss, leather 1mm thick between iron and wood. Ash, surface TLS	*c.* 11mm	-

Table 5 Shields: construction details

the leather by heating to fit on the wood and also to harden the surface is possible (Cameron 1991). A thin leather skin would also take up the form of any decoration applied to the surface of the wood (Cameron 2000).

In Grave 1, the shield appears to have been placed against the wall of the chamber. The rivets on the flange of the shield boss do not appear to be robust, and with the garnet embellishment, may indicate an object for display. This shield boss also has two layers of leather preserved on one side.

Grave 1
Adult skeleton: found with seax, spear, bronze bowl and iron-bound tub. The boss is 130mm high (omitting the button) with a curved profile, high neck and modest flange. The grip is a Dickinson and Härke 1a1, short with expanded terminals. The boss and shield-board are remarkable for the elaborate button and studs or rivets. The button is an iron 'mushroom' on a shank — all encased in silver sheet. The domed rivets on boss and shield board are of iron with a twisted wire surround, all silvered. The exception is boss rivet (2b), with cabochon garnet.

The five board mounts (objects 2c–g) are larger than the rivets on the boss, but otherwise very similar with silvered domes and encircling silver beaded wire. The board was about 600mm or more in diameter.

The shield boss may be compared with several other bosses figured by Evison (1963), especially Hadleigh Road, Ipswich (fig. 24h), Loddington, Northants (fig. 25a) and Cavecastle, Yorks (fig. 25f), and three with tall curved cones (figs 26a, b, g). It should be noted that these all had buttons, although buttons are generally absent on continental bosses (Evison 1963, 51).

The silvered rivet heads may be compared with the studs with beaded collars seen on large triangular 7th-century buckles and with similar rivets on continental bosses. From Kent, Finglesham grave 95 produced a buckle (of the early 7th century) with three sizes of stud, in gold, and from Crundale, another buckle in gold with three studs, of mid-7th-century date (Webster and Backhouse 1991, 22, 24). The late grave from Ford, Wiltshire, contained a buckle with three rivets, each with a cabochon garnet with gold filigree circlets or collars (Evison 1969). The mount on the Hadleigh Road hanging bowl is of 'buckle' shape, with similar domed rivets (Bruce-Mitford and Raven 2005, no 86).

Grave 24
No skeleton: buried with spear (or arrowhead), bronze bowl, imported pot. The boss is an unusual shape, moderately tall (130mm) with short neck and vestigial flange, and no sign of a button. The grip is short and flat, also 1a1. Three iron rivets or pegs are probably from the board: they are about 16mm long overall, with tall 'heads'. Their shanks indicate a board some 12mm thick.

One of the distinctive features of the continental sugarloaf boss types is the lack of a button, and one might compare the rounded apex of 24/1 to the Walsum type, found in the lower Rhineland (Evison 1963, 51, fig. 35e–f). Both bosses in Graves 1 and 24 hint at a connection with continental types, although their differences may indicate insular development. It may be that this object belongs at the rather more individualistic end of what is usual for England in the mid-7th century (J. Hines pers. comm.). However, it is interesting that Buttermarket, Ipswich has two bosses with continental parallels, in graves 1306 and 3659. Grave 3659 has a similar sugarloaf form to Grave 1, also lacking a button and with a convex dome and distinctive domed rivets, in linked sets (Scull 2009, 254). The shield in Grave 24 also has domed or 'mushroom-headed' rivets (drawn from X-ray), and similar 'mushroom' rivets in a shield were found in the barrow 2 burial at Ford, Wilts. Here, Evison (1969, 62) noted the association of such studs or rivets with the late, *i.e.* 'sugarloaf', type of shield bosses.

Lacking an apex button, this boss could also fit Theune's category of continental shield boss with high 'skull-shaped' dome (or sugarloaf), found in the latest accompanied Phase V (J–K) (Theune 1999), and in this respect is like Buttermarket 1306 'of a form otherwise unknown from burials in England' (Scull 2009, 254).

III. Bag or belt fittings in Grave 30

In Grave 30, jewellery (beads, rings, toilet sets) was found in the neck/chest area in the remains of a leather bag or purse excavated as Soil Block 0345, besides several small bronze fittings (9a–c), with expanded circular terminals, with a rivet or an open ring, in an area of dark staining close to the knees excavated as Soil Block 1140 (Figs 34–5; Plate 11).

Such bronze fittings were once seen as box catches or fittings (Lethbridge 1931, 48; West 1998, fig. 21, 17–21), but have more recently been identified as bag or girdle fittings (Geake 1997, 81; Penn 2000, 66; Scull 2009).

Similar fittings were found at Harford Farm, Norfolk (grave 19A), associated with leather, and were interpreted as fittings from a bag or purse (Penn 2000, 66). Local examples include Boss Hall, Ipswich grave 93, whose fittings are interpreted as evidence for a bag or girdle (Scull forthcoming). In Cambridgeshire, similar objects have been found at Burwell, graves 3, 83 and 97 (Lethbridge 1931, figs 22, 33 and 35) Holywell Row, grave 85, and Shudy Camps, grave 11 (Lethbridge 1931, figs 18; 1936, fig. 2). At Shudy Camps, they were found below the knees, with beads and a coin (Lethbridge 1936, fig. 2). Others come from several cemeteries in Kent, including Kingston (Faussett 1856, 133, 152, 154; Brown 1903, pl. XCVII; Evison 1956, fig. 18).

Recent excavations in Cambridgeshire have added to this list: Melbourn grave 93 has produced a pair of such fittings with a 'girdle group', but are reconstructed as belt fittings, and called 'bar-shaped strap stiffeners' (Duncan *et al.* 2003, fig. 21). In Cambridge itself (Cambridge Backs), another example has been found, with an elderly female, associated with a buckle and a possible pendant (Dodwell *et al.* 2004, fig. 19).

Of the six possible bags at Coddenham, only the bag in Grave 30 had such fittings, but no knife or steel. The other possible bags were associated with knives and their typical accompaniments.

The contents of bags are sometimes little more than collections of odds and ends, sometimes of Roman or earlier date, with a preference for open or ring-shaped objects, and some may have had an amuletic function (Ager 1989, 223). It could be that such items were no more than stray finds, kept as 'collectable' items, rather than functional objects.

IV. Knives in Graves 1, 2, 3, 5, 8, 9, 13, 19, 25, 26, 30, 32, 40, 44, 45, 47

Knives were found in a third of the graves, all as single finds, except Grave 44 (two), and include the odd knife and tool in Graves 30 and 47. Here, they have been classified according to Evison's types, so far as condition allowed (Evison 1987, 113).

There are seventeen knives and most have traces of mineral-preserved organic material. Thirteen were found

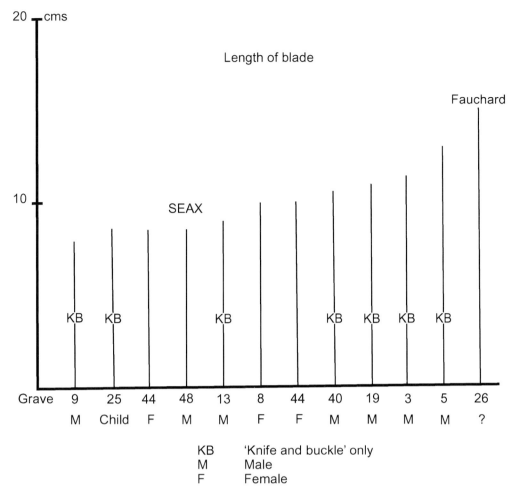

Figure 78 Knives: blade-lengths

to have horn handles and on several it was possible to see where the handle extended onto the blade to keep it firmly in position. Thirteen had traces of leather on their blades, the remains of a leather sheath or bag. On some of the knives a leather sheath can clearly be seen to cover part of the handle. Five of the knives are closely associated with a steel or awls, and may have been in the same bag, case or sheath (Graves 3, 5, 8, 48 and 50).

Härke has noted that males tend to have longer knives (blades) than females (Härke 1989), but here the sample is too small for much significance. Of the burials with a knife, the majority were probably males. However, amongst the shortest blades was that from Grave 25 (a child's burial), and the largest blade was in Grave 26, with the fauchard, but with an individual of unknown sex.

Of the sixteen burials with a knife, ten were in essence 'knife with buckle' burials, and these were probably all males. This is a pattern seen at Harford Farm, Norfolk, where knife and buckle burials were a distinctive group

(Penn 2000), at Carlton Colville, Suffolk (Lucy et al 2009, 418), and at the 6th-century cemetery of Morning Thorpe, Norfolk, where unweaponed males were mostly 'knife and buckle' burials (Green and Rogerson 1987).

V. Tools

Fauchard in Grave 26

Grave 26 contained a knife and buckle, and an object like a billhook, a continental type known as a fauchard, placed at the head. This item appears to be the same type of object as that from grave 437 at Buckland, Dover, the burial of an adult male, aged 35–40 (Parfitt and Anderson forthcoming). The fauchard (buried alongside sword, knife, buckle, Roman coin, pursemount/firesteel, coin and glass vessel) was found lying on its edge, outside the left thigh, pointing towards the foot of the grave. An unpublished provisional list of the grave finds (Haith 1997) states that this is:

A unique find, the first to be securely recorded in an Anglo-Saxon context (although earlier excavation accounts such as Faversham occasionally describe iron 'billhooks', unfortunately no longer extant, amongst the finds), is the iron fauchard from Grave 437 (listed as a billhook in the category tables below), a single-edged, hafted weapon with a right-angled hook projecting from the back of the blade. This is a rare Merovingian weapon-type known from a handful of Continental sites such as Hamoir, (Belgium),

Type	Date (Evison 1987)	Grave
1	5th into 7th	2, 3, 5, 25, 26, 45
2	450–600 onwards	8, 32? 47?
3	7th century	9, 13, 44
4	7th century	30
5	7th century	19, 40
6	7th /8th century	-

Table 6 Knives: types and dating

Douvrend (Seine-Maritime), Lieven (Pas-de-Calais), Breny and Vendhuile (Aisne), Vers-sur-Selle, Marchelpot, Macornay, and Nouvion-en-Ponthieu (Piton 1985, 242–3).

In further discussion of the grave 437 example, Axel Kerep says that these are usually regarded as agricultural tools rather than weapons, and are well-known on the continent (mostly in north-west France), with a date-range from the mid-5th to the mid-6th centuries (Kerep in Parfitt and Anderson forthcoming).

In her discussion of grave-goods from the earlier excavation at Buckland, Dover, Evison had also referred to single-edged weapons and the example from a weapon-grave at Hamoir, Belgium, describing it as a 'cutlass with a right-angled hook on the back' and saying that 'this cutlass and similar bill-hooks are sometimes of more practical solidity like tools and would not be suitable as show pieces' (Evison 1987, 28).

Tools in burials are rare, but not unknown: grave 21 at Harford Farm, Norfolk, contained what may be part of a flax or woolcomb (heckle) (Penn 2000), as did grave 14 at Lechlade, Glos (Boyle *et al.* 1998, fig. 5.39; Miles and Palmer 1986, 17), while the lavish burial at Prittlewell, Essex, contained what may have been a scythe (Blair *et al.* 2004). The object in Grave 26 may thus be considered a tool rather than a weapon, although its significance is uncertain.

Small tools (Graves 3, 5, 8, 9, 47, 48, 50)

Five graves contained 'spatulate tools' or 'steels', each associated with a knife and found close to the waist area, and perhaps in a bag. These are small iron objects with tangs or handles, with a blunt end, parallel-sided and with a rectangular section; that is, no edge. Graves 3, 5 and 48 were probably of males, Grave 8 a female. A small iron object in Grave 44 might be a point or an 'awl', like that in Grave 5, but appears to be round-sectioned, with a head, and is therefore probably a rivet or even a miniature anvil.

Iron objects are not always easily identified; Grave 47 contained a knife with another iron object, which may be a distinct tool or object type. A similar object was found at Chamberlain's Barn, Bedfordshire in grave 15, with a knife and key (Hyslop 1963). In Grave 50, (1) was a possible tool, placed together with (2) and (3) in a sheath or bag, and may be a knife and 'steel'.

Spatulate tools are usually found singly with knives, and are often known as 'steels'. There have been questions about their function, whether they are too soft for sharpening tools and whether they are firesteels (Hirst 1985, 88; Penn 2000, 56–8). Geake, in her discussion of 'spatulate tools', noted the lack of evidence for handles and cited the recent suggestion (P. Ottaway) that these are firesteels and not sharpening steels, although their

associations are not entirely conclusive. Geake also noted that of her sample of forty-eight, thirty-nine were with a knife, and of twenty-three with recorded positions, seventeen (75%) were apparently in a sheath with a knife (Geake 1997, 92–93).

Spatulate tools have been found in 6th-century burials (for example, at Morning Thorpe graves 37, 350 and 351, and Sewerby, Yorks), but most are 7th-century, for example Polhill, Kent (Hawkes 1973), Harford Farm, graves 4, 28 and 42 (Penn 2000). The example in Harford Farm grave 28 was in a bag with shears (Penn 2000, 27–29).

At Coddenham, Graves 5 and 50 each contained an iron object which, if a firelighting function is admitted, might be strike-a-lights. They were found close to knives and were possibly in bags, evident in Graves 8 and 48. Grave 47 contained a pair of iron objects, one a knife, the other a small tapering bar with a nibbed end.

Spatulate tools have been found with males and females. Mostly, they have been found in moderately-equipped burials, associated with a knife and buckle, although Grave 8 also contained a bag and coins, and Grave 48 had a seax and elaborate buckle, with perhaps a bag or purse.

VI. Buckles (Graves 1, 2, 3, 5, 8, 9, 13, 19, 24, 25, 26, 30, 40, 45, 46, 48)

Sixteen of the graves contained buckles, some graves had two, and nearly all were associated with a knife, suggesting belt and buckle as standard kit; of the sixteen burials containing buckles, eleven were probably males and two were females, with the burials in Graves 25 (six years), 26 (no skeletal remains; with fauchard) and 46 (15–16 years) of unknown sex.

At the 6th-century cemetery at Morning Thorpe in Norfolk there was a strong pattern of weapon burials with knife and buckle, burials with knife and buckle only (possibly males) and accompanied females with bags/ purses, often without a buckle. Burials with knife and buckle are therefore more likely to be of males than females, and this may also have been true at Harford Farm, Norfolk (Penn 2000). A similar situation may be seen at Coddenham (see Knives, above).

In Grave 1, the buckle (4), found at the side of the grave, had leather over the top of the tongue and part of the frame, which suggests that the belt was threaded through the loop (JW). In Grave 2, a buckle with linear decoration was found. Buckles with similar decoration have been found at Shudy Camps in graves 67 and 87 (Lethbridge 1936, fig. 1). Grave 3 contained a buckle (1c) with double tongue; Geake has drawn attention to the 'type-fossils' of the later 7th century, typically the small and narrow

Grave	3	5	8	9	30	47	48	50
Skeletal remains	Adult M?	Adult M?	F	M	F	?	M	F
Coin	-	-	*	-	*	-	-	-
Knife	*	*	*	*	-	*	*	-
Buckle	*	*	*	*	-	-	-	-
Spatulate object/steel	*	*	*	-	-	-	*	-
Tool	-	-	*	-	-	*	-	*
Awl/point	-	*	-	-	-	-	-	*

Table 7 Possible bag/tool groups

buckles, the double-tongued buckle and buckles with three rivets, examples including Ford, Wilts (Geake 1994; 1997, 77). More recently, the whole corpus of buckles has been studied by Marzinzik (2003), who has set out a useful typology. Marzinzik discusses continental influence on buckle types in the late 6th century onwards, which then seems to have waned, although some new buckle types were taken up (types II 23 and 24), possibly as England looked to the continent past France towards the east (Marzinzik 2003, 88–9). Her typology allows all the Coddenham buckles to belong to the 7th century.

A few tiny plain triangular buckles were still around in the second half of the 7th century (Geake 1997, 76–77). Examples of the small buckles were found in Grave 30 (10a–c, 10d) at the ankles and in Grave 46 (2) at the hip.

The buckles from Grave 1 (1d) by the seax and Grave 30 (10ci and 10d) by the ankles, may be compared with those from the 'princely' burial at Prittlewell, Essex, identified as shoe buckles (J. Watson, pers. comm.). Shoe buckles are rare, and Geake noted just six to eight examples from her sample, all matched pairs found by the lower leg, and all found in Kent, except for a possible single find from Hadleigh Road, Ipswich (Geake 1997, 65). A similar buckle, with a strap-end, comes from Shudy Camps grave 57, buried with a knife, steel and triangular 'pursemount' (Lethbridge 1936, fig. 1). At Harford Farm, two very small buckles were found in grave 19, with tag and leather, found at the ankles (Penn 2000, 58, fig. 89). These recent finds extend the known distribution into East Anglia.

Grave 48 (male, young-middle-aged) contained a large iron buckle, inlaid with silver wire, buried with a seax. The rivets remain, but the three bosses are missing, as is most of the inlay; however, the design is fairly clear on the X-radiograph and consists of curved panels, hatched to create a skewed ladder pattern. This elaborate inlaid buckle is clearly a Frankish import, and this type of large triangular buckle with shield on tongue and inlay in dense geometric patterns makes its appearance in England in the 7th century, being used to fasten heavy belts at the waist, and mostly worn by men. Like the Coddenham example, such buckles generally had all-over decoration, with the rivets part of the decorative scheme. They are made of iron or bronze, the Coddenham example being of iron, and are mostly 70–75mm long (the Coddenham example is 105mm). They are found in the earlier part of the 7th century, but continue in use for some time (MacGregor 1997, 90, 162–75).

In England such buckles are rare and are mostly found in Kent. In 1981, Hawkes listed a handful of inlaid buckles from England, all from two sites in Kent, Finglesham and

Updown (Eastry III), where the number of such buckles was held to reflect the high, even royal, status of the latter cemetery (Hawkes 1981).

Inlaid buckles of other shapes also occur: a U-shaped plate at Updown (Eastry III) (Hawkes 1981, fig. 3.3) and an oval buckle from Monk Sherborne, Hants (Teague 2005, 121–4). A recent metal-detector find from Paston, north Norfolk, is of a counter-plate from a belt set, trapezoidal with lobed shoulders and domed stud (NHER 44074).

Hawkes saw a recurrence of inlaid buckles from the late 6th century through the 7th century and later, made in Frankish workshops. Trenteseau saw them as mostly 7th century, with diffusion of the individual workshop products connected with Frisian trading activity (Trenteseau 1966, 196).

In her review of inlaid triangular buckles, Geake suggested an earlier 7th-century rather than a later 7th-century date for them and said there was 'no evidence that the large decorated triangular buckle continued to be buried after the middle of the 7th century' (Geake 1997, 76–7). Locally, Briscoe drew attention to a bronze 'Aquitanian' buckle from Lakenheath, west Suffolk, of early 7th-century date (cf. West 1998, 79, plate VI, 1). Another Frankish bronze buckle came from grave 26 at Hadleigh Road, Ipswich, but with a shield-shaped plate rather than the triangular type (West 1998, fig. 67, no. 7).

The Coddenham example may belong to Siegmund's Rheinland Phase 8 (AD 610–640) or Phase 9 (AD 640–670). Siegmund shows Frankish buckle forms, like that from Grave 48, which might date from the first half of the 7th century or a little later (Nieveler and Siegmund 1999, fig. 26: form 4 or 5). The Coddenham example may be compared with an iron military buckle in a male grave from Lent, Netherlands of around AD 600; this was of bronze with silver inlay (Webster and Brown 1997, catalogue no. 15, pl. 49).

VII. Wire rings, toilet sets, pendants and beads (Graves 8, 16, 30, 38, 44)
by Birte Brugmann

Rings
The silver wire rings from Graves 44 (1), 30 (4a, 3e–i), 38 (3a), 8 (11) and 16 (1) and the copper-alloy wire ring from Grave 8 (11) are made of wire thicker in the middle and thinning towards both ends. The wires are plain with the exception of rings 30/3e and 30/3h with a 'beaded' section (groups of incised lines). The terminals of the silver rings are elaborately wound, some formed into tight coils suitable for suspension (Geake 1997, figs 4.10–11). Ring 30/3e has a bezel and may have been a finger-ring (see below). The silver rings were found in the neck and chest area, in each case associated with beads, and in Grave 30 additionally with pendants and toilet sets, possibly all in a bag (see below). The two graves with sexed skeletal remains (8 and 30) were identified as female.

Wire rings made of copper-alloy or silver were used by women for various purposes throughout the Early Anglo-Saxon period, but silver wire thicker in the middle (in some cases with beaded sections) and with terminals tightly wound back on the ring are exclusively found in graves of the Final Phase. See, for example, Boss Hall and Buttermarket, Ipswich (Scull 2009), Harford Farm, Norfolk (Penn 2000, 50), Edix Hill, Barrington A, Cambs

Type	Grave/object	
I b,c,d	9/1b	
I 10di	3/1c	Wide date range
I 10dii	13/1, 24/4	?7th century
???	30/10a–c, 30/10d	
II 19	40/3	Almost any date
II 22a	5/3a, 46/2	6th or 7th century
II 22bii	1/4	Late 6th/7th century
II 24a	1/1d, 2/4, 25/2, 26/2, 40/2	Mostly late 6th/7th century and later
II 24b	2/3, 19/2, 45/1	6th century or later

Table 8 Buckles: Marzinzik types

(Malim and Hines 1998) and Winnall, Hants (Meaney and Hawkes 1970, 37). In Frankish and Alamannic regions, 'spiral rings with coiled ends' (*Spiralringe mit Federenden*) were used for female fashion in the 5th century (*c*.420/30 to 460/70 AD) and again in the 7th century (Burzler *et al.* 2002, 88). The continental 7th-century evidence suggests that the Anglo-Saxon 'Conversion-period silver ring necklace' was not as independent a fashion statement as suggested by Geake (1997, 111).

The possible finger-ring from Grave 30 (3e) was found with the other 'necklace' rings, and as it is of the same manufacture and differs from the other rings only in that the wire forms a bezel shaped as a spiral, it seems possible that this ring was an elaborate necklace ring rather than a finger-ring of a type well known from Anglo-Saxon 5th- and 6th-century graves (see Parfitt and Anderson forthcoming). Associations of wire rings with and without coiled bezels from two graves at Chamberlain's Barn II, Bedfordshire, and Burwell, Cambridgeshire, were judged by Hyslop (1963, 199) to be original parts of the necklaces rather than associated finger-rings. For re-used finger-rings on necklaces from Final Phase contexts see Geake (1997, 49).

Toilet sets

Toilet sets positioned on women's chests together with dress accessories are not only known from Final Phase contexts, but also from 5th- to 7th-century continental and Anglo-Saxon graves (see Parfitt and Brugmann 1997, 66; Penn 2000, 59). While toilet sets from 6th-century contexts are usually made of copper-alloy, the silver sets from 7th-century contexts are more delicate (Penn 2000, 60).

Coddenham contained two silver toilet sets, both from Grave 30 (3b and 3c). The rings used for the suspension of the 'implements' (SF 1118 and 1125) are made of plain wire with the typical tightly wound terminals (see above). The implements of the larger set (3b) are all made with the same technique. Their suspension loops are formed by a double loop; the terminal was then tightly wound back on the shaft. In the 7th century, this technique was widely used for wire both in Anglo-Saxon England and on the continent under Frankish influence (*e.g.* chatelaine links in Wieczorek *et al.* 1996). The toilet implements are all decorated with incised lines resembling the incised lines or 'beaded' sections on two of the necklace wire rings in the same grave (see above). The implements of the smaller set (3c) have plainer loops but one object has its handle marked with incisions ('knife' SF 1233). It seems possible that the wire rings, the finger-ring and the toilet sets were made together as a set. This may also apply to the pendants discussed below.

The smaller of the two toilet sets in Grave 30 (3c) combines a pick, a possible 'hand'/nail cleaner, and a knife-shaped object, presumably a razor or a scraper. The larger set in Grave 30 has an ear scoop or spoon and, as it seems, two picks or spears. The function of the object with five terminals on 3c is not clear because Roman nail-cleaners are only bifurcated. For a more detailed discussion on the practical function of implements from Roman and Early Medieval toilet sets see Martin (1984, 126ff) and Riha (1986, 26ff), for possible amuletic functions see Meaney (1981, 148 ff.).

Bifurcated and knife-shaped objects are not a regular part of toilet sets from 6th-century Anglo-Saxon contexts but they are found on Roman sets. For a copper-alloy example of both on the same set from London Wall see Wheeler (1930 pl. 39). This supports the notion that toilet sets from 7th-century Anglo-Saxon contexts follow Roman rather than early Anglo-Saxon tradition (Penn 2000, 60).

None of the implements from Grave 30 would have been used with excessive force and the fact that they are made of silver therefore does not necessarily speak against their functionality (contra Penn 2000, 60). Three picks, however, would seem excessive if merely functional and therefore support evidence that Early Medieval toilet sets were displayed as status symbols (see Penn 2000, 60), signalling that the owners could afford to eat meat (Martin 1990, 95).

Pendant and spangle

The silver wire ring (3d) in Grave 30 is of the same manufacture as the associated wire rings (see above). It is thicker in the middle and the terminals are tightly wound back on the ring. Attached to it were a silver scutiform pendant and spangle, both unusual for their square shapes with rounded corners. The pendant (SF 1227) has a pyramid-shaped central boss, is decorated with triangular punch-marks comprised of smaller triangles and has a ribbed loop soldered on for suspension. The spangle (SF 1228) has a domed boss, is decorated with lines of punched dots and perforated at one corner for suspension. A similar pendant has been found in the valley below the cemetery (Plunkett 2005, pl. 28; West 1998, fig. 19.11).

Scutiform pendants show Scandinavian influence on Anglo-Saxon dress fashion (see Hines 1984) and were worn mostly during the mid-6th century onwards (Bead Phase B: Parfitt and Anderson forthcoming). The two objects in Grave 30, however, are not only unusual because of their shape, but also because they were suspended from the same ring. Spangles are found mostly in 5th- and early 6th-century graves such as grave 13B at Edix Hill, Barrington A, Cambs, with seven copper-alloy wire rings (Malim and Hines 1998, fig. 3.36). It could be thought unlikely, though, that the Coddenham set is an heirloom because of the unusual square shape of the pendant and spangle and Final-Phase-type wire ring (see above), and the existence of a parallel among the objects found at Vicarage Farm CDD 022 (*cf.* Plunkett 2005, pl. 28; West 1998, fig 19.11).

Beads
(Table 9)
A gradual change in Anglo-Saxon bead fashion from the 5th to the 7th centuries can be divided into three main phases corresponding with the conventional division of metal grave-goods into an *Early Phase* (Bead Phase A) and a *Final Phase* (Bead Phase C). The change in bead fashion suggests an intermediate phase (Bead Phase B) between the *Early* and the *Final Phase* that explains difficulties in joining the *Early* and the *Final Phase* directly (for a recent survey on Anglo-Saxon chronology see Hines (1999)). Comparison with continental frameworks suggests that Bead Phase B was introduced in the mid-6th century and Bead Phase C in the mid-7th century (Brugmann 2004). With the exception of Graves 6 and 16 the bead types and type combinations from Coddenham date all graves containing beads to Bead Phase C. While Grave 6 may date in the late Phase B, the

combination of a bead type of Phase B with a Final-Phase-type silver wire ring in Grave 16 (see below) suggests a date for this grave in Bead Phase C.

The change from the bead fashion of Phase B to that of Phase C corresponding with the Final Phase is marked not only by a change of bead types, but also by a change in bead numbers. In Phase B, some bead combination groups comprised more than a hundred beads, including large numbers of polychrome beads. In contrast, the group of twenty-eight beads from Grave 30 is large for an assemblage of types that can be dated in Bead Phase C. Most polychrome beads used in this bead phase are heirlooms, such as the 6th-century mosaic (millefiori) beads from grave 33 at Harford Farm, Norfolk (Penn 2000, 91).

Amethyst
According to Koch (1987, 346), two types of amethyst beads were imported to the Frankish and Alamannic regions via Italy. Small almond-shaped amethyst beads mostly of a strong purple colour were traded from the last third of the 6th century onwards, longer amethyst beads paler in colour and of a lower quality were traded in the mid-7th century. Most amethyst beads from Anglo-Saxon contexts are of the long type and therefore presumably part of the mid-7th-century amethyst bead trade. For a distribution of amethyst beads in Anglo-Saxon England see Huggett (1988, fig. 2). The few examples of small amethyst beads from Anglo-Saxon contexts datable before the Final Phase / Bead Phase C suggest that Anglo-Saxon England was not much involved in the earlier trade (see Brugmann 2004).

Coddenham produced five almond-shaped amethyst beads. The two beads from Grave 44 (2c, 7) are 8mm and 11mm long and may have been part of a 6th-century import, but as they are pale and associated with a Final-Phase-type silver ring (1), they may have been extensively exposed to daylight and old at the time of burial, or are possibly just smaller than most of the beads traded in the mid-7th century. The three pale, large amethyst beads from Grave 30 (4b, 4c, 4d) are 20–29mm long and were probably part of the 7th-century trade that provided Anglo-Saxon England with the amethyst beads typical of the Final Phase.

Ivory/bone
Visual examination of three beads from Grave 30 (3m, 4e, 4f) suggests they are made of ivory, or possibly bone in the case of bead 4f (Sue Anderson, pers. comm.). At the time, ivory and bone were used for bag rings, combs and playing pieces, and beaver teeth were worn as pendants, but Geake (1997, 47) in her survey of grave-goods in Conversion-Period England lists only two bone beads and no ivory beads at all. This may to some extent reflect difficulties with the identification of badly preserved ivory, bone and shell on the basis of visual examination.

Copper-alloy
The copper-alloy barrel-shaped beads from Grave 30 (3k, 3l) are made of beaded wire. Biconical or barrel-shaped beads made of copper-alloy, silver or gold wire are found mostly, but not exclusively, in graves of the Final Phase (Geake 1997, 42f; Parfitt and Anderson forthcoming). Two examples of late 7th/early 8th-century date were found in coin-dated graves in Ipswich, grave 44 at

Buttermarket and grave 93 at Boss Hall (see below). Geake (1997, 43, table 6.1) argues for a main use in the second half of the 7th and early 8th centuries.

Of the fifty-nine metal beads in Geake's sample of 7th- to 9th-century graves, only nine were made of copper-alloy (Geake 1997, 42). In Grave 30 the two beads are the only bronze objects among the silver rings, pendants and toilet sets found on the chest. In comparison to graves of the 5th and 6th centuries, few objects made of copper-alloy are found in graves of the Final Phase. The predominant use of iron and the more extensive — if economic — use of silver in this period may suggest a shortage of copper-alloy that would make the two beads from Grave 30 comparatively cheap, but nonetheless special substitutes for gold beads rather than substitutes for silver wire beads.

The obvious way to produce a hollow bead out of wire seems to be to wind it around an organic core, possibly made of wood. This would have been a simpler way of producing a bead than using a tube made of sheet metal for a core (Parfitt and Anderson forthcoming). Geake (1997, 112) ascribes the use of metal beads to the influence of late antique jewellery on 7th-century Anglo-Saxon fashion. The use of beaded wire for the gold filigree beads in 6th- and 7th-century Frankish fashion seems to form another possible source of inspiration, which in turn may show Lombard influence and thus be traced back to Italy (Koch 1990).

Silver
The silver sheet fragments from Grave 30 (3j) originally formed a double-bell bead, a type not only used in Anglo-Saxon but also in Frankish fashion, for example, the well-equipped 'girl's grave' at Frankfurt Cathedral, Germany (Wieczorek *et al.* 1996, 940, fig. 12). The introduction of double-bell beads to Anglo-Saxon fashion in the late 6th century (Bead Phase B) precedes the Final Phase, but most finds date to the 7th century (Geake 1997, 43). Bell-shaped objects made of sheet silver are often found in graves as separate objects, and it would therefore seem possible that not all of them were halves of double-bell beads. The halves from Grave 30 by themselves, however, are so fragile that is seems unlikely they were worn other than joined.

Glass
The terms wound, drawn and folded are defined in Brugmann (2004, 21). The earliest datable Anglo-Saxon bead type among the monochrome glass beads from Coddenham is an opaque yellow biconical bead from Grave 6 (2). Small and mostly translucent biconical beads were a regular part of late Roman bead fashion (see type *Roman Biconical* in Brugmann 2004), but the shape was introduced to Anglo-Saxon glass bead fashion only in Phase B. Though it was also used for bead making in Phase C, the Coddenham bead is likely to be of an earlier date because opaque yellow glass was a common colour in bead combinations of late Phase B (Parfitt and Anderson forthcoming) but rare in later contexts. Associated with this bead was a translucent turquoise (green/blue) coiled bead (1) (two fragments of the same bead), an unusual type in an Anglo-Saxon context. The colour combination of yellow and turquoise is best known from Kentish bead fashion of late Phase B (Parfitt and Anderson forthcoming) and it seems likely that Grave 6 is of the

grave	Sf	material (body)	larger perforation	smaller perforation	diameter (body)	length (body)	manufacturing technique (body)	shape (body)	colour (body)	translucency (body)	manufacturing technique (decoration)	decoration
04\2a	1049	glass	3.5	4	8	5	wound, spiral traces on perforated sides	biconical	red	opaque		
06\1	1016	glass	2.5	3	5	5	wound	coil	turquoise	translucent		
06\1	1017	glass	2.5	3	5	4	wound	coil	turquoise	translucent		
06\2	1018	glass	5	5	8	6	wound, no spiral traces on perforated sides	biconical	yellow	opaque		
07\1	1046	glass	5	5	8	5	wound, spiral traces on perforated side	cylindrical	green	opaque		
08\1	1206	glass	6	7	16	13	?wound	globular, ribbed cross section	turquoise	opaque		
08\2	1208	glass	3.5	4	8	6	wound, spiral traces on perforated sides	barrel-shaped/cylindrical	red	opaque		
08\3	1209	glass	3.5	4	8	5	wound, spiral traces on perforated sides	biconical	blue (petrol)	semi-translucent		
16\2	1212	glass	4	5	13	11	wound	globular	petrol	semi-translucent	applied	three red dots on three white dots on equator
30\3j	1128	silver			9	8	fragmented halves	bell-shaped				
30\3k	1226	cu-alloy	3.5		8	18	Ae beaded wire coil	barrel-shaped				
30\3l	1230	cu-alloy	2	2.5	7	14	Ae beaded wire coil	barrel-shaped				
30\3m	1241	ivory?						fragment				
30\3n	1108	crystal					missing					
30\3o	1117	glass					missing					
30\4a	1119	glass & silver	9	9	21	7	wound; in silver double sling with twisted coiled terminals	annular	blue-green	translucent	applied	opaque white and light blue twisted trail(s?) around perforation on both sides and on equator, loopy trail on top lost
30\4b	1110	amethyst	2	2	13	20		almond-shaped	pale			
30\4c	1243	amethyst	2	2.5	19	29		almond-shaped	pale			
30\4d	1245	amethyst	2	2	18	28		almond-shaped	pale			
30\4e	1246	ivory?	2	2			fragment; remaining diam. 11mm, L. 12mm					
30\4f	1235	ivory/bone?					inside of perf. tinged green from contact with cu-alloy? L. 6mm; diam of perf. 2mm	fragment				
30\4g	1112	glass	5.5	6	11	9	wound, no spiral traces on perforated sides	barrel-shaped	orange	opaque		
30\4h	1115	glass	4	5	10	9	wound, glass badly preserved	barrel-shaped	orange	opaque		

30\4i	1236	glass	3	4	9	8	wound or folded, glass badly preserved	barrel-shaped	orange	opaque
30\4j	1109	glass		4	4		drawn, fragmented, probably 7mm in diam	globular	red	opaque
30\4k	1242	glass	3	4	9	6	drawn, one perforated side ?marvered flat, other ?crimped	globular	red	opaque
30\4l	1244	glass	4	4	7	6	folded; glass badly preserved	barrel-shaped	red	opaque
30\4m	1113	glass	3.5	4.5	8	6	drawn, perforated sides cut; glass badly preserved	barrel-shaped, wedge-shaped cross section	red	opaque
30\4n	1129	glass	4	4.5	8	6	folded; glass badly preserved	globular	red	opaque
30\4o	1240	glass	3	3	5	9	drawn or folded	polyhedral (cylindrical with square cross section and marvered edges)	red	
30\4p	1114	glass	3	3.5	7	6	wound, perforated sides ?marvered flat; cross section slightly facetted (marvered?)	barrel-shaped	red	opaque
30\4q	1239	glass	4	4	9	6	drawn, perforated sides ?crimped	globular	green	semi-translucent
30\4r	1111	glass	3.5	4	8	7	wound, cross-section slightly facetted (marvered?)	globular	green	semi-translucent
30\4s	1237	glass	4	4	8	6	drawn, perforated sides ?marvered flat; cross section slightly facetted (marvered?)	barrel-shaped/cylindrical	green	semi-translucent
30\4t	1238	glass	3	3.5	9	6	wound, slightly concave perforated sides, cross section slightly facetted (marvered?)	barrel-shaped/cylindrical	green	semi-translucent
30\4u	1130	glass	2.5	3	8	6	wound; perforated sides ?marvered flat; cross section slightly facetted (marvered?)	barrel-shaped	green	semi-translucent
30\4v	1116	glass	3	3.5	8	5	drawn, perforated sides crimped	globular	white	semi-translucent
30\4w	1248	glass	5	5	8	6	wound or folded	cylindrical	white	semi-translucent
30\4x	1249	glass	4	4	8	6	drawn	globular	green	semi-translucent
38\3b	1190	glass	3.5	4	8	5	wound, spiral traces on perforated side(?s) (not cleaned)	cylindrical	green	opaque
38\2	1191	glass	4	4	8	6	wound, perforated sides ?marvered flat	barrel-shaped	red	opaque
44\2b	1050	glass	2.5	3	9	9	wound?	globular	green	semi-translucent
44\2c	1051	amethyst	2	2	9	11		almond-shaped	pale	
44\7	1058	amethyst	1.5	2	8	8		almond-shaped	pale	

The cross section of all perforations is round

Table 9 Beads in graves

71

same date. The position of the two beads in Grave 6 could suggest they were worn on a string, another indication of a date for this grave before Phase C (see below).

The only other bead grave at Coddenham that does not include any types dated in Phase C is Grave 16 with a polychrome globular bead (2) with three red dots on white dots applied to a petrol-blue body. It seems likely that the production of greyish or petrol blue beads with red on white dots is related to that of white beads with blue crossing trails and red dots typical of Phase B (Brugmann 2004, type *Dot 34*). The type with layered dots is found in six graves dated on the basis of their bead combinations, which all fall in the later part of Phase B (Phase B2): Eriswell (Suffolk) grave 0310; Hadleigh Road (Ipswich) grave 98; Morning Thorpe (Norfolk) graves 216 and 288; Driffield (E. Yorks) grave 26 and Alton (Hants) grave 39 (Brugmann 2004, table 11). A bead of the same type in grave 27 at Harford Farm (Norfolk) was found in a later context (Penn 2000, 91 bead 7b). Coddenham Grave 16, however, seems to be of a later date than Grave 6 because the bead was positioned inside a silver wire ring (see below).

The *Roman Melon* bead (1) from Grave 8 at Coddenham is an antique 'heirloom'. This type of 'melon' bead is quite different from any other type of bead with a ribbed cross-section found in Anglo-Saxon contexts in that it is made of material looking like blue/green (turquoise) Egyptian faience and has narrow shallow ribs, sometimes worn down to the core. In Anglo-Saxon contexts, *Roman Melon* beads are remarkably common for a Roman type and were used throughout the 5th to 7th centuries (Brugmann 2004). The Coddenham find is the only bead from the site that was actually on a ring (silver wire), suggesting a different use from the other beads found in association with rings. A Roman Melon bead from Harford Farm grave 27 (Penn 2000, 94) was found on an iron ring as part of a chatelaine and may have been used as an amulet (Meaney 1981, 192).

The *Melon* bead in Grave 8 was associated with two *Wound Spiral* beads (2, 3) dating the bead group in Phase C (Brugmann 2004), a blue biconical and a red cylindrical bead. The perforated sides of *Wound Spiral* beads are not smooth but retain the trace of a spiral from the winding process and have larger perforations than earlier types of monochrome beads of their size. At Coddenham, they are also found in Graves 7, 44 and 38 (see below).

Grave 7 produced a green cylindrical *Wound Spiral* bead (1) that dates the grave in Bead Phase C, Grave 44 contained a biconical red *Wound Spiral* bead (2a) and a globular green bead of unknown date. The amethyst bead and the silver wire ring in the same grave (see above) support a Final Phase date for the grave. In Grave 38 a cylindrical green *Wound Spiral* bead (3b) was associated with a barrel-shaped red bead (2) of unknown date. As with the polychrome bead in Grave 16, the *Wound Spiral* bead was found inside a wire ring.

The earliest datable bead types in Grave 30 are the three barrel-shaped *Orange* beads (4g, 4h, 4i) a type linking the late Bead Phase B2 with Phase C (Brugmann 2004). Other than in continental row-grave cemeteries, almost the only orange beads found in Anglo-Saxon contexts are the barrel-shaped *Orange* beads, probably imported from the continent since their main distribution lies in Kent (Brugmann 2004, fig. 68).

The most spectacular bead type among the beads of Grave 30 is an *Annular Twist* bead (4a) in a silver suspension loop. It has two types of the fine twisted trail, which may relate this type to reticella glass (see Brugmann 2004), applied to a translucent blue-green body. One trail is made of white and light blue glass, the other one, set on the edge of the perforation, lost. The Coddenham bead raises the number of known *Annular Twist* beads to twenty (see Brugmann 2004, fig. 119). Among the graves with *Annular Twist* beads, which have an exclusively Anglo-Saxon distribution and can all be dated in the Final Phase, are the coin-dated grave 93 at Boss Hall with a *terminus post quem* of 680/90 AD (Scull 2009, 114) and the bed-burial at Swallowcliffe Down (Speake 1989, no. 15).

In the Final Phase, elaborate silver suspension loops were not only used for *Annular Twist* beads, but also for other types of polychrome beads (Scull 2009, 92–7). The coil formed of the terminals of these loops, presumably for suspension from a thong, suggest that their production is related to that of Final Phase silver wire rings (see above) and that a bead suspended in this way was worn in the Final Phase, even if the bead itself was manufactured at an earlier date, such as a number of mosaic beads from Harford Farm (Penn 2000, 91ff).

Five beads from Grave 30 (4p, 4r, 4s, 4t, 4u) do not have a round but a slightly facetted cross-section. Four of these beads appear to be wound, one drawn. It seems possible that the slightly irregular cross section of these beads is the result of some bead-making process in which the bead body was slightly marvered before the glass solidified. Four of the beads, including the drawn one, are semi-translucent ('cloudy') green, one is made of opaque red glass. Green beads of this type are also found in grave 93 at Boss Hall (see above) and graves 22 and 33 at Harford Farm (Penn 2000, 95). Beads of this type are not found in Bead Phases A or B, and systematic analysis might show that they are found in later rather than earlier Bead Phase C.

Three globular drawn beads with round cross-sections, two made of green and one of white semi-translucent glass (4q, 4v, 4x) have parallels in the same graves at Boss Hall and Harford Farm as the beads with irregular cross sections discussed above. Bead 4w seems to be made of the same semi-translucent white glass as bead 4v, but may not be drawn but folded. Detailed research would probably show that the three drawn and two folded opaque red beads 4k, 4l, 4m and 4n, and possibly also fragment 4j, are made by the same workshop(s) as the green and white beads and were the output of a Final-Phase production of wound, solid drawn and folded beads which at first glance looked very much the same.

Polyhedral beads in Anglo-Saxon contexts are usually either Roman or 6th-century mosaic beads (see Brugmann 2004). Bead 4o in Grave 30 presents a rare case of an opaque red bead of this shape in an Anglo-Saxon context and is probably a stray import from the continent. This also seems to be the case with a couple of green polyhedral beads from the 6th-century grave 92 at Deal, Kent (Parfitt and Brugmann 1997, no. 12).

Position of objects

At Coddenham, all silver rings were found in the (presumed) neck and chest area, together with beads.

Copper-alloy ring (11) in Grave 8 was found in the area of the pelvis together with a suspension hook (10) and fragments of comb (12). The position of the rings, beads, pendant, spangle and toilet sets in the neck and chest area of the woman in Grave 30 may indicate that they were positioned in a bag rather than worn and jumbled when the body decayed. Evidence for rings, beads and a toilet set being buried in a bag comes from Harford Farm grave 33 (Penn 2000, 66). However, none of the objects in Grave 30, including the toilet sets, would be out of place in a necklace and therefore it seems equally possible that the objects were on a necklace, and were dislodged when the body decayed.

Evidence from Chamberlain's Barn II, Bedfordshire suggests that the wire rings found in neck and chest area in four graves were tied together with a single thread to form a necklace and that beads were strung across them (cf. Hyslop 1963). Organic evidence from other sites suggests that rings were sewn onto clothing or some leather backing (see Penn 2000, 50). Evidence for such a fashion at Coddenham is supported by a bead found inside a ring in Graves 6 and 16, although Grave 30 had five silver rings and twenty-eight beads which suggests some other arrangement (if the objects were in fact part of a necklace and not kept in a bag).

Conclusion

With the exception of Grave 6, the beads, rings, pendant, spangle and toilet sets date the Coddenham graves in the Final Phase / Bead Phase C (covering roughly the second half of the 7th century). The combination of silver wire rings and beads, presumably forming necklaces, is a well known type of dress accessory of the Final Phase. Evidence for beads being strung, as was common in the preceding Bead Phases A and B, comes from Grave 6, where two beads were found very close together. This grave is likely to date in the late Bead Phase B (first half of the 7th-century). Grave 30 with twenty-eight beads, silver wire rings, a ring with silver pendant and a spangle, and two silver toilet sets is particularly well furnished. Apart from the scutiform pendant and spangle, the association of objects matches well-furnished East Anglian graves at Boss Hall, Ipswich, and Harford Farm, Norfolk. The dating of Coddenham Grave 30 suggested by the beads is consistent with the *terminus post quem* provided by the looped coin in the same grave.

VIII. 'Safety-pin' brooches in Grave 11

Grave 11 contained two silver 'safety-pin' brooches, the only certain brooches found at Coddenham, and these add to a small number already known, all simple safety-pins with catchplate. Most are decorated with bands of incised lines. They come from 7th-century burials, although Geake has suggested that their inspiration came from Iron Age and Romano-British brooches (Geake 1997, 54, 113), and they include 'kite-shaped' examples like one from Cherry Hinton, Cambs (White 1988, 40–1).

Cessford and Dickens have mapped the findspots of both silver and bronze examples of these brooches (thirteen findspots) to which Coddenham now adds another (Cessford and Dickens 2005, fig. 11). The other finds are widely spread: Swallowcliffe Down, Wilts (Speake 1989); Uncleby, Yorks (Smith 1912); Shudy Camps, Cambs (Lethbridge 1936); and Mucking, Essex

(Hamerow 1993, 61). They are all from well-furnished female graves of 7th-century date and can be seen as 'distinctive to the dress and fashion of aristocratic seventh-century females' (Speake 1989, 49). The 'rich' grave at Kingston, Kent (grave 205) contained a disc brooch, drop-handled bronze bowl and safety-pin brooches (Webster and Backhouse 1991, 50–1).

Geake also noted that these brooches have been found in various positions in the grave, but were possibly kept in boxes or bags rather than worn, and an amuletic aspect might be reflected (Geake 1997, 55). The Coddenham brooches were found widely separated on either side of the burial in Grave 11, which, if they were worn, suggests some movement of the burial (Fig. 17).

IX. Possible penannular brooch in Grave 44

Grave 44 contained a female with beads, key and latch-lifter. Objects sieved out included a small curved iron bar or point (6). This appears in X-ray to have an expanded terminal, which could suggest a penannular object, even possibly a penannular brooch c. 25mm diameter. Penannular brooches are found widely in the 7th century (Hines 1984, 263; Leeds 1936, 98–9), and are well represented at Uncleby, Yorks (Smith 1912), but the material of the object from Grave 44 makes this less likely.

X. Iron keys/latch-lifters in Graves 30, 38 and 44

Three graves of females contained remains of iron keys or latch-lifters. Grave 30, the bed-burial, contained a collection of objects (5–8) suspended from the waist, including a knife, two possible tools, chain link and parts of an iron key. Textile remains suggest that these were possibly kept in a bag.

Grave 38 contained an iron key (4), besides a pot and beads. In Grave 44, knife and possible finger-ring (4a–b), and key (5), were found together at the ?left side in the waist area. The wire ring with beads (1 and 2) suggests this burial was also that of a female.

In Early Anglo-Saxon graves, females were often buried with objects at the waist, suspended from a belt or contained within a bag. These girdle groups often included a knife and girdle-hangers and/or keys.

Bronze girdle-hangers were apparently non-functional objects and belonged to the 6th century, whilst iron keys seem to be functional and mostly belong to the later 6th or 7th centuries. At Morning Thorpe cemetery in Norfolk, the occurrence of the two types was almost exclusive, but found in much the same phases, although keys went on in use later than girdle-hangers (Geake 1997, 57–8; Penn and Brugmann 2007, 43). At Hadleigh Road, Ipswich, keys were found but no girdle-hangers, wrist-clasps, cruciform or small-long brooches, typical of the 6th century (Layard 1907; Ozanne 1962).

A characteristic of women's graves in 'Anglian' areas in the 6th century, 'keys' may reflect married status, as 'mistress of the house' or keeper of the marital 'treasure', a signal of status as wives or hosts, or even have some sexual connotation (Evison 1987, 117–8; Hawkes 1973, 195–6; Hirst 1985, 87–8; Meaney 1981, 178–81). They are sometimes found in pairs, which suggests an element of display rather than a solely functional purpose. Most have been found with adult women (Stoodley 1999, 111), but some have been found with children (Geake 1997, 58), making them perhaps a sign of inherited status rather than actual role. Ager has discussed the little evidence that they might indicate the 'free born' individual (Ager 1989, 224).

The other adult females in Graves 4, 8, 11 and 14 were not so provided and may have been of a different social status.

XI. Vessels

Horn or wooden vessel in Grave 1

Grave 1 contained a bucket by the feet and within the remains of the bucket, three small clips (8a–c), one of decorated bronze sheet. Objects 8 a and b were two small strips of bronze sheet, one edge lipped; object 8c was a rim clip with incised decoration and a small rivet hole, and was associated with fragments of horn. The clip would fit a rim 4mm thick, and comparison with the clips from possible drinking horns seems to confirm identification as a clip from a similar vessel (C. de Vegvar, pers. comm.).

At Castledyke, Barton-upon-Humber, grave 124 produced a loop, whilst grave 183 produced another clip, like that from Coddenham, with a 'wavy' outline and a slight lip along the edge. These are also interpreted as coming from drinking horns (Drinkall and Foreman 1998, 296, figs 91, 113). The Coddenham clip is thinner and thus might be from a thinner-walled vessel but being associated with fragments of horn and placed within the bucket, objects 8a–c seem most likely to come from a drinking horn.

Drinking horns are best known from the high-status graves at Sutton Hoo, and from the late 6th-century 'princely' burial at Taplow, Bucks. The latter had a rim binding and foils held on by four clips (though unlike the Coddenham clips in detail). Other possible examples come from Broomfield, Essex, Little Wilbraham and Holywell, Cambs, and Loveden Hill and Caenby, Lincs (East 1983).

Pottery vessels in Graves 24, 35 and 38
by Sue Anderson

Introduction

The only pottery which could be positively identified as Early Saxon was collected from three graves. The 490 sherds (2,300g) represent three vessels, one from each burial. None of the pottery identified as Iron Age had similar fabrics, but some were similar to material from other Saxon sites. However, all of these vessels were associated with identifiably Iron Age sherds. Sixteen handmade sherds (112g) remain unidentified, but it is possible that some or all could be Saxon.

Methodology

Quantification was carried out using sherd count, weight and estimated vessel equivalent (eve). A full quantification by fabric, context and feature is available in the archive. All fabric codes were assigned from the Suffolk post-Roman fabric series, which includes Norfolk, Essex, Cambridgeshire and Midlands fabrics, as well as imported wares. A ×20 microscope was used for fabric identification and characterisation. Form terminology for Early Saxon pottery follows Myres (1977) and Hamerow (1993). Recording uses a system of

letters for fabric codes together with number codes for ease of sorting in database format. SCCAS pottery quantification forms were used and the results were input onto an Access 97 database.

Results

The three vessels were identified as follows:

Baggy jar (60 sherds, 627g) with upright plain tapered rim above a slight shoulder (150mm diameter, 50% complete) and flat-rounded base. Sand and organic tempered (Fabric ESO2). Oxidised pale buff to brown externally, reduced black internally. Rough surface. Internal burnt residue. Context 0338 (Grave 35).

Baggy jar (30 sherds, 533g) with upright plain tapered rim (130mm diameter, 25% complete) and flat-rounded base. Organic tempered (Fabric ESO1) with occasional sand. Oxidised red externally, reduced black internally. Rough surface. Context 0515 (Grave 38).

Bottle or narrow-necked jar (c.400 sherds, 1140g) with rolled rim, short neck, sub-biconical body and flat base. Wheelmade, decorated with rouletted cabling. Medium sandy greyware (Fabric ESIM), soft and abraded, rough feel, containing clear and white quartz sand up to 0.3mm, and occasional fine to coarse red grog. Grey-black surfaces with reddish brown core, occasionally with an inner reduced core in thicker sherds. Context 0168 (Grave 24).

The two plain baggy jars are typical of pottery grave-goods found at other recently excavated Early Saxon cemetery sites in Suffolk (*e.g.* Eriswell, Flixton, Sutton Hoo). Their organic fabrics suggest a date in the 6th to 7th centuries. The third vessel was an import whose form was difficult to reconstruct due to the fragmentary and abraded nature of the sherds, but part of the rim and neck were present, there were decorated sherds with very shallow rouletting from the upper half, and partial reconstruction of the lower body indicated a globular profile on a flat base. The closest parallels would appear to be bottles from Sarre and St Peter's, Kent (Evison 1979, *e.g.* figs 3c, 5c and 8d). Imported vessels are relatively rare in Suffolk, but are known from Lakenheath, Sutton Hoo and Ipswich (Evison 1979) and recently an example was excavated from a grave at Hadleigh (Anderson, unpub.). None of these is the same type as the Coddenham vessel, although the Hadleigh pot, a biconical jar with girth-grooving of the upper half, is in a similar fabric. Further discussion of the Coddenham and Hadleigh vessels is provided by Alan Vince (below).

Characterisation of wheel-thrown Anglo-Saxon vessels from Coddenham Grave 24 and Hadleigh (HAD059)
by Alan Vince
(Figs 79–80, Tables 10–11)

Introduction

Amongst the grave-goods from the Coddenham and Hadleigh cemeteries were two wheel-thrown pottery vessels. A binocular microscope study of each vessel was carried out and samples taken for thin section and chemical analysis. The thin-sections were stained using Dickson's method in order to differentiate carbonate inclusions (which, as it happens, were not present in either section). The chemical analysis was carried out using Inductively Coupled Plasma Atomic Emission Spectroscopy (ICP-AES). A range of major elements were measured together with minor and trace elements.

The pot in Grave 24

The vessel is fragmentary, but it is possible to see that the sherds come from a bottle with a globular body, tall neck (with a slight cordon about halfway down the neck) and a rolled-out rim. The vessel has a cable roulette pattern roller-stamped on the body, both above and below the girth. The vessel belongs to Evison's Group 1e and is particularly close to a vessel from St Peter's, Kent (Evison 1979, fig. 6b).

The fabric is oxidised and a dark brown colour with dark grey surfaces and contains abundant well-sorted quartz of fine sand or silt grade together with moderate rounded inclusion-less red clay pellets up to 2.0mm across.

In thin section (V1627) the main visible feature is a sand consisting of well-sorted quartzose grains, some angular, some sub-angular and a few rounded, ranging up to 0.3mm across. Some of these grains have a coating of haematite. Sparse red clay pellets, some of which were angular and some rounded, up to 2.0mm across, were present. Most of the grains are monocrystalline quartz, but chert was also noted. Sparse muscovite laths up to 0.2mm occurred in an anisotropic groundmass of baked clay minerals.

The Hadleigh pot (HAD 059)

This vessel, excavated from a grave, one of four around a ring-ditch at Aldham Mill Hill, is also fragmentary, but can be reconstructed to reveal that it is a beaker or bowl with a biconical body and a corrugated upper half with a simple, rolled-out rounded rim. The vessel belongs to Evison's group 3e, and is similar to the two vessels from Prittlewell, Essex (Evison 1979 fig. 16 a and b). The fabric and petrology are identical to that of the Coddenham vessel.

Discussion

Both methods of study confirm the close similarity of the two vessels both in petrological and chemical composition and clearly demonstrate that the two vessels were the products of the same centre, if not the same kiln. The thin-section shows that no distinctive rocks or minerals are present, but suggest that the sand used for tempering was loosely cemented with haematite, or an iron-rich clay. The red clay pellets might be from the same source although the absence of quartz inclusions within them suggests otherwise.

A survey of wheel-thrown pottery vessels found in Anglo-Saxon graves was carried out in the 1970s by Prof. V. Evison (Evison 1974; 1979). This survey concluded that the majority of these finds were from a single source and that this source lay in the Pas-de-Calais, on the basis of the distribution of vessels decorated with cable rouletting found in Merovingian graves. Evison pointed out that there was a small number of vessels from other sources included in her corpus and that the majority of the vessels in her Fabric I (Pas-de-Calais) group were found in Kent. In order to confirm that these two Suffolk pieces were indeed from the same source as Evison Fabric 1 those vessels in the British Museum, a total of 26 vessels out of Evison's total of 131, were re-examined using a binocular microscope. In addition, a chemical analysis of most of the vessels in Evison's corpus had been carried out by M. Cowell of the Department of Scientific Research (Cowell 1979) using Atomic Adsorption Spectroscopy. This data was re-examined together with that from other early to mid Anglo-Saxon imports studied by the author using ICPS-AES.

Fabric
The fine quartz sand seen in the Coddenham and Hadleigh vessels is a feature of sixteen of the vessels examined in the British Museum. In addition, two vessels have a very similar appearance, but without the sand inclusions. This leaves six vessels with different fabric characteristics, one of which Evison thought was unlikely to be an Anglo-Saxon import. One vessel from Faversham dismissed by Evison as being Romano-British did, however, contain this same sand and may therefore be re-instated into the corpus. Of the sixteen vessels with this fine sand temper, only four have red clay pellets of the type seen in the Coddenham and Hadleigh vessels (Table 10). In addition, two of the vessels without sand had similar red clay pellet inclusions.

It is also interesting to consider the temperature and kiln atmosphere in which these vessels were fired. The British Museum (BM) vessels show a range of colours which indicate both firing temperature and redox conditions (ranging from dark grey to a steel grey for reduced vessels and from dark brown to salmon pink for oxidised vessels). The redox and firing temperature of the eighteen Fabric I vessels examined in the BM is shown in Table 11. Low firing is defined as that insufficient to remove all the carbon, giving a dark brown or black core. Moderate firing is defined as that giving a brown or grey core and high firing as giving a salmon pink or light grey core. The Coddenham and Hadleigh vessels would be classified as moderately fired, placing them in a small subgroup of the BM samples. These two vessels both have oxidised cores with reduced surfaces, the most common firing pattern in the BM samples shared by six out of the sixteen vessels. However, only one BM vessel (Evison Ig4) shared both the moderate firing and the firing pattern of the Suffolk finds whilst two others (Evison 4a1 and 4a2) have a lower firing temperature.

Evison fig.	Evison type	Site	Fabric	Form
10b	1i2	Wingham	EVISON FABRIC I	bottle
15e	3c5	Bishopbourne	ESAXIMP	bowl
2c	1c2	Strood	ESAXIMP	bottle
2e	1d2	Faversham	EVISON FABRIC I	bottle
4a	1e1	Sittingbourne	EVISON FABRIC I	bottle
7e	1g4	Broadstairs	EVISON FABRIC I	bottle

Table 10 Vessels and fabric groups, with red pellet inclusions (from Evison's Corpus)

Redox	?	high	low	moderate	**Grand total**
Oxidised	1	3	1	-	**5**
Oxidised core; reduced surfaces	-	3	2	1	**6**
Reduced	1	3	-	-	**4**
Reduced with oxidised surfaces	-	-	-	1	**1**
Grand Total	**2**	**9**	**3**	**2**	**16**

Table 11 Redox and firing temperature of sixteen Fabric I vessels in the British Museum

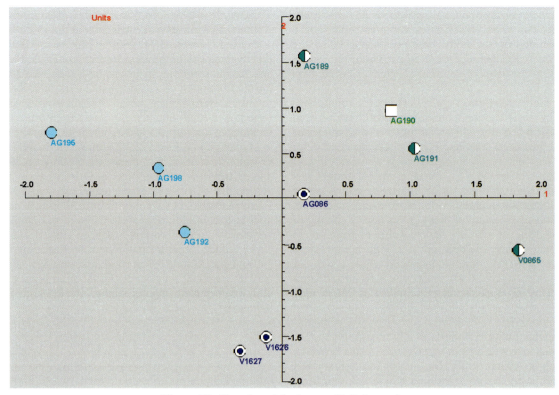

Figure 79 Grey burnished ware (full dataset)

A statistical analysis of the chemical data was carried out in two stages. First, the full range of measured elements could be compared with a small number of analyses of early and mid Anglo-Saxon vessels. These consist of possible Badorf ware vessels from Flixborough and Whitby, grey burnished ware vessels from Flixborough and a single example of Evison Fabric I, a jug from the Castledyke South cemetery, Barton-upon-Humber (Whitwell 1990). A Principal Components

Analysis of this dataset indicates that the grey burnished wares have a chemically similar composition, as do the Badorf wares.

A sherd of a black-surfaced vessel with a light-coloured body and fine quartz sand temper from Flixborough falls within the Badorf group. The three Evison Fabric I samples plot mid-way between these two groups, with the two Suffolk pieces being more similar to each other than to the Barton-upon-Humber sample (Fig. 79).

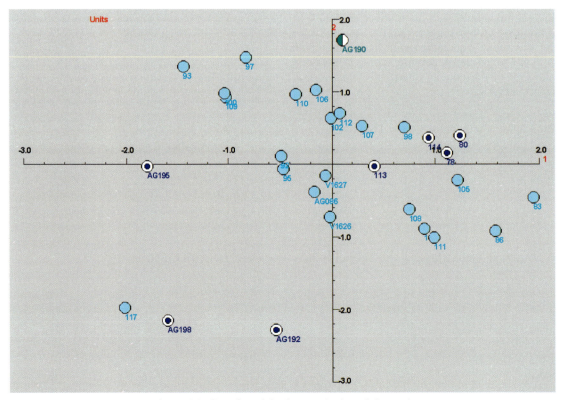

Figure 80 Grey burnished ware (reduced dataset)

Since only the major elements were examined by Cowell, a reduced dataset was analysed. This included Cowell's data for those vessels examined in the BM which had the standard fabric together with the Suffolk and Barton pieces and the Flixborough grey burnished samples. The results of this analysis show that the Suffolk and Barton samples fall within a cluster of results from the BM vessels with one BM sample and the Flixborough standard grey burnished wares falling outside this cluster on one side and the Flixborough light-firing sample falling outside the main cluster but on the other side. The BM untempered vessel samples form a coherent group within the main cluster (Fig. 80, Nos 78, 80, 113 and 114).

The results of this re-analysis suggest that the Suffolk and Barton vessels have the same chemical composition as those in Evison's Fabric I group but that whereas the untempered grey burnished wares from Dover are indistinguishable in composition from the sand-tempered ones, those from Flixborough are chemically different. Given that the analysis includes material analysed using two different techniques, AAS and ICP-AES, the difference in composition between the grey burnished wares needs to be confirmed by re-analysis of the BM samples using ICP-AES. Nevertheless, it seems clear that the Suffolk and Barton samples are made with the same raw materials as those studied by Evison.

The BM vessels with red clay pellet inclusions include the outlier (Fig. 80 No. 117), and three with compositions indistinguishable from the remainder (Fig. 80 Nos 95, 102 and 109).

To conclude, although the Suffolk vessels fall within ranges for fabric, firing temperature and firing conditions found in the standard Evison Fabric I group they fall into minor subgroups for each trait. Thus, although it might be chance that both the Suffolk vessels are moderately fired with oxidised cores and reduced surfaces and that both contain red clay pellets it does suggest that there is a stronger link between them than simply coming from the same centre. It may be that they actually formed part of the same cargo.

In her discussion of the distribution of these imports, Evison suggests that whereas those from the remainder of Anglo-Saxon England occur in such small numbers and are of such disparate types that they may be casual imports resulting from generalised contact with Frankia, those from Kent include a large proportion of bottles and occur in larger numbers in cemeteries. These, she suggests, may be the result of a trade in the bottles' contents. If this is true, then perhaps the Suffolk finds should be seen as part of the same process.

Bronze vessels in Graves 1, 24 and 30
Bronze vessels were found in Graves 1, 24 and 30, all apparently wrapped in textile. Grave 1 contained a trivet-base bowl, with bucket and possibly a drinking horn, Grave 24 held a trivet-base bowl and a pot, whilst Grave 30 contained fragments of a hanging bowl.

The two bowls from Graves 1 and 24 are of Frankish design and manufacture, and probably made in the 6th century, but buried much later. Both hanging bowls and other bronze bowls are sometimes found associated with other vessels, and with food or other items, such as combs, as here in Grave 24. Some ritual connection is likely.

In his review of the Sutton Hoo Ship Burial publication, Werner argued that all such vessels (hanging bowls, 'Coptic' bowls, tubs) were tableware for use in the rituals of drinking and feasting, and drew attention to Bede's report on King Edwin's feast and mention of tableware. Werner also saw a link between some of these vessels and the washing of hands after a meal, perhaps linked to the combs occasionally found with them, as in Grave 24 (Werner 1992, 5). Grave I at Barton-upon-Humber, Lincs, contained a hanging bowl, fragments of Frankish bowl, relic box, scales and weights, and comb, and grave 205 Kingston Down, Kent, produced a similar assemblage of objects. Since then, further excavation at Sutton Hoo has revealed a 'princely burial', in Mound 17, probably of the 6th century, accompanied by a horse in a separate pit, weapons, bronze bowl, bucket, cauldron, pottery vessel and a comb (Carver 2005) strengthening the perceived association between high status and bronze vessels, and emphasizing combs as an associated object type.

Trivet-base bowls (Graves 1 and 24)
Imported bronze bowls were found in Graves 1 and 24, both probably of males, each with a spear (Grave 1 a seax, shield, spear, bucket; Grave 24 a shield, spear, comb). The two bowls are very similar, each about 340mm in diameter and 104mm deep.

Each vessel is of raised bronze sheet, with sides flaring gently outwards to a narrow rim, and cast omega drop-handles on soldered-on lugs, and a cast foot-ring, also soldered on: Grave 1 foot-ring is tripod; Grave 24 foot-ring is tetrapod. The drop-handle in Grave 1 is more rectangular; the bowl in Grave 24 has a curved loop handle, but both handles have 'pads' at the corners and a central moulding. Grave 1 bowl is very similar to that from Kingston, Kent (grave 205), with rectangular handle and triple moulding; Grave 24 bowl has a quadruple moulding, more like the bowl from Uncleby, Yorks (Geake 1997; Richards 1980, app. 4, nos 39 and 42), but this bowl is a large plain globular vessel with flat out-turned rim, with a rectangular omega handle with central mouldings and corner 'pads' (H. Geake, pers. comm.).

The vessel in Grave 1 with tripod foot-ring may be compared to the vessel buried with the Cologne 'princess' in the mid-6th century. This was a shallow bowl (rim diameter 350–360mm) with gently out-turned rim, tripod foot-ring but with plain omega drop-handles (Doppelfeld 1960, taf. 24; Werner 1964, fig. 5.4).

Tripod-ring bowls are Frankish and usually thought to have been made in the Rhineland in the 6th century. They are found north of the Alps, and may be compared with the cast bronze Byzantine (or 'Coptic') bowls from the eastern Mediterranean, whose distribution points to a route through the Rhineland (Richards 1980, figs 15, 46). Richards considered the tripod-ring bowls to be a separate development and a 'class of bronze vessels in their own right', although their similarities and distribution suggest a close relationship (Richards 1980, 19–20).

In his study of trade patterns, Richards concluded that tripod-ring bowls in England and on the continent were mostly 6th-century (*e.g.* Sarre 88, Gilton 8 and 19). He listed eight examples in England (six in Kent, two in Yorkshire), all probably imports (Richards 1980, 19; app. 4). Most were deposited in the 6th century, but English exceptions are Kingston grave 205 (early 7th century), Castledyke, Barton-upon-Humber, Lincs, and Uncleby, Yorks (both deposited in the late 7th/early 8th century) (Drinkall and Foreman 1998, 295; Geake 1997, 87).

These vessels are found in two varieties, those with 'looped feet', mostly buried in the 6th century, and those with 'unlooped feet', possibly buried later. A burial at Coombe, Woodnesborough, Kent, contained a bowl with simple omega-shaped drop-handles, on a low tripod of cast bronze with looped feet (found with a square-headed brooch), thought to be of 6th-century date, and a recent find from Deal, Kent, is a bowl on a looped trivet, of 6th-century manufacture and burial (Parfitt and Brugmann

1997, 82, fig. 46). However, an example from Thaining, Germany, was in a grave dated to end of the 7th century (Ellis-Davidson and Webster 1967, 32–3, fig. 5).

The type with 'unlooped' feet, as here, is found more widely, from Kent to Yorkshire, and in 7th-century graves, raising questions about both their date of manufacture and burial practices (Geake 1997, 87–8). Of Geake's 1997 sample, complete bowls were found in just twelve graves, with a concentration in Kent and East Anglia, and occur with high status males in the late 6th/7th century. It is remarkable that Coddenham should produce two such vessels, usually found in Kent, and buried so long after manufacture.

The hanging bowl in Grave 30
(Table 12)
Grave 30 contained the very fragmentary remains of a sheet bronze hanging bowl and its cast escutcheon or mount. The remains consist of two fragments of rim, four larger and several small pieces of the body, and part of a simple openwork cast mount. There is no surviving indication of solder, and no basal fragments. This object may be reconstructed as a bowl with a narrow T-shaped rim, and a shallow concave neck above a softly carinated shoulder. The rim pieces suggest a diameter between 170mm and 210mm. The absence of so much of the bowl, and the presence of just one of the assumed three (or four) suspension mounts, suggests the possibility that only part of the vessel went into the grave.

The cast openwork mount, although broken, shows that this bowl clearly belongs to the distinctive class of A type bowl, which contains all the openwork mounts, both plain and decorated. Fifteen with openwork mounts (or single mounts) were listed in the recent *Corpus*, eight of which were decorated and seven of which were quite plain, like the Coddenham mount reconstruction (Bruce-Mitford with Raven 2005, 10–11, 20).

The mount (whose integral hook is missing) can be simply reconstructed as a circular mount with curved shapes creating two pelta-shaped voids, like those from the mould found at Craig Phadrig, Inverness, in Scotland, which may therefore be their place of manufacture (Youngs 2008, 209, fig. 9.3a). Besides the Craig Phadrig mould, two bowls with similar plain mounts have been found in Scotland, and another (enamelled) by the River Bann, Northern Ireland (all in non-funerary contexts).

The Coddenham mount is very close to the two-pelta mount from Castle Tioram, Highlands (*Corpus* no. 112), whose bowl has a similar A rim and is also small/medium, at *c*. 170mm diameter. The fragmentary bowl from Tummel Bridge, Tayside (*Corpus* no. 117) is much larger, at 300mm diameter, and has a four-pelta mount.

Besides these examples from northern Britain, a number of examples of Craig Phadrig openwork peltate mounts come from across the Anglo-Saxon world, including East Anglia (Youngs 2008, fig. 9.6).

In England, what in some respects may be a very similar bowl, judging by the mount and the remains of the rim, comes from Field Dalling, in north Norfolk. It has a similar T-shaped rim and four-pelta openwork mount (Bruce-Mitford with Raven 2005, no. 66, 221, 257–264, figs 259–261). However, besides being much larger and made of brass, it is a 'very solid piece with massive fittings' (S. Youngs pers. comm.), and the parallel is thus far from exact.

More locally, from 'Ipswich', come fragments of a bowl with cast openwork mount with integral bird-head hook, probably similar to the Coddenham mount, but with four pelta (Portable Antiquity Scheme SF 9336). The bowl has a similar diameter, *c*. 170mm, to the Coddenham bowl. From further afield, other examples of bowls with openwork mounts include one at Wilton, Wilts, with diameter 270mm and out-turned rim (Bruce-Mitford with Raven 2005, 291–3, no. 97). A stray find of a single mount with hook comes from Eastwell, Leics (no. 45), the mount a plain two-pelta design.

All these mounts may be products of the Craig Phadrig workshop (Bruce-Mitford with Raven 2005, 20–1), and it is likely that the Coddenham and 'Ipswich' bowls are also products, although varying in detail. Besides the bowls with plain mounts, there are other mounts, or bowls with mounts, related in form, but decorated. These include the bowl with four decorated mounts of Craig Phadrig type from Baginton, Warks (no. 93), and the mount from Coleraine, River Bann, Northern Ireland (no. 119). A fragment of a hook with mount comes from Wighton, Norfolk (no. 69). This has four voids and is decorated with an enamel scroll, but the general form is not unlike the Coddenham mount.

Corpus No.	Location	Pelta	Description
Plain mount			
13	Hildersham, Cambs	2	Bowl, 251mm diameter
45	Eastwell, Leics	2	Mount with hook. Stray find
66	Field Dalling, Norfolk	4	Complete bowl, 257–264mm diameter, brass
97	Wilton, Wilts	4	Bowl with out-turned rim, 270mm diameter
-	'Ipswich', Suffolk	4	Fragments of hanging bowl, *c*. 170mm diameter, with bird-head hook. (Portable Antiquities Scheme SF 9336)
-	Coddenham, Grave 30	2	Fragments of hook and bowl, 170–210mm diameter
112	Castle Tioram, Tummel Bridge, Scotland	2	Bowl, *c*. 170mm diameter
117	Tayside, Scotland	4	Bowl, 300mm diameter
Decorated mount			
93	Baginton, Warks	2	Bowl, 300mm diameter, with four enamelled mounts
119	River Bann, Coleraine, Northern Ireland	2	Mount, enamelled
69	Wighton, Norfolk	4	Fragment of hook with mount, enamelled

Table 12 Openwork mounts (plain and decorated) related to Craig Phadrig form (*Corpus* numbers from Bruce-Mitford with Raven 2005)

In recent excavations at Tranmer House, immediately north of Sutton Hoo, an Anglo-Saxon cemetery with 19 inhumations and 17 cremations was found; cremation burial 491 was placed in a hanging bowl (with a comb as accompaniment). The bowl, about 250–263mm wide, belongs to type A, but with an enamelled crescentic openwork mount, unlike the simple circular peltate Coddenham mount (Fern 2007; Newman 2005, 486) but with some decorative links to the bowls from Coleraine, Hildersham and Baginton.

Hanging bowls may derive ultimately from late Romano-British bowls (Geake 1997, 11) but their dates of manufacture and burial remain the subject of debate, and in Geake's survey, both manufacture and burial in her 'Conversion Period' was thought possible (Geake 1997, 115).

The Coddenham bowl was in a grave radiocarbon-dated to AD 605–655, whose mounted coin gives a *terminus post quem* of AD 629, whilst the Anglo-Saxon 'coin' points to a date at the very end of the radiocarbon range, or a little beyond (see Chapter 8).

Stevenson (2005) has suggested a date in the early 7th century for the bowls with openwork mount. In his discussion of the dating of type A bowls, Bruce Mitford refers to the openwork mount, and the fact that they are confined to type A bowls, 'which is in itself a conclusive argument against the dating of plain openwork escutcheons to the late seventh or eighth centuries' and thought that the latest deposition of an A bowl was possibly Sutton Hoo Mound 1, where it was already old, and said 'no openwork bowl has occurred in a firm seventh-century context' (Bruce-Mitford with Raven 2005, 19, 22).

South-east Suffolk is something of a 'hotspot' for hanging bowls (or parts). Fragments of hanging bowls also come from the settlement site at Vicarage Farm and elsewhere in Coddenham, and from the important 'productive' site in Barham, the adjacent parish, at BRH018. The settlement site at Vicarage Farm CDD022 has produced an enamelled mount (no. 82) which exactly matches a pair (no. 80) from the Barham site and the basal mounts of Kingston grave 205 (no. 42). The Barham site also produced an enamelled disc (no. 79) and an appliqué mount in the shape of a fish (no. 81). Elsewhere in Coddenham, site CDD019 near the Roman site to the south-west, produced a fragment of hook and openwork mount (no. 83), the animal hook being very similar to the hook recorded from the lost Badley Bridge bowl (no. 78).

Other finds of hanging bowls, of various types, come from elsewhere in the region, most notably the three bowls from Sutton Hoo (nos 88–90). The list includes the composite bowl found at the Hadleigh Road cemetery, Ipswich (no. 86) and the odd bowl at Badley Bridge (no. 78).

The deposition of hanging bowls may reflect the identity of the individual as a host or hostess, and their role in feasting and drinking (Geake 1997, 87), but a frequent association with such objects as combs suggests a more specialized function and context.

Deposition of vessels as fragments may be a deliberate practice, with records of bowl fragments, especially mounts, rather than complete vessels, being deposited, although these occur more often with female burials and may have been recycled as ornaments before burial

(Brenan 1984–5; 1991; Bruce-Mitford with Raven 2005; Geake 1997, 114).

Iron-bound bucket/tub in Grave 1

Grave 1 produced two vessels: a bronze bowl (3) and an iron-bound bucket or tub (7) built of oak staves. This was a simple affair of four hoops, with a twisted handle hooked onto a fairly plain pair of hooked escutcheons. The vessel was probably about 260mm high, and slightly flared from top to bottom, from 250mm rim diameter to 260mm base — the rim diameter placing it towards the top of Geake's sample of twenty-one buckets from fifteen graves (Geake 1997, table 4.17).

A similar vessel (also with oak staves) from Barrington grave 18B, was in a bed burial, of a female between 17 and 25 years old (Cook 2004, 48; Malim and Hines 1998, 52). This bucket compares closely to the Coddenham bucket in size, the twisted handle, and the shape of the escutcheon or mount, and it is tempting to postulate the same manufacturer.

Iron-bound buckets are found with both males and females, mostly placed at the lower end of the grave, whereas bronze-bound vessels were usually by the head. In Grave 1 the bucket was placed in the lower left side of the grave, possibly with a drinking horn (Fig. 6).

Although iron-bound buckets appear from the middle of the 6th century onwards, Geake's sample suggests a 7th-century context for most of them (Geake 1997, 91), and Cook also noted that iron-bound buckets were usually later than their bronze-bound counterparts and usually larger (Cook 2004, 43–4).

Cook also included in her *Corpus* a similar vessel from Broomfield, Essex (no. 18) and Hadleigh Road, Ipswich (no. 96). At Broomfield, two buckets with iron mounts accompanied a male (Cook 2004, 41, 52–3; Geake 1997, 151).

Many buckets were built of yew, including the bucket from Sutton Hoo Mound 14 (Carver 2005, 216, fig. 105), and the use of oak at Coddenham may be a little unusual. The general use of yew, with its known toxic and prophylactic qualities, may place their assumed role in the feasting hall in a different light.

XII. Combs in Graves 8, 24 and 30

Three graves contained the remains of combs. Grave 8 contained a bag and its contents, in the waist area, with a comb amongst the arm bones. The burial was that of an adult, probably female. Grave 24 was a male burial, with shield, bronze bowl and imported pot. The comb was found within the bowl, by the right side. Grave 30 was the bed burial of an adult female. The comb was found at the side of the grave, away from the other grave-goods.

Combs are not naturally part of 'dress', some have been found as part of a bag/box group, and others alongside the body. As noted above, bronze bowls are sometimes found associated with combs, and a ritual significance may be suspected in these cases, which now includes Coddenham Graves 24 and 30.

Combs are usually found in high-status graves, with examples coming from Sutton Hoo, Buckland (Dover), Harford Farm (Norfolk), Whitby (Yorks), and another buried with St Cuthbert's body in the later 7th century at Lindisfarne, Co Durham. However, not all combs have been found with adults; a recent excavation at Melbourn,

Cambs, recovered a hump-backed comb buried with a 13-year-old, along with shears and firesteel/pursemount (Duncan *et al.* 2003), and amongst the seven combs from Barrington, the young woman in the grave 18B bed burial was provided with a comb (Malim and Hines 1998, 218). A comb in a bronze bowl is recorded at Brightwell Heath, Suffolk, in a burial mound. The comb was in a triangular-lugged bronze bowl, which also contained a cremation burial, a decorated bone disc and ivory bracelet (West 1998, 12–13, fig. 11). Most recent is the comb and hanging bowl found at Tranmer House, Sutton Hoo (above).

With the high-status associations, some special significance is often suggested, with especial reference to sculptural depictions of combs on tombstones, for example, the mid-7th-century gravestone at Nieder-dollendorf, Germany, which shows a man combing his hair (Lasko 1971, 86–9; Penn 2000, 62). The comb placed in the grave of St Cuthbert must have some special significance for the burial of a tonsured monk.

The combs
by Ian Riddler

Three single-sided composite combs were retrieved from separate graves within the cemetery (Comb 1: Grave 30; Comb 2: Grave 24; Comb 3: Grave 8). All three combs survive in poor condition, but elements of their shape and decoration can be reconstructed. They are generally similar in terms of their materials, design and decoration, albeit with some differences. They are all made of antler, with rivets of iron. In each case, they include connecting plates with doubled framing lines, apparently unbounded at their ends, although the terminals of the connecting plates do not survive for Comb 3. Within the bounding lines lie single ring-and-dot patterns, disposed either in a single line (Comb 1) or in groups of four, separated by paired crossing diagonal lines (Comb 2). The patterning for Comb 3 is less clear, but it appears to utilise an alternation of single ring-and-dot patterns, arranged in a single line, and doubled crossing diagonal lines, as with Comb 1. In all cases the decoration is the same on both connecting plates and on Combs 1 and 2 it extends also to the end segments, filling the space beyond the connecting plates and the comb teeth. No end segments survive for Comb 3.

The end segments for Combs 1 and 2 project beyond the line of the back of the connecting plates, allowing both to be described as 'winged' combs. Comb 3 would almost certainly have been winged as well (very few combs of this period are not winged). The precise shape of the end segments from Comb 1 is not apparent, but the surviving end segment from Comb 2 is serrated, running in a curve from the end, to a pointed projection in the middle, with another curve beyond.

The riveting for Comb 1 follows a conventional Anglo-Saxon pattern, with the majority of the tooth segments secured on one edge and the end segments fastened through their centres. With Comb 3 the central part of the comb follows a similar arrangement, but one tooth segment is secured both at the edge and at its centre. Comb 2 is a little more complicated. The rivets are spaced at 20mm intervals and each one coincides with the centre of the pattern of crossing diagonal lines. The whole arrangement of the comb is therefore very well planned, and the decoration determines the riveting, which determines the widths of the tooth segments. With many other Anglo-Saxon combs, the widths of the tooth segments determine the rivet spacing, and this is often irregular. In this case, however, the riveting in effect forms a part of the decoration. The other two combs incorporate the same decorative motifs, but they are set out in a different manner. Fine diagonal patterning lies across the top of all three combs, cutting into the upper part of each connecting plate and running across the tooth segments.

The three Coddenham combs belong with a series of winged single-sided composites of 7th-century date. They may all belong to the second half of that century. Most of these combs have been found in graves, although some have come from contemporary settlements. Several distinct types can be identified within the series as a whole. They include a number of combs with decoration confined within panels, from Barrington, Burwell, Ducklington, Ipswich, Kingston, Thetford and West Stow (Malim and Hines 1998, fig. 3.63; Lethbridge 1931, figs 25.1, 34 and 36; Faussett 1856, pl. XIII; Dallas 1993, fig. 159.2; West 1985, fig. 272.2).

Closer parallels for the Coddenham combs are provided by those with continuous sequences of ring-and-dot patterning and decorated end segments, as with examples from Sutton Courtenay House IX, and particularly from Swallowcliffe Down (Leeds 1923, 167 and fig. XXVIII.1b; Speake 1989, 53–4 and figs 43 and 47).

Two further elements of the Swallowcliffe Down comb are also significant. Firstly, the riveting is systematic and is related directly to the decorative scheme. It is independent of the widths of the tooth segments, as with Coddenham Comb 2 and perhaps also with Comb 3. Secondly, the end segments are modelled to provide to inward-facing beasts. The profiling of the top of the end segments is essentially a feature of the Middle Anglo-Saxon period and it is one reason, incidentally, why the celebrated comb from Wharram Percy is of Middle Anglo-Saxon date, and does not belong to the early Anglo-Saxon period (MacGregor 1992, fig. 29; Riddler and Trzaska-Nartowski). The undulating end segments of Coddenham Combs 1 and 2 survive in fragmentary condition but may also have been intended to represent stylised beasts.

A comb from Canterbury also provides an important parallel (Blockley *et al.* 1995, 1167 and fig. 515, 1183). It has been placed in the 6th century on the basis of the broad dating of accompanying ceramics from its context, but the comb itself is certainly of 7th-century date, and probably belongs to the middle of the century. It is a doubled connecting plate comb, decorated with a continuous sequence of ring-and-dot motifs and with a riveting system that respects the decoration. The tops of the end segments are sinuous, rising to rounded apices in the middle, although they are undecorated. As with the Swallowcliffe Down comb, there are significant parallels between the design of the comb and the Coddenham series.

The closest parallel of all for Coddenham Comb 2, however, is provided by another comb from West Stow (West 1985, fig. 272.1). Indeed, there can be little doubt that this single-sided composite was made by the same comb maker. Only the central portion of the West Stow comb survives, but the decoration is the same, and it is integrated with the riveting. Moreover, it extends also to diagonal line patterns across the top of the comb, which occur across all three of the Coddenham combs, if more elaborately at West Stow. That also is largely a Middle Saxon feature, which can be seen on several combs from Ipswich, as well as the single-sided composites from Barrington and Burwell grave 83, and further combs from Wharram Percy and York (Riddler, Trzaska-Nartowski and Hatton forthcoming; Malim and Hines 1998, 3.38; Lethbridge 1931, 65; MacGregor 2000, fig. 70.27; Rogers 1993, fig. 682.5704, 5710 and 5723). It occurs also on a comb from Sutton Hoo Mound 1 (Care Evans and Galloway 1983, fig. 582).

The West Stow comb was recovered from the cemetery, where grave groups were not recorded, rather than the settlement, and it is not closely dated. The cemetery was a 19th-century discovery and the surviving objects cannot be assigned to individual graves (West 1985, 64–5). It does not help, therefore, with the dating of the Coddenham combs. Parallels provided here with combs from Swallowcliffe Down and Ipswich suggest that the Coddenham combs belong to the second half of the 7th century. Speake, following Hawkes, noted that the type, in general, became more common after the middle of the 7th century. The Swallowcliffe Down comb has been dated to the late 7th century (Hawkes 1973, 198; Speake 1989, 54). By that time, however, other single-sided composite comb designs were becoming prevalent in East Anglia, and particularly those with bands of lattice patterning, with an emphasis more on the ends of the connecting plates than the centre (Riddler 2001, 66; Riddler, Trzaska-Nartowski and Hatton forthcoming). The Coddenham combs prefigure these designs and accordingly belong perhaps to the period *c*.AD 650–675.

XIII. Textiles
by Penelope Walton Rogers

For technical terms, see Walton Rogers (2007, 60–67). Textiles were recorded in eleven graves, which may be classified by their accessories as five male-gender (Graves 1, 2, 24, 26, 32), three possibly male-gender (Graves 3, 5 and 13) and three female-gender (Graves 8, 30, 44); and on one unstratified object in a small pit (565). Changes in women's costume during the later 6th and early 7th century, had led to fewer metal brooches, clasps and buckles being worn, and, since textiles in burials are mostly preserved by their association with metalwork, correspondingly fewer clothing textiles survive. At Coddenham, however, soft-furnishings are present and the bed in Grave 30 is of particular interest.

Clothing: men
(Fig. 81)
A fine textile woven in tabby repp, 28/Z x 24/Z per cm, was preserved in a man's grave, Grave 2, in association with the small buckle and leather strap, (3), and on both faces of the knife, (1). The knife lies on the diagonal at the man's left waist and the buckle is immediately below. Tabby repp is a solid plain weave sometimes used for bedding, but when it appears in clothing it is almost always at the waist. In Grave 2, as elsewhere, the folds and the rib of the weave run across the knife and therefore across the body. It may be tentatively suggested that this is some form of cummerbund, comparable with the Roman *fascia ventralis*, which soldiers wore under the military belt and in which they kept small personal items tucked

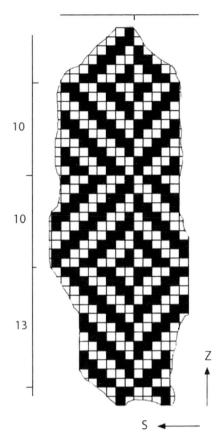

Figure 81 Grave 26, the pattern of the wool diamond twill

into the folds (Ubl 1989). A second tabby weave, a medium-weight piece, 16/Z x 10/Z per cm, was situated in a double layer against one face of the knife, where its function is unclear.

The buckle (4) found at the edge of Grave 1 had traces of poorly preserved textile running from the back of the buckle and falling over the edge of the buckle loop, with remains of a leather strap pierced by the buckle pin. Although no technical details of the textile could be recorded, its position and orientation are typical of textiles preserved on belt-buckles and it may be suggested that this object has been displaced from the man's waist. In Grave 26, textile was found on the back of a buckle (2) that was certainly in the region of the waist,. In this instance it was a medium-weight tabby made from hemp (or possibly low-grade flax), 14/Z x 12/Z per cm, which, unusually, still has brown fibres present, indicating that it has not been bleached. The natural fawn of the garment and the unremarkable quality of the weave tend to suggest working clothes.

In the same grave as the brown hempen garment, Grave 26, textile was preserved on one face of the iron fauchard (1). The textile was a thick wool diamond twill, 10/Z x 9/S per cm, made from a naturally dark brown or black fleece (for the weave structure see Fig. 81). The thread-count, weave and the use of a naturally coloured fleece are all typical of Anglo-Saxon cloaks (Walton Rogers 2007, 170). To judge from the position of the object in the grave, the fauchard may have been resting on the man's shoulder, but if not, the cloak may have been laid out as a grave lining comparable with those at Snape graves 36, 37 and 43 (Filmer-Sankey and Pestell 2001).

Clothing: women

In Grave 44, traces of a poorly preserved plain fabric, probably woven in tabby, were found on the iron latch-lifter (5), along with fine parallel S-ply cords, which represent either a tablet-woven band or a fringe. Similar remains have been found in 7th-century graves at Buckland II, Kent, in adult women's graves (353, 413) and a child's burial with female accessories (grave 376), where they were interpreted as the end of a woven girdle (Walton Rogers forthcoming). A warp-faced tabby running through a chatelaine complex at Harford Farm grave 22 may also represent the end of a girdle (Crowfoot 2000, 86). Long fringed girdles can be seen in a number of images of women of the Byzantine court (Owen-Crocker 2004, fig. 99; Marzinzik 2003, fig. 16A, 16B) and their presence in 7th-century graves probably reflects the arrival of Mediterranean fashions in Britain. The plain fabric in Grave 44 may represent any part of the woman's clothing — the robe, long veil or mantle.

Soft furnishings in the grave

In Grave 24 the shield lay towards one end of the grave, probably above the man's head to judge from the position of other objects in the grave, and imprints of textile were recorded on the outer face of the boss. One of the textiles is a relatively coarse, slightly ribbed piece, 12/S x 6/?. It is not possible to identify the fibre from an imprint, but the thick S-spun yarn suggests wool. This does not resemble Anglo-Saxon clothing fabrics and it is more likely to be some form of blanket or coverlet. A second piece interfolded with the first seems to be plain tabby, comparable with both clothing and bedding textiles of the period.

In Grave 1, the shield had been tilted over so that the conical boss lay touching the sword next to it. The organic remains now visible on the upper outer surface of the boss almost certainly represent the area caught between shield-boss and sword and the outermost layer of skin or leather will be from the sword scabbard. The textiles lie in two layers, the first and closest to the sword a thick wool textile with a twill-like texture, and the second a relatively coarse tabby, 12/Z x 12/Z per cm, with the appearance of linen, which covers a wider area of the boss (Plate 1). Crumpled layers of a medium-weight textile preserved on the grip at the back of the shield may represent the same linen tabby, or possibly something finer. The thread-count (7/Z x 7/Z per cm) and general characteristics of the textile are reminiscent of the different types of wool coverlet recorded elsewhere. Representative examples include the weave known as 'summer-and-winter' on top of a shield in 6th-century grave 85 at Wakerley, Northants (Crowfoot 1989), a variant of the same from under the body in 6th-century grave 37 at Snape (Crowfoot 2001, 208–9; re-classified in Walton Rogers forthcoming) and a warp-float tabby weave under the helmeted head of a man buried in the 7th century at Wollaston, Northants (Walton Rogers unpublished). The sword lay next to the body and it is possible that the Coddenham example represents a coverlet placed over the dead. If this is correct, then the sword was placed in the grave alongside the body, the coverlet laid on top, and then the linen-wrapped shield put in alongside.

The textile on undated iron object SF 1224 in Context 565 (a small pit), is represented by a coarse ground weave with swirls of animal fibre on top and has been interpreted as a pile weave. Pile weaves are found in women's graves in the 6th century but the three recorded from 7th-century barrows, Sutton Hoo Mound 1 (SH10) (Crowfoot 1983, 442–4), Broomfield Barrow (B4) (Crowfoot 1983, 471–2) and Banstead Down (Crowfoot 1976), are from men's burials, and there is a growing body of evidence that specialist textiles became a male preserve in the 7th century (Walton Rogers 2007, 240–1). The pile weaves are generally interpreted as cloaks, but the Coddenham example is unusually coarse, at 6 threads per cm, and may represent some sort of rug or cover. Where the 6th- and 7th-century pile weaves were made is unclear, but they are found in Vendel and Viking Sweden and they were certainly an export from the Nordic world in later centuries, although Ireland may have played a part in their production (Geijer 1938, 131–2; Guðjónsson 1962, 70–1). It is possible that they are the textiles termed *villosa* or 'shaggy' which were traded by Frisians in the 8th century. Even coarse examples such as the Coddenham piece were probably very valuable.

Wrappers for metalwork

In Grave 24, the fragments of the copper-alloy bowl, (2), have extensive areas of medium-weight linen tabby, 14–16/Z x 14–16/Z per cm, over the outer surfaces. Long strands of yarn underneath the foot-ring suggest a fringed border and some thick threads dipping into the weave at this point indicate some form of needle-worked binding or decoration next to the fringe (Plates 5 and 6). These remains may be reconstructed as a plain linen cloth draped over the bowl and its fringed ends tucked in under the foot-ring. Other pieces of similar tabby weave inside the bowl may be the same or perhaps a different fabric, used to wrap the bowl contents. Large flat areas of a finer tabby, 18/Z x 22–24/Z per cm, lie underneath the bowl (Plate 6), and probably represent sheeting underneath bowl and body. Similar remains — a fine textile and parallel cords which may be a fringe — were recorded on the copper-alloy bowl from the bed burial, Grave 30. This covering of bowls with linen cloths has been recorded at several other sites, including Banstead Down, Surrey (Crowfoot 1976, 71), where the linen had been stretched over the mouth of the vessel and tied with a cord, and Brightwell Heath, Martlesham (Crowfoot 1967, 38), Snape cremation 68 (Crowfoot 1973; 2001, 157), Sutton Hoo Mound 4 (Crowfoot 1983, 466–7), Wreningham, Norfolk (E. Crowfoot, pers. comm.), and Croydon (Park Lane) grave 6, Surrey (Walton Rogers 2003, 95).

A linen chevron or diamond twill, 16/Z x 14/Z per cm, was preserved on the socket of the spearhead (6) in Grave 1. There is good evidence that spears were wrapped for burial (Walton Rogers 2007, 228), usually in coarser cloths than the one preserved here, but the position of the fabric close up against the socket, where in other graves there is sometimes a cord binding, is typical of a spear wrapper. Folds of medium-weight linen tabby on a sharp steel (6) from Grave 3 and on a fragmentary iron object (1b) from Grave 8, may also represent wrapping fabrics.

Cords for stringing and binding

Cords and threads had been used for a number of different purposes. There was a section of a necklace cord inside two beads (3k and 4a) from the bed burial, Grave 30: it was 1.5–2.0mm diameter, multi-stranded and almost certainly flax. A cord had been used to bind together a knife and a sharpening tool (5a b) in Grave 8: it was S-cabled (cabled means plied and then re-plied) and it was over 1.0mm thick. Some Z-spun linen threads had also been used to bind the handle of an awl (3c), from Grave 5 and with it was a medium-fine tabby, 18/Z x 16/Z per cm, probably hemp: these remains are similar to the binding on an awl from Harford Farm grave 18, which was a tabby-weave 20/Z x 14–16/Z per cm, bound with a multi-strand cord (Crowfoot 2000, 84). Finally, an S-spun thread of naturally grey wool that spirals along the cutting edge of a knife (3) from Grave 44, is likely to represent the remains of stitching from the sheath (J. Watson, pers. comm.).

Textiles from the bed burial, Grave 30
(Plate 14)
The same textile was recorded repeatedly on the iron bands that form the upper and lower rails on the left and right of the bed. It is a coarse textile woven in 2/2 twill and made from plied yarn, 9/Z2S x 7/Z2S per cm (Plate 14). The fibre is grey wool, identified first by transmitted-light microscopy and then confirmed by scanning-electron microscopy by J. Watson. The textile is in all instances exactly square to the iron bands, on one face only, and it must be assumed that it forms part of the bed structure rather than the bedding. It is curious, however, that this is a wool twill. Plied yarn gives extra strength to the fabric, but wool is more elastic than linen and twill more elastic than tabby. There must have been a reason for the choice of a strong textile with plenty of 'give'. Other textile items included a fine tape, 6–7mm wide, twisted tightly round one of the metal fittings from the upper left side rail (SF 1094), and a fine linen tabby on one of the attachment plates of a copper-alloy ring (9g). The function of these is unknown, but a fine twill on the lozenge-shaped studs of the headboard and footboard may represent some form of fixed fabric cover.

At Swallowcliffe Down four textiles were associated with the bed, of which three were probably blankets and sheets, but the fourth was a poorly preserved twill on the eyelets which may be comparable with the Coddenham twill (Crowfoot 1989, 116–7). George Speake thought it

Plate 14 Grave 30: Textile on bed

lay between the suspended latticework and a mattress of straw or grass, for which there was evidence on nail heads and eyelets, and drew comparison with the Shudy Camps bed with similar coarse cloth and straw (Speake 1989, 98). Elisabeth Crowfoot refers to these twills as from the 'body support area' in her description of another example of 2/2 twill of about 10/Z x 10/S per cm on the bed in grave 18, Edix Hill, Barrington (Crowfoot 1998, 240–1, 246). It is possible that the Coddenham twill is a form of support for the mattress, pinned to the rails of the bed and originally resting on the cords strung between the eyelets.

Chapter 6. Human Skeletal Remains

by Sue Anderson

I. Introduction

Human remains from thirty-four Early Anglo-Saxon graves were available for analysis, the remaining sixteen excavated graves having contained no bone. A full list is provided in Table 14.

II. Method

Measurements were taken using the methods described by Brothwell (1981), together with a few from Bass (1971) and Krogman (1978). The maximum mesio-distal and bucco-lingual dimensions of teeth were also recorded. Non-metric dental traits were recorded based on figures published by Hillson (1996). Sexing and ageing techniques follow Brothwell (1981) and the Workshop of European Anthropologists (WEA 1980), with the exception of adult tooth wear scoring which follows Bouts and Pot (1989). Stature was estimated according to the regression formulae of Trotter and Gleser (Trotter 1970). All systematically scored non-metric traits are listed in Brothwell (1981), and grades of cribra orbitalia and osteoarthritis can also be found there. Pathological conditions were identified with the aid of Ortner and Putschar (1981) and Cotta (1978). Material from regional and national contemporary groups has been used for comparison (see below), but note that in some cases the figures used are not as published because they have been recalculated in order to make them directly comparable (for example, in terms of age group).

III. Comparative material

Comparisons are made with Early to Middle Anglo-Saxon groups where possible (shown in Table 13).

Very few large contemporary groups have been analysed in East Anglia, due to the typically poor preservation of Anglo-Saxon cemeteries located on the acidic sandy or gravel soils.

The four 5th- to 7th-century groups are rural in nature, the best comparator in terms of status being Barrington, where two bed burials were excavated. The four later groups are thought to be either monastic or 'proto-urban'.

IV. Number of individuals

The thirty-four graves contained a minimum of thirty-five articulated skeletons — there was one double burial (Grave 6). No disarticulated bone was found.

V. Condition

An assessment of condition of the bone was made for each skeleton, although it is recognised that this is fairly subjective. The assessment of condition took into account the preservation of the bone, not the completeness or otherwise of the skeleton. Three skeletons were considered to be in 'good' condition, six were 'fair', six were 'poor' and twenty were 'very poor'. Generally there was a high degree of surface erosion in this assemblage, many bones consisting of flaky fragments of the outer layers which had been separated from the thicker cortical bone and had often either disappeared or were the only part to survive. All skeletons were fragmented, even those in good condition, although it was possible to reconstruct a few skulls for measurement.

VI. Demographic analysis

A summary list of skeletons with age and sex is included in Table 14.

Juveniles

Six children below the age of 16 years were present in this assemblage, a proportion of 17.1%. A further sub-adult was identified as a possible male, although he was probably aged 16–18 years. If he is included, the percentage of juveniles is increased to 20%. This is still relatively low and may be attributable to the generally poor condition of juvenile (and adult) bones in this group. Five of the six child skeletons were categorised as 'poor' or 'very poor'. If the graves which produced no skeletal material are considered, at least another six children could be added to the total, which would give a proportion of 24% children to 76% adults. This is within normal limits for Early to Middle Anglo-Saxon groups — generally between one fifth to one third of the burials are juvenile — although still at the lower end of the range.

Site name	Location	Date range	MNI	Analyst
Great Chesterford	Essex	M.5th–6th century	167	Waldron (1994)
Barrington A	Cambs	6th–E.7th century	148	Duhig (1998)
Norton	North-east	6th–E.7th century	109	Marlow (1992)
West Heslerton	Yorkshire	5th–7th century	192	Cox (1990)
Burgh Castle	Norfolk	7th–10th century	167	Anderson and Birkett (1991; 1993)
Nazeingbury	Essex	L.7th–M.9th century	153	Putnam (1978)
Brandon Cemetery 1	Suffolk	8th–10th century	153	Anderson (1990)
Caister-on-Sea	Norfolk	8th–11th century	139	Anderson (1991, 1993)

Table 13 Early to Middle Anglo-Saxon burial groups

Grave	Skeleton	Sex	GG sex*	Age	Condition	Stature	Cranial Index	Pathology
1	0198	Unsexed	Male	Adult	Poor			
2	0173	?Male	Male	c.16–18	Fair	175.7		
3	0215	?Male		Adult	V. poor			
4	0191	Female		Adult	V. poor			
5	0179	?Male		Mature	V. poor			OP
6a	0176	Unsexed		Young	V. poor			
6b	0192	Unsexed	Female	Young	Poor			Misc
7	-		Female		No bone			
8	0554	?Female	Female	Adult	V. poor			
9	0199	Male		Y-MA	Fair	176.7	73.8	OP, Trauma
10	0227	?Male		Adult	V. poor			
11	-		Female		No bone			
12	0207	Unsexed		Adult?	V. poor			
13	0221	?Male		Adult	V. poor			
14	-		Female		No bone			
15	0611	?Female		Young	V. poor			
16	-		Female	Child?	No bone			
17	-			Child?	No bone			
18	0232	Male		Middle-aged	Good	176.8	77.6	Dental, Trauma, Degeneration, Deficiency, Misc
19	0206	Male		Old	Fair-good	177.0	76.0	Dental, Trauma, Degeneration, Infection, Misc
20	0660	Male		Young	V. poor			
21	-				No bone			
22	-				No bone			
23	-			Child?	No bone			
24	-		Male		No bone			
25	0547	Unsexed		c.6	Poor			
26	0542	Unsexed	Male	Adult?	V. poor			
27	0342	Female		Young	Poor-fair	157.4		OP
28	0332	Unsexed		c.3	V. poor			
29	0553	Male		Young?	Fair			
30	0337	Female	Female	Mature	V. poor	178.2		Degeneration
31	0325	Unsexed		c.7	V. poor			
32	0348	Unsexed	?Male	c.11–12	Poor			
33	0343	Unsexed		c.4	V. poor			
34	0483	Unsexed		Adult	Poor			
35	-			Child?	No bone			
36	-			Child?	No bone			
37	0317	Unsexed		Adult	V. poor			
38	-		Female	Child?	No bone			
39	-				No bone			
40	0301	?Male		Old	Good	170.9	71.9	Dental, Infection, Degeneration, Trauma
41	-				No bone			
42	0288	Female		Middle-aged+	Poor			Dental, Trauma, Degeneration
43	0324	Unsexed		Middle-aged?	V. poor			Dental
44	0293	Unsexed	Female	Unknown	V. poor			
45	0314	Male		Y-MA	V. poor			
46	0428	Unsexed		c.15–16	Fair			
47	0455	Unsexed		Adult	V. poor			Infection?
48	0448	?Male	Male	Y-MA	Fair			Dental
49	-				No bone			
50	-				No bone			

*GG Sex — grave-good sexing

Table 14 Summary of graves and skeletons

Of the Early Anglo-Saxon groups, West Heslerton produced the smallest proportion, 17.7% juveniles; Norton 30.2%; at Barrington, 31% were below the age of 18; but at Great Chesterford, where child mortality seems to be unusually high, 50% were below 15 years. Amongst the Middle Saxon groups, Nazeingbury had the unusually low figure of 11.1%; Burgh Castle had a proportion of 18.0%; Caister 23.0%; at Brandon, 20.3% of the fully excavated (but poorly preserved) cemetery were children. Unfortunately, non-random distribution of child burials in some sites, together with the fact that so few cemeteries are completely excavated, makes interpretation of these figures difficult. The expected proportion of children would be around one third of the group, so a lower figure *may* be significant in interpreting burial practices.

Four of the juveniles died between the ages of 3 and 7 years, one was aged 11–12 years at death, and one was 15–16 years old. The fact that there are no infants in the assemblage is almost certainly related to preservation of bone at this site. Based on other groups, approximately 5–10% of all child burials might be expected to be below the age of 2 years in the Early Saxon period, and around 15–20% in the Middle Saxon period. However, sometimes the figures can be skewed by clusters of child burials. For example, at Hartlepool Church Walk, 62.5% of children were under 2 years (Anderson 2007), and at Great Chesterford the figure was as high as 80%. In most other groups, the highest death rates are in the 2–5 year or 6–11 year ranges.

Adults
Twenty-nine individuals were over the age of 16 years at death. Of these, thirteen were male (including seven ?male), six were female (two ?female) and ten were unsexable. As some grave-good sexing was possible, the skeletal evidence was compared with that from the artefacts and, where sexing was possible from both methods (only four individuals), the results were the same. Four unsexed adults had gender-specific grave-goods, adding a further two males and two females, and one of the children had male artefacts. The graves which did not contain bone added a further adult male, three adult females and two juvenile females. The total for adults, based on both sexing methods, was fourteen males and nine females, a sex ratio of 1 M : 0.6 F. This is not statistically significant. Clearly the excavated area represents only the edge of a much larger cemetery, which could account for the difference.

There were some problems in the sexing of this group which were not entirely related to the poor condition of many of the skeletons. It has been noted in other Anglo-Saxon groups that the sexing features of the skull can be indeterminate (*e.g.* Duhig 1998, 157). In two of the female skeletons at Coddenham (Graves 30 and 27), it was observed that the occipital crest was large, a male trait in most populations, although in both cases features of the pelvis indicated a female. The skeleton in Grave 40, sexed as ?male, had a large femoral head and robust cranial features but the sciatic notch of the pelvis was wide. This individual could have been wrongly sexed, and unfortunately the grave-goods were equally ambiguous — two buckles and a knife. In this cemetery, however, for those graves where biological sexing is available, all individuals with only a buckle and a knife are male.

Table 15 shows the distribution of adult age at death. Categories of age rather than actual age ranges are employed because estimation of adult age at death is difficult with currently available techniques. The data should be taken to represent *biological* rather than chronological age at death.

Only 59% of these skeletons could be aged more closely than 'adult'. If the 'Middle-aged' category is assumed to include individuals over approximately 40 years of age, then almost two-thirds of the group (58.8%) were younger than this at death. The lack of people in old age, however, may again be a reflection of the poor overall preservation of the assemblage, as the thinner, more porous bones of the elderly might be expected to disappear more quickly than the stronger bones of younger individuals.

In other Early Anglo-Saxon groups, perhaps surprisingly, the proportion of individuals in the younger adult categories is even higher. At Norton, 81.8% of individuals were below *c*.40 years, at West Heslerton 84.3%, at Barrington 63.1%. Only Great Chesterford was lower, with 47.4%. There were fewer older adults, proportionally, at Norton and West Heslerton than at Coddenham, but more at Barrington and Great Chesterford. The Middle Saxon groups all had lower proportions of young adults than Coddenham, the highest being Brandon at 53.0%, then Nazeingbury at 43.0%, Caister at 31.1% and Burgh at 31.1%. This tends to suggest that Coddenham was moving towards the Middle Anglo-Saxon pattern, as might be expected in a Conversion Period cemetery of relatively high status.

VII. Metrical and morphological analysis

Tables of measurements and non-metric traits are provided in the site archive.

Stature
Estimated living stature could be calculated for five men and two women. The mean of the male group was 175.4cm

Age group	Male No.	Male %	Female No.	Female %	Total incl. unsexed No.	Total incl. unsexed %
Young	3	30.0	2	50.0	7	41.2
Young/Middle-aged	3	30.0	0	-	3	17.6
Middle-aged	2	20.0	1	25.0	4	23.5
Old	2	20.0	1	25.0	3	17.6
Total aged	10		4		17	
Unaged adult	3		2		12	
Total	**13**		**6**		**29**	

Table 15 Distribution of adult age at death

(5' 9") and the range was 170.9cm to 177.0cm (5' 7" to 5' 9½"). The tallest individual in the group was the woman from the bed burial (Grave 30), who measured 178.2cm (5' 10"), the other female being only 157.4cm tall (5' 2"). All five men and the taller of the two women were above the male and female averages for contemporary groups. This may be a reflection of status, as these people appear to have been better able to approach their genetic potential.

The tallest groups in East Anglia are those associated with possible monastic houses. Burgh Castle, for example, has a male mean of 175.9cm, Nazeingbury 175.3cm. A group from a possible Middle Anglo-Saxon monastic graveyard in Hartlepool (Anderson 2007) were in the same range, at 175.2cm. At Barrington, the overall male mean was 173.3cm, but it is interesting that the mean for ten men buried with shields and spears was 175.3cm. Other Early Anglo-Saxon groups were shorter, the male mean at Great Chesterford being 166cm, at West Heslerton 173.7cm, and at Norton 173.5cm. Middle Anglo-Saxon groups at Brandon and Caister-on-Sea were also shorter, their male means being 171.6 and 170.8cm respectively.

Cranial indices

Only four skulls were reconstructable, all male, and it was not considered worthwhile to record the full range of measurements for these. Only the maximum length, breadth and height of the vault were recorded for each, and cranial indices calculated. The average breadth/length index was 74.8, and the range was 71.9 to 77.6. The skulls were all dolichocranial (narrow) or mesocranial (medium width), which is as expected for an Anglo-Saxon group. Most groups tend to have around two-thirds of skulls in the narrow range.

Non-metric traits

Non-metric traits are small asymptomatic deviations from the 'normal' skeletal anatomy and are scored on a present/absent basis. A number have been shown to be of genetic origin, and this may be the case for others. Tables of scores and percentages for each trait are included in the Appendix.

The maximum number of individuals for which any one trait could be scored was eight. A statistical study using mean measure of divergence (MMD) showed no significant difference from several groups in Norfolk, Suffolk and York, probably due to the small sample size. However, it is interesting that the closest group was the Anglo-Saxon population from School Street, Ipswich. Nothing unusual was observed in those areas which could be scored most frequently, and unfortunately it was not possible to identify family groups on this basis. It may be of interest, however, that the three individuals with lambdoid wormian bones (in Graves 9, 19, 18), all of which were located in similar positions in the suture, were also very similar in height and cranial dimensions, and two of these men were buried in adjacent graves. Of course, as the individuals for whom these metric and morphological traits could be recorded were so few, the possibility that these traits were common in the group cannot be discounted. Non-metric traits of the teeth are discussed below.

VIII. Dental analysis

Twenty-three individuals had complete or partial dentitions. Of these, sixteen were adults and seven children. The sixteen individuals consisted of nine males, four females and three unsexed adults of various ages at death, but the group was too small for separation into sex or age categories.

If complete dentitions from all the adult individuals had been present, there would have been a total of 512 observable positions. However, 177 teeth/positions were missing, leaving 335 observable positions, 103 of which consisted of the enamel part of the tooth only, the roots and alveolar bone having dissolved. This means that there were 232 positions which could be assessed for abscesses or ante-mortem tooth loss. Ante-mortem loss was recorded in 16 positions; the ante-mortem tooth loss frequency for this group is therefore 6.9%. Ten abscesses were recorded, which gives a frequency of 4.3%. Post-mortem loss from assessable alveoli totalled 36. No teeth in this group were unerupted, including the third molars of the youngest individual (Grave 2, c.16–18 years). A total of 283 teeth were present. Fourteen carious lesions in the surviving teeth gave a frequency of 4.9% for this dental pathology. This data is summarised in Table 16, along with prevalences from other groups.

Site	% caries	% abscesses	% A–M loss
Coddenham	4.9	4.3	6.9
Norton	3.4	0.7	4.1
Barrington	3.2	?	7.1
West Heslerton	2.4	0.1	1.2
Burgh	1.9	2.0	6.1
Caister-on-Sea	1.8	5.4	6.5
Brandon	1.0	2.5	6.1

Table 16 Dental disease frequencies at Coddenham and contemporary sites

The prevalences of the three main types of dental disease at Coddenham are very high in comparison with most other contemporary groups. This is probably due in part to the small size of the group. Overall frequencies are in any case difficult to compare, since dental disease always affects the older members of a group to a greater degree than the younger. For example, West Heslerton had a very high proportion of young adults, which could account for the low frequencies of dental disease seen there. At Coddenham, all ante-mortem tooth loss affected three middle-aged and old individuals, and all caries and abscesses were present in four of this age group (one had caries, but no alveolar bone survived so abscesses could not be scored).

The carious lesions seen in this group all appear to have originated in interstitial cervical positions and often affected adjoining teeth as a result. In five cases the caries had spread to affect a large part of the crown. This is typical of Anglo-Saxon groups.

The seven juvenile dentitions added a further 20 deciduous teeth, and 53 erupted and 41 unerupted permanent teeth. No caries was present in any of these teeth, reducing the prevalence in erupted permanent teeth to 4.2%.

The poor condition of the teeth generally made recording of calculus and enamel hypoplasia difficult, but both conditions were present. Calculus was particularly heavy in at least four middle-aged or older men. Slight enamel hypoplasia had affected the anterior mandibular teeth of Grave 40 between the ages of *c*.4–6 years, the lower left first incisor of Grave 32 at *c*.3–4 years, and the lower canines of Grave 48 between *c*.3–6 years. The presence of this condition suggests that periods of illness or malnutrition had occurred in these individuals.

Maximum mesio-distal and bucco-lingual measurements of the teeth were recorded for all extant teeth, to determine whether these data could aid in sex determination. An attempt was made to apply principal component analysis to the data, but unfortunately the number of individuals for whom both measurements could be taken for any one tooth was no more than sixteen, and often much less. Several of the larger groups of measurements were used, but it was clear that the overlap between the sexes was too great in this small group for the data to be used in sex determination.

Epigenetic traits of the teeth were recorded systematically following Hillson (1996, partial information on ASU Dental Non-Metric Recording System). Unfortunately, as for tooth measurements, there was a high degree of missing data. Recording of this type has not been attempted on previous groups studied by the author, so no directly comparable data sets were available. A study of non-metric traits of teeth from Middle Anglo-Saxon Brandon and Roman Icklingham has been undertaken (Lloyd-Jones 1997) and this was compared. Based on nine traits using the mean measure of divergence (MMD), both sites were found to be statistically significantly different from Coddenham, although they showed no significant differences between each other. As so little data was available, it is uncertain whether this difference is real or simply a result of inter-observer error. Few traits of note were present at Coddenham; Carabelli's cusps were present on the first upper molars of two children (Graves 28 and 33), protostylids were present on the lower right third molars of two adults (Graves 6a and 9), and Grave 31, a 7 year-old child, had unerupted permanent barrel-like upper lateral incisors.

IX. Pathology

In general, the condition of these skeletons, with so much surface erosion and post-mortem breakage, was not conducive to the preservation of pathological changes and few were observed.

Arthropathies and degenerative disease
Five men and three women had changes which were related to degenerative disease, ranging from slight osteophytosis to Grade III osteoarthritis.

A fairly well-preserved young to middle-aged male (Grave 9) had slight osteophytosis of some left zygapophyseal joints of the vertebrae, but no other degenerative changes. A mature adult ?male (Grave 5) in very poor condition had slight new bone growth on the border of the right acetabulum (hip joint). A young female (Grave 27, age based on tooth wear) had slight new bone growth on both femoral head borders. In general, most of these changes were minor and would have had little impact on daily life. Grave 18, a middle-aged male in good

Plate 15 Grave 42, channel in distal right radius

condition, had osteophytosis of the proximal left zygapophyseal facet of one mid-thoracic vertebra and slight porosity of the sixth and seventh cervical vertebral bodies, but no other degenerative changes.

A middle-aged or older female (Grave 42) in poor condition had Grade I–II arthritic changes on some mid-thoracic vertebral joints and one rib, which may have caused her some discomfort. She also had osteophytes at the distal end of the right radius, and a channel had formed in the articular surface with a groove opening at the anterior edge (Plate 15). This may be related to an arthritic condition or an infection.

The mature adult female from the bed burial (Grave 30) had osteophytosis of all surviving vertebrae (T9–S1), which were largest on the right sides of the third to fifth lumbars. There was Grade II osteoarthritis of the fifth lumbar and first sacral bodies, but most other joint surfaces were not assessable. There were osteophytes at the superior edge of the anterior facet of the calcaneus.

Most joint margins of an old male (Grave 19) had slight lipping, but it was most noticeable on the femur and humerus heads. Osteophytes were also present on his mid-thoracic to lumbar vertebrae, some large. These, together with new bone formation on several joints and ligament attachments, specifically the right femoral greater and lesser trochanters and both tibiae joints for the proximal fibulae (calcification of the interosseous membrane), suggested the possibility of diffuse ideopathic skeletal hyperostosis (DISH), although the individual was probably well-muscled and some of the changes could simply be adaptations of the skeleton as a result of this.

The most pronounced degenerative changes in this group were seen in Grave 40, an old ?male in good condition. There were osteophytes of all thoracic to first sacral vertebrae and some mid-rib heads. The margins of both scapular glenoids were also affected. Osteoarthritis was present in both hip joints, with large osteophytes around the femoral heads, patches of eburnation on the articular surfaces, and sclerosis of the acetabular floors. In the spine, the first and second cervical vertebrae were affected with Grade III osteoarthritis, there was sclerosis and osteophytosis of the left zygapophyseal joints of the first to fifth cervical vertebrae, Grade II osteoarthritis of the fifth to seventh cervical bodies and the seventh

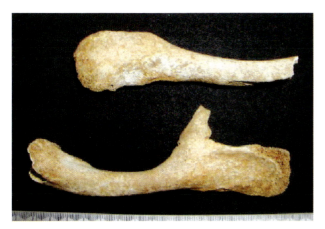

Plate 16 Grave 19, bony spur on left clavicle, with right for comparison

Plate 18 Grave 19, oval lesion in right fifth metatarsal

cervical and first thoracic left zygapophyseal facets. The vertebrae, particularly the mid to lower thoracics, were cod-like and there may have been some compression anteriorly in the lower thoracic region, with kyphosis.

Trauma and stress indicators

Major trauma was rare in this group and consisted only of a few fractured bones. No cuts, either healed or unhealed, were seen. Most physical trauma was in the form of minor stress-related lesions such as Schmorl's nodes of the spine, or evidence for torn ligaments or muscle attachments.

Most individuals were not assessable for the presence or absence of Schmorl's nodes due to poor preservation of the vertebral column. Individuals who were affected by them included a middle-aged male (Grave 18, T10–12), an old ?male (Grave 40, T8–L3), and a mature female (Grave 30, T9–L1). Grave 19, an old man, had none.

The left clavicle of Grave 19, an old male, had a large bony spur at the conoid tubercle and roughening of the posterior surface over the trapezoid line (Plate 16). The most likely cause of this is a torn muscle followed by myositis ossificans. The attachments for the deltoid and pectoralis major of this individual suggest that he was very well muscled, perhaps indicating that he was involved in an occupation which required greater than average strength, such as blacksmithing or woodworking. There

was also a small, healed, osteochondritic lesion in the centre of the proximal end of the right proximal hallucial phalanx (the big toe joint)

Small fragments of two mid-rib shafts, one right and one left, indicated that healed fractures had affected Grave 18, a middle-aged man (Plate 17). The left side seemed to be slightly more advanced in terms of callus formation, the right side still having a visible fracture line. This could indicate two episodes of injury. A small stress fracture was observed on the proximal end of the tibia, on the posterior edge of the lateral side. It was semi-circular and 12mm across.

A young to middle-aged male, Grave 9, appeared to have had a fracture of the right clavicle, although the only evidence was a marked thickening of the shaft in comparison with the left. This individual also had a small stress lesion at the distal articulation of the tibia next to the medial malleolus. The roughened edge of the anterior of the right calcaneus suggested that there was also some damage here, which had been followed by osteophyte formation and pitting.

Plate 17 Grave 18, fractured ribs

89

Grave 40, an old male, also had stress lesions at the anterior facet of both calcaneii (heel bones), which were semi-circular and had roughened edges. The inferior margin of the chin was roughened, irregular and asymmetrical, possibly indicating a torn muscle attachment. There appears to have been spondylolysis and spondylolisthesis of the fifth lumbar vertebra, but the arch is missing.

A torn muscle attachment was the likely cause of new bone on the right radius around the radial tuberosity, of middle-aged female Grave 42.

Deficiency disease
Generally skulls were in too poor condition for the presence or absence of cribra orbitalia and porotic hyperostosis to be recorded. However, cribra was present to a mild degree in the orbits of middle-aged male Grave 18 and *c*.15–16 year-old sub-adult Grave 46. These conditions are associated with iron deficiency anaemia.

Infections
Maxillary sinusitis was present in two old males, Graves 19 and 40, both in the left side and as a result of abscess draining. The facial bones of Grave 40 were partially reconstructed, and the left maxilla appeared to have an unusually deep fossa in the region of the infra-orbital foramen in comparison with the right (not complete). This area seemed slightly pitted, although it was affected by post-mortem surface erosion, and it seems possible that the infection within the sinus could have affected it. One other possibility is a healed trauma followed by inflammatory changes.

A small patch of grained periosteal bone was present on the medial surface of the left tibia shaft of Grave 40, which could be the result of inflammation. However surface erosion had removed most of the surrounding bone so the diagnosis is tentative.

Grave 19 had an erosive lesion in the proximal end of the shaft of the right fifth metatarsal, on the superior surface *c*.13mm from the proximal facet. It was oval and measured 10 x 7mm x 4.5mm deep. The sides were smooth and curving, and the base opened into the medullary cavity (Plate 18). The cause is uncertain: it could be a very localised infection, or perhaps a bone cyst.

A proximal fragment of the right tibia shaft was one of the few surviving fragments of unsexed adult Grave 47. A large oval cyst with a smooth floor, *c*.13.5mm long x 7.5mm wide x 7.5mm deep, was present internally, and the cancellous structure appeared slightly thickened around it. This may have been caused by an osteomyelitic infection, but preservation was too poor to be certain.

Miscellaneous lesions
Slight abnormal curvature of the tibiae medio-laterally was seen in both Grave 6b (young unsexed adult) and Grave 48 (young to middle-aged ?male). This may have resulted in genu valgum (knock knee) and can be a result of rickets or scurvy in childhood, or of unknown cause.

There was slight coxa valga of the right femur of Grave 18, a middle-aged male, which had resulted in sclerosis of the superior edge of the femoral head. The cause, in this case, is unknown.

X. Summary and discussion

The remains of thirty-five individuals were examined. The majority were in poor or very poor condition. The group consisted of six children under the age of 16 years, thirteen adult males, six adult females and ten unsexed adults. A further six children, one adult male and three adult females were suggested for graves which did not contain any bone. The male to female ratio was not statistically significant.

There was no particular pattern to the distribution of juvenile ages at death, probably due to the small size of the group. No infants were present, but this was probably a result of poor preservation. Only seventeen adults could be aged, and of these the majority were probably below the age of 40 years at death. Again the lack of very elderly individuals may be a consequence of the acidic soil conditions. Although the evidence is tentative due to the size of the group, it appears that the pattern of adult age at death is closer to that found in Middle Anglo-Saxon, rather than earlier, populations.

Six of the seven adults for whom stature could be estimated were above average height for the period. They compared well with Middle Anglo-Saxon monastic groups and high status Early Anglo-Saxon males. This suggests that at least some of the Coddenham population were able to achieve their genetic potential. Few other metric characteristics could be analysed, but the four skulls which could be measured were in the normal range for an Anglo-Saxon population.

Cranial and post-cranial non-metric traits were recorded and compared statistically with other local groups. Although the figures were too small to show any significant difference, it was interesting that the Coddenham group bore the closest similarity to an Anglo-Saxon population from Ipswich. The possibility exists that three of the males were related, based on the presence and position of extra-sutural bones of the skull and other physical factors. Non-metric traits of the teeth indicated a difference between this population and late Roman and Middle Anglo-Saxon groups to the west of the county, Icklingham and Brandon respectively. The skeletal non-metric traits also indicated a large difference, very close to being statistically significant, between Coddenham and Brandon.

Dental disease prevalences were relatively high in the Coddenham populations, but this is often the case in small groups, since one or two badly affected individuals can skew the figures. This is the case here — all examples were found in four middle-aged or older adults. Even so, the number and size of carious lesions affecting these individuals appeared unusual for an Anglo-Saxon group, and could indicate a diet rich in carbohydrates.

Pathological conditions identified in this group consisted largely of degenerative disease, trauma and stress-related injuries. Most were typical of a rural Anglo-Saxon population, where it might be expected that accidental injury and the general physical stresses of daily life would be represented in the bones. There was nothing to provide any evidence for violent death or trauma, although a possible fractured clavicle and a pair of fractured ribs may have been caused by intentional blows. Evidence for deficiency diseases and infections was also slight, but traces of these may have been removed by post-mortem erosion.

Although the group was relatively small and many of the skeletons were poorly preserved, it is possible to provide some tentative conclusions about the physical nature of this population. There is some evidence that they were relatively well-nourished — few signs of deficiency (such as enamel hypoplasia), a diet rich in carbohydrates, and above average stature for example — which may indicate high status. However, even those buried with the most lavish of grave-goods, such as the woman from the bed burial, showed signs of physical stress.

Whilst similar in many respects to their contemporaries throughout the Anglian area, the group appears to have been genetically closest to populations living to the east of the region, around Ipswich and the East Norfolk coast.

Chapter 7. Burial Practice

I. Introduction

Whilst the distribution of individual objects types in Early Anglo-Saxon cemeteries could suggest regions with differing material culture, changes in burial patterns were synchronous across England outside Kent. Cemeteries in the 6th century are notable for their strong patterns of accompaniment, and little evidence for ranking, a situation which changed around AD 600, with the dropping of accompanied burial and a dearth of accompanied burials until the middle of the 7th century. From about this period, cemeteries such as Coddenham are found, characterised by mostly unaccompanied or modest burials but with a proportion of burials more lavishly provided. These burials were acompanied by grave-goods from a distinctive range of objects, some imported, and found across the whole country, irrespective of kingdom. Across the whole country, too, cemeteries with such burials came to an end around the 720s.

In the later 7th century, modest or unaccompanied burial was the dominant mode, and amongst accompanied burials there was no strong pattern of provision, in part a reflection of access to material culture (Hyslop 1963, 189; Meaney and Hawkes 1970, 45). Local conventions appear to have been stable, perhaps even enforced or controlled by special individuals (Geake 1999b; 2003).

II. Location

The cemetery stood on a ridge or bluff with a minor stream to the north, overlooking an occupation site in the valley below at Vicarage Farm (CDD 022). Burial in such locations was probably typical of Anglo-Saxon cemeteries in the 6th century (Penn and Brugmann 2007), and was still the case with many late 7th-century cemeteries. At Coddenham, as at Harford Farm and many other places, the existence of a prehistoric barrow (219/220) may have been another determinant of location.

The ridge with its prehistoric barrow provided a perfect location for a monument intended to be seen from the valley below, and the establishment of a visible and permanent presence may have been a primary reason for the location of the cemetery at this point on the skyline, next to an existing barrow.

III. Use of barrows

By the end of the 7th century, the mortuary landscape included minster churches and 'monasteries' for the elite, whilst other individuals were buried elsewhere, sometimes in prominent places, often marked by a burial mound. There may have been four barrows at Coddenham: those around Graves 1, 2, and 17, and ring-ditch 219/220 with no identified central burial, possibly a prehistoric barrow.

The association of prehistoric barrows and Anglo-Saxon cemeteries is well-known in 5th- to 6th-century cemeteries, and appears to have been especially marked in the later 7th century, in particular in certain areas of England, especially Kent, Wiltshire and the Peak District (Meaney 1964, 18–19; Shephard 1979), but also further north, *e.g.* at Uncleby and other sites, on the Yorkshire Wolds (Lucy 1999; Smith 1912).

The reason for the building and reuse of barrows has been much discussed, especially in relation to social and religious changes through the 7th century. It has been held that barrows may have been built to announce ownership of land (Shephard 1979, 77), or as a way of using the past 'to promote the interests of a social elite' (Bradley 1987, 14–15).

In his review of the reuse of earlier monuments, Williams saw the practice as a deliberate appropriation, to create a burial landscape and to use and enhance existing places already invested with special qualities and symbolism (Williams 1997). The creation of communal burial places with major landscape features may have ensured an enduring and respected presence in the landscape and in communal consciousness — in essence, a memorial — and further, ensured proper burial for the living in their turn.

There may be both local and personal traditions at work, with burial in a barrow at this period being seen both in England and in the Rhineland, but not France (Van de Noort 1993, fig. 2). Van de Noort also saw barrow building as an expression of pagan identity in opposition to Christian ideas, a view strongly expounded by Carver, who saw the Anglo-Saxon impulse to raise barrows as a response somehow connected to the presence, even 'threat' of Christian missions:

'later, in the 7th century, mounds were used in the rest of England, in more majestic isolation, as the flagship of the unconverted' and at Sutton Hoo, 'the use of burial mounds, ships… are seen as deliberate allusions to the enterprise politics of Scandinavia, as opposed to the imperial programme of Latin Europe' (Carver 2002, 140).

Carver's argument invokes the spread of barrow building from the Lower Rhine in the 5th century to the Upper Rhine by the 8th century, argued to reflect an aristocracy in formation or under threat (Carver 1998, 53–4). Since barrows also occur in 5th- and 6th-century cemeteries, it may be doubted whether this fully explains the building of barrows late in the 7th century.

At Harford Farm, Norfolk, the cemetery contained both barrows and burials with probable Christian significance, and was close to Caistor St Edmund, possibly a site with some 'official' status, given the evidence for trade or exchange here (Penn 2000). At Coddenham, the evidence suggests an elite presence, and at Ipswich and Southampton Anglo-Saxon barrows are found in cemeteries within or adjacent to royal *wics*. With minster churches and a 'royal' presence locally, it must seem unlikely that burial in barrows was pagan or not nominally Christian.

Whereas an individual burial might quickly become invisible and anonymous, a monument and the cemetery as a whole would retain a presence in the landscape and thus in communal memory: barrows were 'a major investment which celebrates an individual and provides a permanent message for the living' (Carver 2002, 139).

IV. Orientation and layout of the graves

The excavated graves represented the eastern part of the cemetery and development within the cemetery as a whole is not evident from them, since they lay on the periphery. No evidence of any boundary was found, and it is likely that the cemetery was 'open'. There was no evident zoning within the cemetery, and males, females, unaccompanied and well-furnished burials were found juxtaposed. The three barrows lie together close to the edge of the ridge.

Based on surviving bone and grave-goods, the burials were probably all west–east with head to the west, or approximately so. The exceptions were Graves 6, 7, 10 and 14, all closer to north-west–south-east, but their alignments may have been influenced by the nearby barrows.

There was a strong preference for west–east burial in Early Anglo-Saxon cemeteries (Faull 1977; Hirst 1985, 27), as seen at Spong Hill, Bergh Apton, and Morning Thorpe (Hills *et al.* 1984; Green and Rogerson 1978; Green and Rogerson 1987), but with no necessary connection with Christian influence.

The Coddenham graves were well-spread with no attempt at burial in rows or even a close and well-ordered arrangement.

Organisation within Anglo-Saxon cemeteries varied greatly, with a contrast between Morning Thorpe in Norfolk, where overcrowding and orderliness by its last phase of use was a striking feature (Green and Rogerson 1987; Penn and Brugman 2007), and at, for example, Lakenheath in Suffolk (Caruth 2006), Barrington, Cambs, (Malim and Hines 1998), or Buckland, Dover (Evison 1987), where graves were quite widely spread over a large area. At Shudy Camps, Cambs, about 150 graves lay in two areas, on quite different alignments (Lethbridge 1936, 83), which was also the case at Lechlade, Glos (Boyle *et al.* 1998), whilst at Harford Farm, Norfolk, graves 1–31 were dug in several short loose rows (Penn 2000, fig. 73).

Organisation within cemeteries may correspond directly to the complexity of the contributing community, but this is not evident at Coddenham, and such ideas involve a rather circular argument.

V. Coffins, containers and position of the body
(Figs 82–84)

Of the 50 graves, only 17 (34%) had substantial skeletal remains surviving, whilst 11 (22%) had a moderate amount and the other 22 (44%) were (almost) devoid of bone. Over half (56%), therefore, had a moderate or better amount of bone survival, whilst nearly half were devoid of bone.

Two burials, in Graves 1 and 30, had been singled out for special burial, suggesting that these individuals had some special identity. Both were placed within large wooden chambers and both may have had a cover placed above the body, though the evidence in Grave 1 is not conclusive, based upon the two brackets or staples found above the body. Grave 30 was more dramatic, with the body placed upon a bed that had been dismantled for burial, and then given a curved cover. Bed burials are widely known, but their significance is not properly understood, although they appear to be reserved for females.

The position of the body was only clear in about a third of the cases, around eighteen graves. In all cases, the body was laid out with head to the west, supine, with arms by the side or crossed over the pelvis. There was no evidence for coffins, yet several bodies had a splaying of the limbs, as if within a void, for example, Graves 5, 8, 9 and 27, with some shift or possible collapse in Graves 32, 40, 42, 43, 45, 46 and 48. In Grave 15, the burial was turned to the side, flexed, but otherwise not unusual.

Grave	Arms	Legs
5	splayed	
8	splayed	
9	splayed	splayed
27	splayed	
29	splayed	
45		splayed
46		splayed

Table 17 Positions of limbs

Other burials remained quite constrained, however, as if bound or confined, with little subsequent movement after deposition, and may have been buried in shrouds. These were Graves 2, 18, 19 and 32, and possibly 40, 42 and 48.

The use of coffins in any cemetery seems to have been first a matter of local practice and second the status of the individual, with coffins more often found with better-provided adults. At Coddenham there was no evidence for coffins, although Grave 1, with two iron brackets (evidence of a 'canopy'), and Grave 30, the bed burial, were 'enclosed' burials, each placed in a chamber.

Grave 20 contained a young male, unaccompanied, with three large flints behind the head but no other sign of 'enclosure'. At Spong Hill, where several burials were in coffins, grave 12 had flints placed around the coffin, and grave 31 (disturbed) had large flints within the grave, possibly outlining or supporting the coffin (Hills *et al.* 1984). This is likely therefore, to represent a practical function, although at Sleaford, the lining of a grave with stones was apparently a 'fairly common feature in this particular cemetery' (Brenan 1984–5, 126), and probably a local practice.

Such 'packing stones' have been recorded elsewhere, and in later cemeteries. For example, at the Middle Saxon cemetery at Caister-on-Sea, Norfolk, about 15% of the burials were found with packing stones, nine with stones around the head, four with stones around the feet, and three with stones around both head and feet (Gurney and Darling 1993, 253).

It is possible that local practices govern the general manner of burial, in the varying provision of coffins, the incidence of barrows, the use of 'mats' under the body, and the laying out of the body to reflect such things as age and gender.

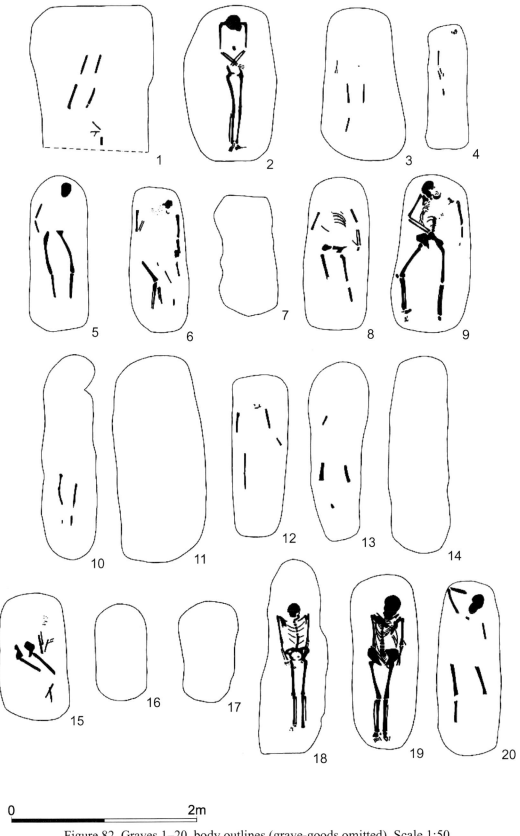

Figure 82 Graves 1–20, body outlines (grave-goods omitted). Scale 1:50

Grave 6 contained two individuals, both young and one possibly female. On the subject of 'multiple burials', Stoodley maintains this scenario as a 'way of dealing with situations which were out of the control of these communities' rather than burial of kin (Stoodley 2002, 121), although there is no other reason to think this was the case.

The textiles hint at some elaboration of the burials, although it is notable that the man in Grave 1 had 'working clothes', which is at odds with the general character of the

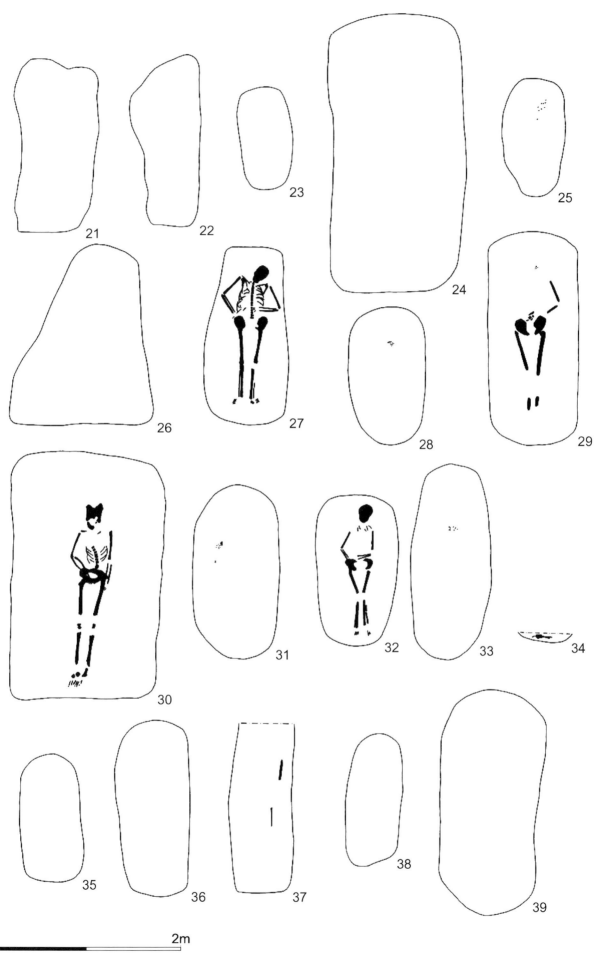

Figure 83 Graves 21–39, body outlines (grave-goods omitted). Scale 1:50

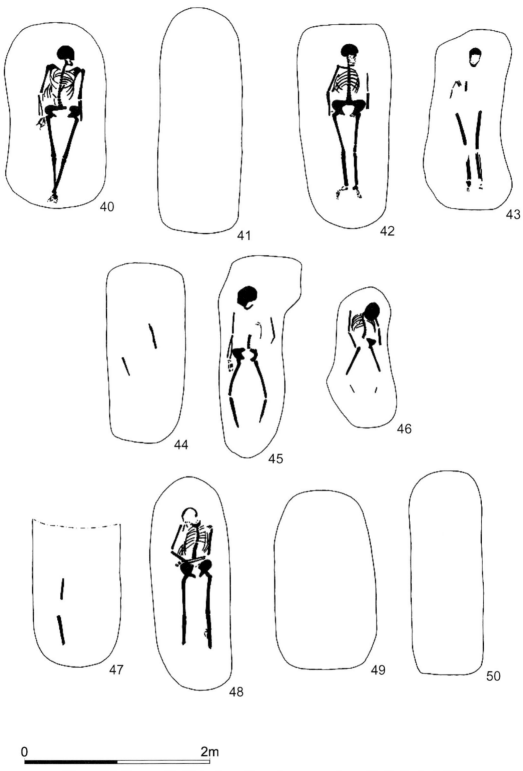

0   2m

Figure 84 Graves 40–50, body outlines (grave-goods omitted). Scale 1:50

burial. Care was taken over screening the body from the soil, with blankets or coverlets over the body in Graves 1 and 24. In Grave 1, it would appear that the shield was then placed over the coverlet, within the chamber. There was some evidence that objects were wrapped for burial, for example, the large bronze bowls in Graves 24 and 30.

In Graves 1 and 30, samples were taken for analysis of macrofossils and plant material. In Grave 1, soil in the bronze bowl (3) and soil in the bucket (7) produced charcoal, mineral-replaced wood, a black 'corky' material and fragment of bone, possibly cremated. A similar result was found in a sample from Grave 30. It was thought that 'some reworking of earlier deposits may be indicated by the presence of small fragments of cremated bone', possibly from Iron Age occupation and burial nearby (Fryer n.d.).

VI. Deposition of grave-goods

By the late 7th century, the material culture seen in cemeteries across England was unlike that of the 6th. The character of the object types, their distribution across the whole country, and the frequency of imported items has changed. Distinctive types can be found in graves from north to south, and appear at Coddenham: seaxes and stud, buckets, certain buckle types, combs and the deposition of combinations such as knives with steels (*cf* Geake 1999b; 2002; Meaney and Hawkes 1970, 45). The same is true of particular burial practices, with bed burials seen across the whole country, regardless of boundaries between kingdoms.

At Coddenham, Grave 11 had two 'safety pin' brooches (the only brooches found), a brooch type whose wide distribution is typical of many late 7th-century object types (Geake 1999b).

Grave-goods in Final Phase cemeteries are few, with weapons a rarity, an occasional brooch and light dress fittings with women, and accompaniments such as vessels and boxes. The few more elaborately-furnished burials were provided with items drawn from a wide range of object types, some specific to the late 7th/ early 8th century, after which grave-goods vanish from regular burials. Coin-dated graves belong to the later 7th and early 8th centuries, up to the 720s (Hawkes 1973), and possibly represent 'the propitiation of the dead by a token-payment for the goods that were henceforth reserved for the use of the living' (Rigold 1960, 52).

Notwithstanding a shared culture, there are some interesting differences in burial practice between Coddenham and other cemeteries, in the ranges of grave-goods found, and, for example, in the absence of coffins or 'mats' such as those in use at Harford Farm, Norfolk. At Coddenham the well-furnished graves were a smaller proportion of the whole, and the grave-goods included a different set of items, with an absence of wooden boxes, shears or relic boxes, as recorded at Harford Farm, but instead bronze vessels and pots, and the possible continental shields, and the Frankish buckle in Grave 48.

Compared with Harford Farm, there were more unaccompanied burials at Coddenham (48% to 25%), fewer 'neutral' burials (24% to 56%), but together, they make up 75%–80% of the burials. This may be connected with a shift to unaccompanied burial over time.

At Coddenham, Shudy Camps and Burwell, about 50% of the burials at each site were accompanied, including a few weapon burials and low numbers of accompanied females. As with most later 7th-century cemeteries, burial provision at Coddenham did not follow any strong pattern, except in the tendency for fewer weapons, and for unaccompanied or lightly furnished burial.

	C	%	HF	%
Weapon burials	5	10	1	2
Elaborate females	2–3	4–6	5	12
'Knife and buckle'	12	24	15	34
Other accompanied	6	12	11	22
Unaccompanied	24	48	11	25

Table 18 Numbers and proportions of 'burial types' at C Coddenham and HF Harford Farm, Norfolk (Penn 2000)

Objects were placed on and around the body, usually with a knife and buckle at the waist, with chatelaines, sometimes a bag (*e.g.* Graves 5 and 8). Grave 30, with a probable chatelaine and bag at the waist, and evidence of a bag with toilet sets and jewellery on the chest, may echo the way in which this was done at Boss Hall, Ipswich (grave 93) and Harford Farm (graves 11 and 33), with jewellery and toilet sets in bags at the chest (Penn 2000, fig. 18).

It is tempting to interpret some of these objects as having amuletic qualities (Meaney 1981) but there is nothing to suggest anything in the nature of a magical tool, as was suggested for objects found with a female burial at Bidford-on-Avon, Warks, where 'bucket pendants' in a leather bag at the neck were thought to be the accoutrements of a 'cunning woman' (Dickinson 1993).

Only perhaps in Graves 8 and 30, with coins in bags or fashioned into a pendant, too few for monetary significance, may grave-goods be amuletic. Grave 8 had a simple collection of beads but was also provided with a knife, buckle and steel set at the waist, a purse with coins, and a comb (in a bag?). Grave 30 was the most lavish and elaborate of the Coddenham burials, with chamber or canopy as well as the bed. Grave-goods and furnishings included a bag with coins, beads, coin pendant and toilet sets, a comb and remains of a hanging bowl.

Weapon burials: of the fifty graves, five males were provided with a weapon at burial, and two of their graves were within ring-ditches.

Grave 1: barrow (possible chamber grave), seax, spear and shield; bowl, bucket and possible drinking-horn
Grave 2: barrow, spear, knife and buckle
Grave 24: shield, spear, bowl, comb, pot
Grave 32: spear, knife
Grave 48: seax, knife, buckle, steel, Frankish buckle

Whereas 6th-century cemeteries like Morning Thorpe exhibit a regular provision of weapons, in later 7th- century cemeteries this was not the case. In many cemeteries there are few or no weapons; for example, the fifty graves at Harford Farm, Norfolk, produced in total a seax and a spear.

	Coddenham	Harford Farm	Polhill, Kent	Burwell	Shudy Camps
Number of burials	50	46	100	124	148
	%	%	%	%	%
Weapon burial	10	2	14	1	2
Accompanied females	16	15	19	13	16
Neutral	24	56	41	33	34
Unaccompanied	48	25	26	50	48

Table 19 Proportions of burial types in 7th-century cemeteries

'Well-furnished' females: of the burials with formal grave-goods, only two or three females were well furnished, *i.e.* with more than just a few beads: Graves 8, 30 and 44. These may be the female equivalents of the male weapon burials, but where Graves 8 and 30 were quite well furnished, Grave 44 was more simply provided, with beads and a pair of knives and latch-lifters at the waist.

Although these were 'well-furnished' burials, there were few objects of great intrinsic worth amongst the females, and little to suggest an elite group; the valuable items include the coin pendant in Grave 30. However, arguing for wealth and status from burial practice in the 7th century is notoriously difficult, especially given the variety of available grave-good types.

'Lightly-furnished' females: five graves had light 'female' furnishings such as beads: Grave 6, Grave 7, Grave 11 two safety-pin brooches, Grave 16, Grave 38 beads and a pot.

'Knife and buckle' burials: as noted above, twelve burials (24%) were effectively 'knife and buckle' burials, sometimes with an item such as a steel or 'awl'. Of the twelve burials, seven were identified as possibly males, one was a child (Grave 25), and the others could not be identified to age or sex. Grave 26 was of a male with knife and buckle, and a fauchard *(*possibly a tool).

Unaccompanied burials: of the fifty burials, twenty-four (48%) were buried with no surviving dress fittings or grave-goods. An immediate problem is of identification to sex and age, since few had much surviving bone: four were female, three male, three children and fourteen unidentified. These burials were scattered over the excavated area and one of them, Grave 17, was enclosed by a small ring-ditch.

The unaccompanied burials cover the whole range of grave lengths, perhaps suggesting that these graves included individuals of all ages, although there is a likelihood that younger children were buried or disposed of in other ways and are therefore not fully represented (Buckberry 2007; Crawford 1993).

Graves with pots: three graves contained a pot (but in each case no skeletal remains). The pots in Graves 35 and 38 were quite small, coarse and plain vessels, like those found in 6th-century inhumation graves (*cf* Spong Hill, Norfolk: Hills *et al.* 1984). In Grave 35, the pot was the only grave-good, and placed by the head; the pot had burnt residue internally. In Grave 38 the pot was by the upper right side, the other accompaniments being a silver wire ring and beads, and latch-lifters.

The exception was in Grave 24 which contained an imported pottery vessel. The grave-goods suggest an individual of some status (shield, spear, comb, bronze bowl) and point to a male burial. It may be relevant that at Morning Thorpe, Norfolk (Green and Rogerson 1987), the many pots with children were all undecorated whilst those with adult males, especially with weapons, were decorated, suggesting that decorated (or, perhaps, in this case, imported) pots were linked to identity and status.

VII. Social structure

The size of the contributing group cannot be estimated, given the probable loss of at least as many graves again, but if the excavated burials were made over a 50-year period, then this group could number less than fifty individuals at any time.

Of the fifty burials only eight were well-furnished, with eighteen modestly provided and twenty-four unaccompanied. This last category, one may assume, were also buried dressed, lessening the present apparent difference between them. However, these differences perhaps reflect individuals of different rank within the group, possibly even the 'free' and 'unfree' (Stoodley 1999, 126–35), and include individuals of some wider importance. Their burial together may suggest a single community, even an individual large household or kin group, with some internal ranking. The well-provided graves suggest a few adult individuals of some status, whose households may have had servants, as well as children and juveniles.

However, whilst the proportions of those with grave-goods, or lightly furnished, compares with other cemeteries of late 7th-century date, the elaborate burials in Graves 1 and 30, and the objects with those burials, point to a community or individuals with access to a wide material culture and resources to acquire 'exotic' objects, and a social context for the display of these objects.

Burial together may suggest the primary importance of a shared burial place, creating a recognised and permanent space, and therefore a continuing individual presence and identity.

Chapter 8. The Dating

Two of the graves contained coins. One of three Anglo-Saxon coins in Grave 8 dates the grave to AD 700x710. The three coins in Grave 30 are more varied and include a mounted coin of AD 629–639 and a counterfeit sceatta, whose prototype dates to the mid or later 7th century. For Grave 30 a date after 629 is therefore indicated, whilst the sceatta prototype would most likely date to the 670s. A date at the beginning of the long reign of Aldwulf (AD 663–713) is likely for Grave 30, but the date range for the cemetery is uncertain: it could belong entirely to the later 7th century and early 8th century with Grave 30 as one of the earliest burials. It is true that some objects may be early 7th century, or earlier, but they may not have been acquired and buried until much later, *e.g.* the hanging bowl, the two bronze bowls and the buckle in Grave 48. One should note two other Frankish bronze bowls also found in late graves: at Castledyke, Barton-upon-Humber, Lincs, and Uncleby, Yorks (Drinkall and Foreman 1998, 295; Geake 1997, 87).

Whilst some of the objects may be dated quite late, especially the coins and objects with a 'late' currency, establishing the potentially 'early' burials at Coddenham is not possible with much certainty, although it is well-known that furnished burials are difficult to assign to the period AD 625–675 (Geake 1997, 124).

In her survey of Conversion-period cemeteries, Geake suggested date ranges for their typical objects, although some, like iron knives were always difficult to identify to type, and others had a very long currency (Geake 1997, table 6.1). Based on this dating, all the objects buried at Coddenham could have been buried in the mid or later 7th century and just into the 8th. Shoe-buckles (with just a few known) occurred in Geake's group A, AD 550–650; they were found in a grave at Harford Farm, Norwich (Penn 2000) and at Coddenham they occurred in Grave 30.

All the objects at Coddenham fit the period up to *c.* AD 700 and a little beyond, with seaxes, iron bucket, spatulate tools, bronze bowl, safety-pin brooches all in Geake's group C, that is, AD 600–700. Objects more specific to the second half of the 7th century, group D, were also found, and suggest that many burials, if not all, belong to the period after AD 650: group 7 shield bosses, sceattas, hump-backed combs, bullae, and two-tongued buckles. For this reason, the date range of the Coddenham cemetery may have a possible start date of *c.* AD 650 and an end date of *c.* AD 700–710 for the surviving burials.

Recent work on dating the earlier 'Migration Period' burials, and changes in material culture leading up to the so-called 'Final Phase' burials (a phrase too heavy with cultural and chronological assumptions for easy use) has been reviewed in Scull (2009, 111–2, 257), in the context of the burials at Boss Hall, Hadleigh Road and Buttermarket, Ipswich. There are several turning points in the character of material culture and its use in burial, first at the end of the Migration period around AD 570/580, when certain dress fittings went out of fashion, at least for burial, and objects such as square-head and annular brooches remained in use, for a somewhat indeterminate period. What are called 'Final Phase' burials followed, but whether continuous or after a decrease in accompanied burial remains uncertain.

Although typical 6th-century accompanied burial goes on into the 7th century, the 'end is vague in absolute terms' (Penn and Brugmann 2007, 95). This phase is best represented in Kent, but 'in the rest of England there is a dearth of burials attributed to the first half of the 7th century' (Geake 1997, 11). In Kent, in cemeteries such as Buckland, Dover, the finds indicate sustained use of the cemetery from the 6th to the early 8th centuries. Outside Kent, cemeteries of the 5th and 6th centuries do not appear to have been used much beyond AD 600, with few burials dated to the first half of the 7th century, and with few late 6th/early 7th-century grave-goods, and these mostly 'male' (Geake 2002). There are exceptions: Barrington, Cambs, Castledyke, Barton-upon-Humber, Lincs, and Lechlade, Glos, where continuity of burial from the late 5th to the late 7th century seems likely (Malim and Hines 1998; Drinkall and Foreman 1998; Boyle *et al.* 1998). However, even at Castledyke, continuous use cannot be proved, and at Lechlade, the later 7th-century graves appear to be on a general west-to-east alignment, in contrast to the north-to-south alignment of the 6th/early 7th-century graves, and reuse of an earlier cemetery, rather than continuity, cannot be ruled out.

Although there are other 7th-century cemeteries within the local area, only Boss Hall grave 93, and the latest graves at Buttermarket, Ipswich, with possible date range of AD 610s–690s, are of similar date. The Hadleigh Road cemetery begins in the late 6th century and runs on into the 7th century. The isolated burials from Elm Street and Foundation Street in Ipswich are undated, but likely to be 8th/9th-century, whilst the sixteen unaccompanied burials at White House in Ipswich can only be dated by the sceattas found in nearby pits, which are likely to be of early 8th-century date (IPS 247; Caruth 1996).

A number of typical 'Final Phase' cemeteries, with typical assemblages of men with seaxes, group 7 shields, and women with silver wire rings and few brooches, seem to have begun in the later 7th century, with none of the material distinctive of Brugmann's Phase FB/MB (Penn and Brugmann 2007). This 'separation' has led to suggestions that it was the acceptance of Mediterranean culture and 'Romanising' efforts in the mid-7th century that led to a more deliberate display of the new identity, when a Christian culture and stricter observance were enjoined at the highest levels of society (Geake 1997; Penn 2000), and a resurgence of accompanied burial seems likely.

Both the Coddenham cemetery and the nearby settlement at Vicarage Farm in the valley came to an end in the early 8th century. There is evidence from around the church in Coddenham of activity in the middle Anglo-Saxon period, with finds of Ipswich ware, available from around AD 700 or soon after (Blinkhorn 1999; Newman 2006; 2007), and a permanent shift in this period to the present village is likely.

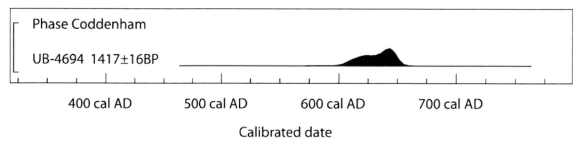

Figure 85 Grave 30 (skull), Radiocarbon result UB-4694

Radiocarbon dating
(Fig. 85)

Dating was carried out by the Radiocarbon Dating Laboratory, Queen's University, Belfast, on a sample of human bone (skull) from Grave 30 (sample UB-4694). This was undertaken as part of the Anglo-Saxon Chronology Project, and kindly submitted by C. Scull on behalf of Suffolk County Council Archaeological Services.

The initial result was a radiocarbon age of 1417 ±16 yr BP; the calibrated date was AD 605–655 at 95% confidence (McCormac *et al.* 2004; McCormac *et al.* forthcoming).

However, from the new calibration date from the Anglo-Saxon Project, a project-specific calibration curve allows this to be calibrated to cal AD 600–660 at 95% confidence (or cal AD 610–655 at 68% confidence).

For Grave 30, an absolute *terminus post quem* is given by the mounted solidus of Dagobert I whose regnal dates of AD 629–639 place this burial after AD 629, and probably some time after that date. Grave 30 can also be dated to some extent by the latest of the three coins found with the burial: a base-metal replica of a sceat, likely to be in the last decades of the 7th century or the first of the 8th century, although the condition of the coin makes identification far from certain, and silver sceattas themselves begin in the 670s at the earliest. A similar situation occurs at Buttermarket, Ipswich where grave 4275, dated by radiocarbon to AD 605–650 (95% confidence), contained a coin unlikely to be earlier than 670 (Scull 2009).

Chapter 9. Discussion and Conclusions

I. The local context

The settlement in the valley at Vicarage Farm CDD 022 produced evidence for an elite group, with access to a wide exchange or trade network, the working of precious metals, and with a remarkable set of early coins, some continental (Everett *et al.* 2003). A folding balance amongst the finds suggests exchange or trade, and certainly a site or community of some importance (*cf* Scull 1990, 209), which came to an end, or shifted, in the early 8th century.

Some of the individuals buried in the cemetery were probably part of this local elite, and, by the late 7th century, presumably moved in high-status and Christian circles. Despite just a few 'rich' burials, the cemetery displays access to continental material culture, whilst the contrast amongst males between weapon burials, the 'knife and buckle' and unfurnished burials suggests some internal ranking within the community. This may be less evident among the female burials, but these include the two burials with coins and gold pendant (Graves 8 and 30). The bed in Grave 30 is of uncertain significance, but its elaboration points to some special status, and bed burial was itself apparently linked to high status, as was use of wooden chambers, and, at this date, burial with weapons. An interpretation of the 'cover' as fragments of boat remains uncertain, but could add to the significance of this burial, and even suggest a deliberate reflection of maritime affiliation.

These individuals may have been special, to judge from their elaborate grave goods, and not represent the majority of the local population. Some of the objects placed with the burials speak of connections with the Rhineland: weapons, shields and buckle, bronze bowls and the pot (and its contents) in Grave 24. Other important graves may be indicated by the two bronze bowls found at Badley (upstream from Coddenham), one a 'Coptic' bowl, the other an unusual globular bowl, and by 'Coptic' bowls at Wickham Market, and possibly Chilton in the Stour valley; these bowls may all be from burials (West 1998, 301–2, fig. 156), and emphasize the continental connections found inland.

Some of these objects have parallels further afield, and suggest a link to other East Anglian cemeteries, and, perhaps, Kent.

II. The geographical background
(Fig. 4)

The distribution of early Anglo-Saxon cemeteries in East Anglia, presumably a reflection of the general settlement pattern, represents a contraction of the Roman pattern of settlement, and echoes the prehistoric pattern, mostly along river valleys, along the fen edge and on the lighter soils (Penn and Brugmann 2007, fig. 9.1). A study of Early Anglo-Saxon settlement in south-east Suffolk shows the sandy coastal strip being extensively settled and the central 'upland' clayland (the till plain) being more thinly

occupied, except where dissected by streams: in south-east Suffolk, 'all of the Early Anglo-Saxon sites are on the light soils of the Sandlings and it appears that the boulder clay areas were abandoned through this period', although it may be significant that 'Early Saxon material is known from all of the larger [Roman] sites' including Coddenham (Newman 1992, 32).

West's map of Middle Saxon metalwork and pottery (West 1998, fig. 158), suggests that even beyond the late 7th century, settlement may still have remained much denser along the coastal strip.

They may be a discontinuous phenomenon, but the distribution and locations of later 7th-century cemeteries in East Anglia, however, echoes that of the 6th-century cemeteries (avoiding the central claylands), and they have been found along the chalk corridor into Cambridgeshire (Lethbridge 1926–7; 1936; Malim 1990; Wilson 1956), near the north Norfolk coast at Thornham (Gregory 1986), in the valley of the River Yare near Norwich at Harford Farm (Penn 2000). Single late 7th-century burials occur at Boss Hall, Ipswich (Newman 1993), and at Bayfield, north Norfolk (Penn and Whitmore 2007).

The contemporary settlement pattern may have been fluid, and there also remains a problem with locating and dating settlement in the 7th century. The settlement pattern up to around AD 600 is largely implied by cemeteries, and after AD 700 is evidenced by Ipswich ware, which appears soon after that date. Between AD 600 and AD 700, a period of change, the evidence is scant and the situation less clear.

The distribution of Ipswich ware, with its start date in the early 8th century (Blinkhorn 1999), 'shows a penetration over two and a half centuries into the heavy clay areas along the inland edges of Newman's survey area and in the central parish of Mendlesham' (West 1998, 317). Newman has noted that 'it is from the early 8th century that the more attractive areas of Boulder Clay were demonstrably settled, and all big Ipswich ware scatters have been found near parish churches' (Newman 2005, 483), but since this is tied to Ipswich ware, an earlier shift is possible.

Whilst finds of Middle Anglo-Saxon Ipswich ware come from around Ipswich and the Deben valley, in Newman's survey (Newman 1992), much less has been found in fieldwork further up the Suffolk coast, or within the Stour valley, possibly suggesting that at all levels, there was greater activity in this 'core' area. Major sites lay along the Rivers Blyth, Alde and Deben, although the pattern of 'productive sites' in East Anglia suggests there was significant trading activity along the north-west coast and fen-edge littoral (Newman 1999b, 39).

III. The mortuary landscape

Whilst the distribution of later 7th-century cemeteries echoes the pattern of earlier (6th—century) cemeteries, from the 630s when the see was established at *Dommoc*, it is likely that royal burial in East Anglia had gradually shifted to churches, some probably built as royal mausolea, and members of the elite had also founded their own monasteries and minsters (for example, Botolph at Iken in AD 654 and Etheldreda at Ely in AD 673).

Outside Kent and Northumbria, there is little evidence for burial next to churches until the 670s, but it was becoming more common from the 680s, particularly for churchmen. For other individuals, or at least some of them, burial continued or began anew, in unenclosed cemeteries located beyond settlement and usually situated on a locally prominent place, often overlooking a river or stream (Penn and Brugmann 2007, 5–6). Some were in established cemeteries; for example, Mound 14 at Sutton Hoo (with bronze bowl, drinking cup and casket) could be of mid–late 7th-century date (Carver 2005, 298), and at Boss Hall, on the boundary of a royal 'estate' (Warner 1996, 121–3), another single burial, of late 7th-century date, was set within an earlier 6th-century cemetery (Newman 1993; Scull 2009). The Boss Hall cemetery lay close to a site later chosen for the construction of a church or chapel with a dedication to St Albright, often taken to be an East Anglian king, Aethelberht, 'martyred' in AD 794 (but see Ridgard in Scull 2009).

Late 7th-century cemeteries are also known from within towns, with several discovered at Southampton, including one associated with a barrow, and individual burials at Winchester and Canterbury (Penn 2000, 100). In Ipswich itself the Buttermarket cemetery contained 71 graves (possibly many more) with about ten small barrows, of which 50% were unaccompanied. There were later isolated burials in Ipswich at Elm Street (IAS 3902) and at Foundation Street (IAS 4601) (Scull 2009), and communal cemeteries of unaccompanied burials in Norfolk at Caister-on-Sea, next to a former Roman shore fort (Darling and Gurney 1993), and inside the shore fort at Burgh Castle (Johnson 1983).

In another contrast, at White House, Ipswich, a ditched enclosure containing two 'halls' and some sixteen unaccompanied burials may date from this general period, and be part of the 'mortuary landscape' (Caruth 1996). This site may illustrate the coming together of cemetery and settlement from around AD 700.

IV. Early land units
(Fig. 86)

By the late 7th century, it is likely that landscape was organised and managed through 'caputs' or central places at the centre of complex 'estates' (see Scull 2009, 312). A division of Suffolk into the Liberty of St Edmund in the west and the Wicklaw Hundreds along the coast is possibly ancient. It has been suggested that west Suffolk (the 8½ Hundreds of Thingoe i.e. the Liberty of St Edmund, first mentioned in a charter of 1044), began as a 7th-century shire and that the Wicklaw Hundreds, centred on the royal estate of Sudbourne (Cam 1944, 185), was another such unit, given to Ely, a royal foundation, at an early date (Davis 1954, xliv–xlv; Scarfe 2002, 20; Warner 1996, 149–152; Plunkett 2005, 13). Between the two, the area known as the Geldable, containing Coddenham and Barham, remained in royal hands (Fig. 86).

A case has been made for another 'regio', or royal estate containing Bramford and Ipswich (Warner 1996, 121–3, fig. 5.3), with a pattern of burial grounds at Hadleigh Road, Boss Hall and Buttermarket, and a church

in Ipswich (St Mildred) (Scarfe 2002, 21, 73–4, fig. 27). This 'estate' had on its margin the cemetery at Boss Hall, next to the site of a possible 'boundary church or chapel' dedicated to St Albright, which had connections with the minster at Bramford and this may point to a special status for the late 7th-century burial at Boss Hall in grave 93 (Scarfe 2002, 173; Newman 1993; Warner 1996, 121–3).

Possibly, activity on this 'estate' had a shifting focus, with Hadleigh Road cemetery arguably attached to a precursor settlement to Ipswich, but set a little way away. In contrast, the Middle Anglo-Saxon enclosure at White House, Ipswich (IPS 247) formerly lay in Bramford parish and also lay on the edge of the 'estate', above the river. It contained two 'halls', various pits and a small cemetery with sixteen burials. An example of such a shift has been noted at Carlton Colville, Suffolk (Lucy et al. 2009). The White House burials were unaccompanied and undated but one of the pits produced two sceattas (Caruth 1996) which may hint at a late 7th/8th-century date.

Neither Coddenham or Barham were part of any known large land unit, and it is possible that they were themselves once separate 'central places' within their own land unit(s), on the east side of the Gipping valley, or had a significance not echoed in territorial arrangements, but evident in the archaeological evidence.

V. Coddenham and Barham

Both Coddenham and the adjacent parish of Barham contained an early settlement associated with many coins and metal objects, far beyond what a 'normal' settlement might produce (CDD 022 and BRH 016/8). The material recorded from these two sites has led to each being named a 'productive' site, and they were possibly seasonal fairs or trading places within the Ipswich hinterland (Newman 1999b, 39).

In the Roman period, a small fort (*Combretovium*) stood on the banks of the Gipping at Baylham Mill, south of Coddenham, on an important junction on the contemporary road network between Roman towns at Colchester and Caistor St Edmund (Moore et al.1988); this fort developed into an industrial centre and small town. Coddenham thus lay close to the river system and road communications.

At Baylham Mill, close to the Roman town and the river (CDD 017/CDD 003), evidence found during roadworks includes 5th- to 9th-century material; this includes Frisian sceattas (AD 700–750) and a silver coin of Offa. The place-name could be 'homestead or enclosure at a river bend' (Mills 1991, 28) and could hint at an early settlement. A landing place here is possible, perhaps connected later with the settlement at Vicarage Farm on the north side of the ridge, via a former Roman road, passing 500m east of the cemetery. The Roman roads are now represented by the modern A140 and fossilised in field and parish boundaries.

It is not impossible that Coddenham took its name from some memory of the Roman name, *Combretovium*, although the place-name is more usually thought to be from 'homestead or enclosure of a man named Codda' (Mills 1991, 85). The –*ham* place-names suggest an early origin, and the existence of two separate 'productive' sites suggests that by AD 700, Coddenham and Barham were distinct entities. The place-name Barham may mean 'homestead or enclosure on a hill' (Mills 1991, 23), which

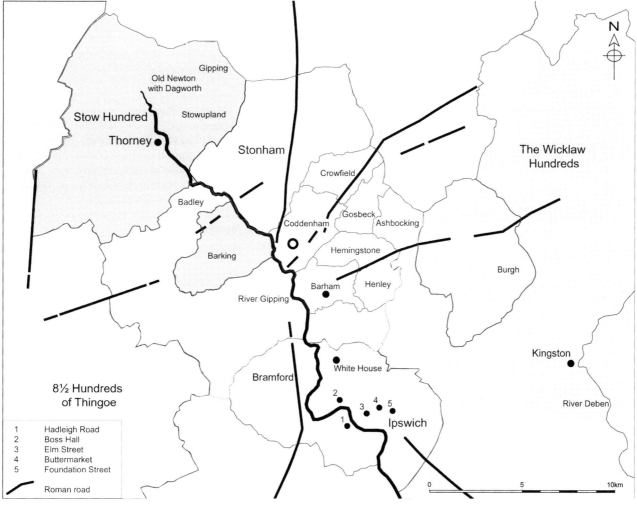

Figure 86 The Ipswich area, showing selected sites mentioned in the text and hundreds in south-east Suffolk. Scale
1.200,000

could relate to the 7th- to 9th-century occupation next to the medieval church, on its elevated site.

The Domesday record for Coddenham may suggest an early minster site (Newman 2003, 106; Pestell 2003, 132–3; Rumble 1986; Scarfe 1999, 52). In 1086, the entries for Coddenham were spread over twelve headings or landowners, with a complex array of freemen and smallholders with their agricultural resources, besides several churches, or parts of churches. The entry suggests holdings in various parishes, that is, a relic minster parish. Blair has commented 'this bizarrely complex case should, however, be seen against the background of rich mid-Saxon metalwork finds which may identify Coddenham as a minster' and suggested 'the extreme fragmentation of earlier ecclesiastical entities' (Blair 2005, 399). Minster churches are also likely at Ipswich, with perhaps others further upstream at Barking, Stonham, and Thorney (Stowmarket) (Scarfe 1999, 52).

Whilst Domesday Book records several holdings under Coddenham, in the medieval period there were just two manors in Coddenham itself, and these survived into modern times. The main manor, later known as Vesseys, Priory or Coddenham Vicarage, became centred on the church. A grant of St Mary's church in Coddenham had already been made to the Augustinian priory at Royston, Herts, to found a monastery here in the early 12th century, which may suggest an intention to found a priory based

upon an old minster church, as was a feature of Augustinian practice (*cf.* Golding 1982). This grant was confirmed in 1184 and 1192 (VCH 1971, 436). The manor of Coddenham Vicarage (most of the parish) was given or confirmed by Hugh de Rickinghall to Royston Priory in the first half of the 13th century and at the Dissolution it came back to the Crown and then to John Atkins (Copinger 1909, 283–4).

The other manor was held by Roger Bigot at Domesday, with a church and a half, and half a mill. This came to be known as Denneys with Sackville Rents (Copinger 1909, 282–3) and came to the Bacon family around 1600. This became the Shrubland Hall estate and came to the Middleton family in the 1780s and then to the de Saumaurez.

The map of the Glebeland in 1773 (SRO HD 1467/1) shows it was concentrated in the area between Vicarage Farm and Glebe Barn, and on the ridge, now covered by modern plantations. The map shows several strips, possibly part of an early field system, around Vicarage Farm, which was probably a manorial holding, and on the hill where the cemetery lay, a situation confirmed by the Tithe map of 1839 (SRO P461/66).

It is possible that a connection existed between the site of the settlement and cemetery and the location of the strips of glebe, but glebe provision was largely a Late Saxon/Norman institution, and in any case, in the early years of Edward IV, the vicar let out 'a considerable part of the glebe which lay in several places in the fields, but some of them are since lost' (Copinger 1909, 285); the glebe mapped in 1773 may therefore be merely the remnant of the original glebe and strip fields.

The 'productive' site at Vicarage Farm, Coddenham
Early Anglo-Saxon settlement in Coddenham began in the 6th century or before. To the east of Vicarage Farm, at CDD 023 (Frontispiece), 6th-century material was found (West 1998, fig. 23), and from CDD 019 and 017, by the river at Baylham Mill, comes a scatter of material, including tweezers and an ansate brooch, and a sceatta of *c*.AD 730–750 (West 1998, fig. 19). Site CDD 021 produced further 6th- to 9th-century material. At CDD 027 material of 6th-century and later date was found; this includes a Merovingian bird brooch (West 1998, fig. 23).

The site at Vicarage Farm (CDD 022) has produced finds of imported coins, Anglo-Saxon gold thrymsas, sceattas and other objects that indicate some special role or status, perhaps with ironworking and craft activities using precious metals, attached to an important household and with a place in the 'commercial' network, although Plunkett speculated on a non-permanent presence (2001, 64). A metal-detector survey carried out over several years has recorded an important assemblage of over sixty Anglo-Saxon coins and other metalwork (this includes 6th- and 7th-century brooches, buckles and coins). The coin group starts in the early/mid 7th century and comes to a halt in the early years of the 8th century.

From close by came other coins and part of a folding balance (Plunkett 2001, fig.6k; 2005, plate 28), which must indicate some use of precious metal as bullion and some 'commercial' aspect to the site, with a function in official regulation of trade. Balances have been found in Kent and in the Upper Thames area, with outliers at Desborough (Northants) and the cemetery at Castledyke (Barton-upon-Humber), and may evidence links to the Merovingian world (Scull 1990).

Not only is the quantity of coins remarkable, but its composition is exceptional; there are three Merovingian tremisses, twelve Anglo-Saxon thrymsas and around fifty early sceattas. These include two East Anglian primary sceattas, three Frisian sceattas, two Kentish types, and four English gold coins (West 1998, fig. 21–2). An 'abrupt' end date, in the early 8th century, may be evidenced by the finds of A series sceattas and the absence of later B series (Newman 1999b; 2003, 102).

The other objects also include gold items: buckles, brooches, a fragment of a late 7th-century 'vandyke' and small bronze 'catches', possibly from a bag or box (like those from Grave 30). The 7th-century English and Merovingian coins also suggest a high-status presence. One of the gold items, a spangle (West 1998, fig. 19.11), is paralleled by a spangle in Grave 30. Other objects include gold jewellery with garnets prised out, possibly for re-use (West 1998, fig. 19.10).

To understand this material and establish its context, the BBC *Hidden Treasures* programme commissioned archaeological fieldwork, a geophysical survey followed by a series of trial trenches. There was extensive occupation debris but few identifiable features. These, however, included a hall house and possibly two sunken-featured buildings. All the pottery (twenty-four sherds) was handmade, that is, there was no Ipswich ware, all

indications of 7th- to early 8th-century settlement (Everett *et al.* 2003; Newman 2003; 2004), and, importantly, an ironsmith's hearth was also found, with other indications of metalworking in gold, bronze and iron, including fragments of gold scrap, bronze items and offcuts, found in earlier metal-detecting survey.

The 'productive' site at Barham
At Barham, the 'productive' site (BRH 016/018) lies next to St Mary's church. The distribution of the finds (within an oval area with the church in the south-east quadrant) suggests an enclosed site, although no ditch was found. Trial-trenching revealed structural evidence and pottery, beginning in the 6th century (Newman 2003; West 1998). A potential parallel might be the manorial enclosure at Livermere, West Suffolk, also associated with a Domesday church.

Like the site at Vicarage Farm, this site started in the late 6th century, but continued into the 8th and 9th centuries, with a peak in the 7th/8th centuries. The fifty or more coins from Barham include an early 7th-century Merovingian gold tremissis of *c*.AD 640 from Quentovic, over forty sceattas, including Frisian types and local R Series (and a few later coins) from the later 7th century onwards, besides an Irish pin, and pottery, suggesting 'a continuous, domestic, rural settlement presence' (Newman 2003, 102; West 1998, figs 6–8). Other finds include many dress fasteners, small buckles, pins, and catches (like those from Coddenham Grave 30), a Frankish buckle plate and mounts from a hanging bowl (Bruce-Mitford with Raven 2005, nos 79–81; West 1998, 6–8). Two of the hanging bowl mounts have a parallel in grave 205 at Kingston, Kent.

Coddenham and Barham may have been 'rural emporia', that is, markets that existed alongside the large-scale *wic* at Ipswich, and may have been associated with some important ecclesiastical centre, perhaps echoed in the Domesday entries (Newman 1999b; 2003).

This picture contrasts with the results of fieldwork in Sutton parish and other places locally where pottery has also been found, indicating intensive occupation, but with no or few coins and little other metalwork, indicating a more obvious subsistence economy (Newman 1999b, 106). In discussion of the Buttermarket site in Ipswich, Scull has seen Coddenham and Barham as 'magnate residences' and 'estate centres', places for collection and despatch of goods to and from Ipswich, 'at the apex of the local settlement hierarchy' (Scull 2009, 309).

VI. Contacts and trade

Rather than a simple hierarchy of sites, with discrete functions and status, and special sites indicated by possession of 'special' objects and activities, Hamerow (1999) saw these special objects as evidence of long-distance trade reaching into rural settlements, and the existence of a market system, also evidenced by the wide spread of Ipswich ware. Seeing Ipswich as a possible 'estate centre' with Christian continental affiliations in the 7th century, Carver also envisaged 'a network of markets (or tribute delivery points) … [but] placed for the most part at sites we know as palaces or monasteries. A role also seems to be played by a new kind of site … which consists of scatters of sceattas in the open, apparently without buildings…"moor markets"…where duty could be discharged or commercial opportunity taken' (Carver 2005, 498). Coddenham and Barham could be regarded in this way, as rural 'emporia', whose contacts are evidenced by objects from France, the Rhineland and Frisia, with occasional fairs or open markets. The number of these sites suggests a sophisticated material culture reaching quite widely.

Given the finds of early coins and other evidence for a high-status presence at Vicarage Farm, Coddenham, it is interesting that the Harford Farm cemetery in Norfolk lies close to Caistor St Edmund, where coin finds and other evidence also point to high-status activity with hints of foreign contact and trade (Penn 2000).

In Ipswich too, the cemetery at Buttermarket lies next to the *wic* itself, and suggests a close connection between an elite, here with foreign elements, and trade.

The material culture seen in cemeteries by the mid-7th century was the same across the whole country, and perhaps had shared external contacts and inspiration. Items such as beads and pendants are found across all England and have parallels with objects in Roman and Byzantine contexts. Parallels for objects from Coddenham can be found widely, with, for example, a site at Uncleby, Yorks also producing a tripod bowl, two-tongued buckle, combs, 'safety-pin' brooches and knives with steels (Smith 1912), some of which types were also found at Kingston, Kent. The fragmentary hanging bowl in Grave 30, the similar bowl at Field Dalling, Norfolk (found buried with a continental bronze bowl), and the fragmentary Ipswich find with its openwork mount, may all reflect widely-shared access to these objects, although themselves of distant manufacture in Scotland.

Some objects are less common types, for example the Frankish ceramic vessel in Grave 24. Other East Anglian examples come from Caistor St Edmund and Bayfield, Norfolk (Penn and Whitmore 2007), Sutton Hoo and Hadleigh in Suffolk, and Prittlewell, Essex, whilst the great majority have been found in Kent, with a handful from elsewhere (Geake 1997, 89–90).

The cemetery also demonstrates connections with other places through burial practice: for example, the Cambridgeshire cemeteries of Shudy Camps, Barrington, Cherry Hinton and Burwell, where the bed burials have similar ironwork, and more distant cemeteries such as Collingbourne Ducis in Wiltshire and Saltburn in Yorkshire. At Saltburn, the bed burial was the focus of the extraordinarily arranged cemetery, and must be of a very special individual.

The material culture seen at Coddenham need not be viewed as the result of 'gift-exchange' (though that may not have been absent) rather than trade. The coins and balance found at Coddenham and Barham must hint at a commercial presence, maybe mediated via Frisia, which had a monopoly of trade around the North Sea in the 7th and 8th centuries (Ellmers 1990). From the 650s, Frisians established 'beach markets' on the North Sea shores, and these may have been one of the stimuli to the trading and manufacturing activity at Coddenham and Barham, and at Ipswich too.

The familiar coastal distribution of 'productive' sites also points to the importance of overseas contacts (Pestell and Ulmschneider 2003), while the burials — such as the single male burial with spear, silver buckles, skillet, bucket, and Frankish pot at Bayfield, north Norfolk (Penn

and Whitmore 2007) — hint at foreign contacts reaching into the coastal hinterland in the early–mid 7th century.

Coddenham and Barham (with earlier sceatta series) may have been active early, whilst the dates for the Buttermarket cemetery, probably beginning in the earlier 7th century, must imply a contributing settlement, that is, the *wic* itself. However, the coins found at Ipswich, with a 50% proportion of R series sceattas (perhaps minted there: Metcalf 1984, 58) point to an economic 'take-off' somewhat later.

VII. Change and abandonment

Around AD 700 or shortly after, both the Vicarage Farm settlement and cemetery were abandoned. The 7th century was a period of dynamic change, fostered in part by new connections, religious, economic and social, established with the continent. By around AD 700 the settlement hierarchy in East Anglia had Ipswich at its peak, and included Barham and Coddenham, other 'productive' sites and ecclesiastical foundations.

There are also reasons to think that a more demonstrative Christianity was a feature of the second half of the 7th century, possibly strengthened by religious reform and consolidation in the 660s and 670s, and increased links to Byzantine Italy, via the Rhineland, rather than France (Bullough 1983, 177–8; Penn 2000, 97, 104). Across England, by the 720s, accompanied burial had generally ended, although the reasons for this are still not fully understood. It may be connected with social changes, the example of royal burial in churches, the growth in the numbers of 'private' churches (and therefore places for private burial) and, from the early 700s, a stronger attention to church dogma with its emphasis on the welfare of the dead through prayers and gifts to the church (Penn 2000, 164–5).

Perhaps the appearance of well-furnished burials in the mid 7th century was the result of economic, as well as religious factors, connected with the establishment of elite households and their 'estates' (Hamerow 2002, 121–3), whilst their disappearance has more to do with religious factors (Bullough 1983, 187; Penn 2000, 105–6). At Coddenham, both the cemetery and nearby settlement came to an end around AD 700 or soon after, possibly replaced by settlement around the present church some 600m to the east, where pottery found in test pits indicates settlement in the Middle Anglo-Saxon period (Newman 2006; 2007).

A similar shift may be observed at the Suffolk site of Carlton Colville, near Lowestoft, a remarkable Early Saxon settlement, possibly an 'estate centre' with many hall buildings, 'sunken-featured buildings' and a small cemetery of twenty-six burials, which was in use from the 6th century until around AD 700, but was then abandoned (Dickens *et al.* 2005; Mortimer 2000; Lucy *et al.* 2009).

This shift may be part of a wider phenomenon in the settlement landscape, involving 'internal' shift of settlements within established territories, and the beginnings of 'external' expansion onto the heavy claylands (Hamerow 1991, 16; 2002, 121–3; Newman 1992; Williamson 1988). Dating evidence in the 7th century from settlements is generally scant, and in East Anglia this shift is best evidenced in the years after AD 700 when the distribution of Ipswich ware pottery can be mapped (Blinkhorn 1999, 8–9).

In this model, many Early Anglo-Saxon sites did not continue into the Middle Anglo-Saxon period, but their replacements then continued, and in time gained a church (Newman 2005, 483, fig. 216). One may speculate that the cemetery at Coddenham represents a relatively small group of people, some of high status, who shifted to a new settlement and began burial anew, on a new site a little upstream where the present church and village now stand, but at some point coming under ecclesiastical control (Newman 2003; Pestell 2003 131–3). In contrast, activity at Barham continued on the same site, but with the later addition of a church.

VIII. Conclusions

The excavation of the cemetery compliments and reinforces the observations made at Vicarage Farm in the valley below, of a community with an elite element and connections with overseas trade, coming to an end or being re-established elsewhere in the early 8th century.

Fieldwork at Barham presents a similar picture of an elite site with overseas connections, (although with no known early cemetery) but with activity carrying on at the same place, perhaps with the later addition of a church, a precursor to the present medieval church.

The cemetery confirms that the community at Coddenham had access to overseas trade, whilst the character of the excavated burials could suggest a small community, even a single large household, with servants and attendants. Not only were they able to acquire exotic objects, they were willing to dispose of them, to recreate and memorialise some of their members at death.

Grave 1

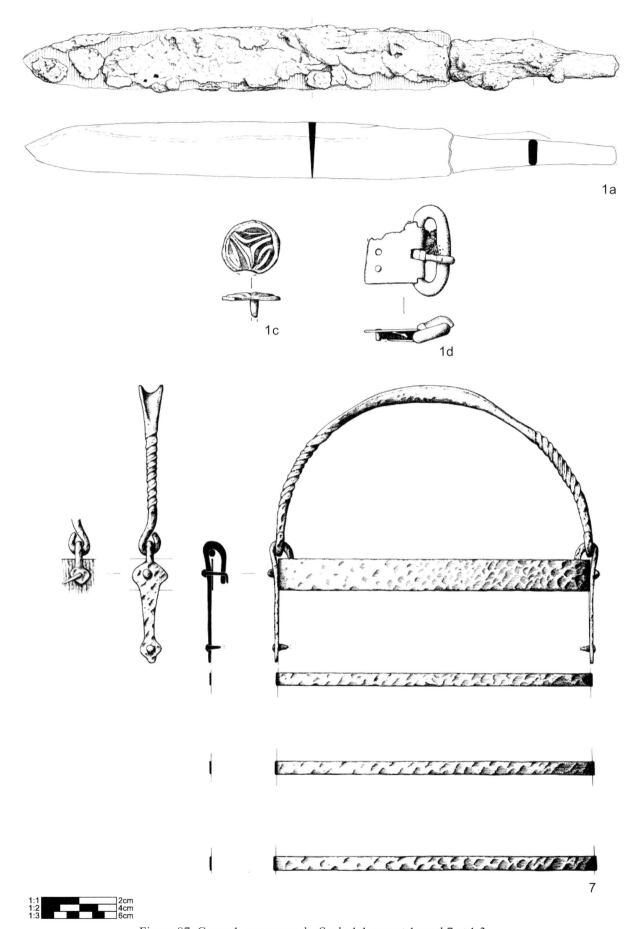

1a

1c

1d

7

1:1 ▬▭▬▭ 2cm
1:2 ▬▭▬▭ 4cm
1:3 ▬▭▬▭ 6cm

Figure 87 Grave 1, grave-goods. Scale 1:1 except 1a and 7 at 1:3

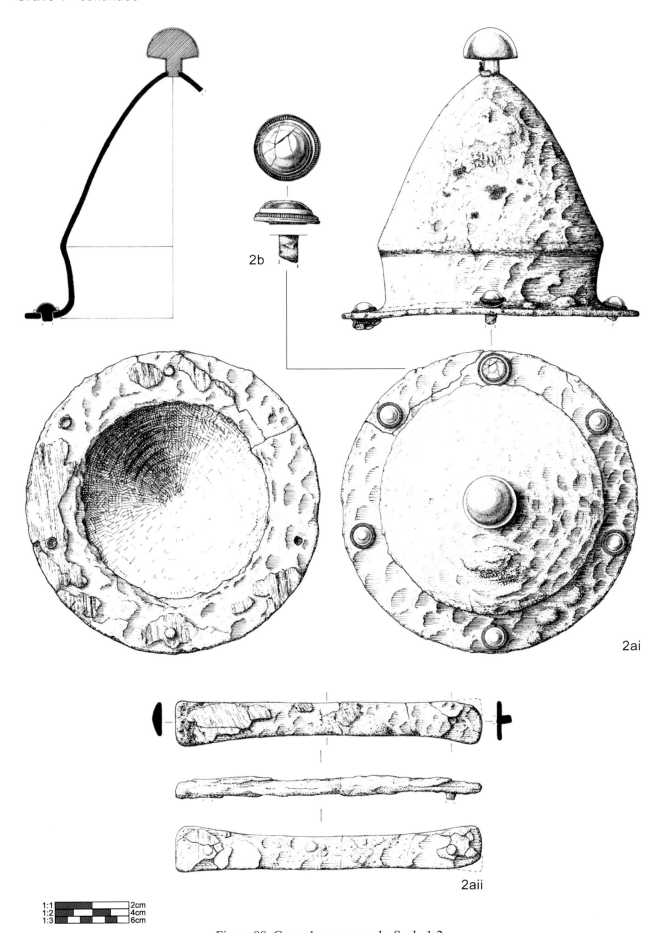

2b

2ai

2aii

1:1   2cm
1:2   4cm
1:3   6cm

Figure 88   Grave 1, grave-goods. Scale 1:2

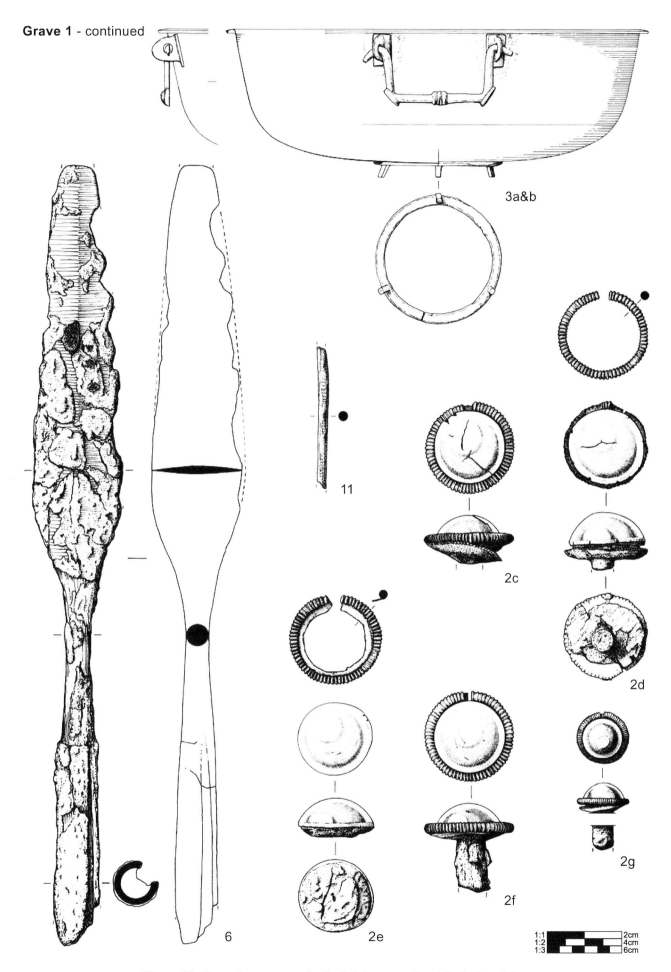

Figure 89 Grave 1, grave-goods. Scale1:1, except 6 at 1:2; 3a, b at 1:3

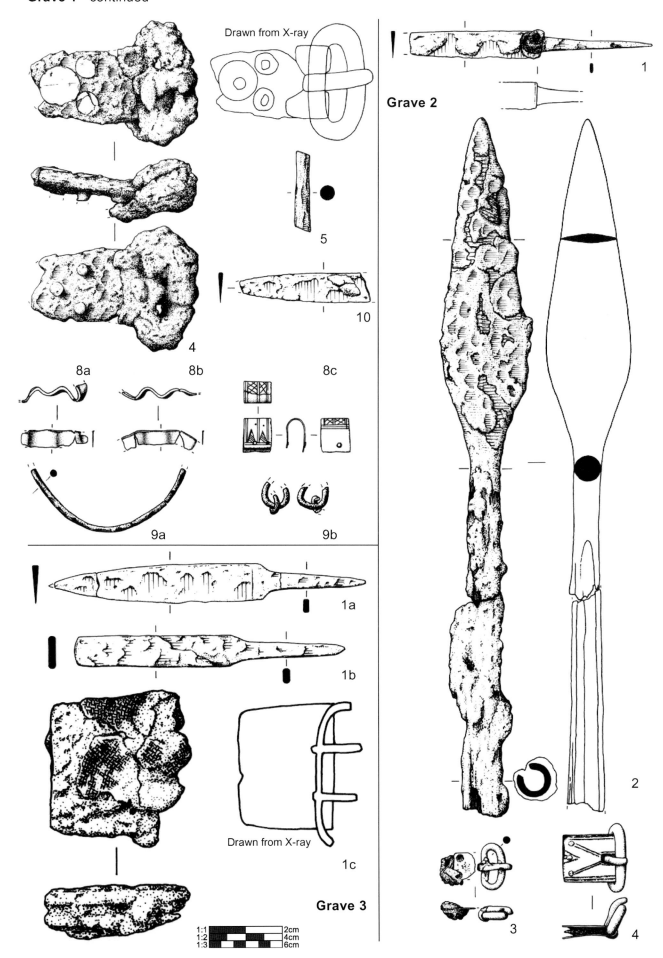

Grave 1 - continued

Drawn from X-ray

Grave 2

Grave 3

Drawn from X-ray

Figure 90 Graves 1, 2 and 3, grave-goods. Scale 1:1, except 1/5, 1/9a, b, 1/10e, 2/1, 2, 3/1a, b at 1:2

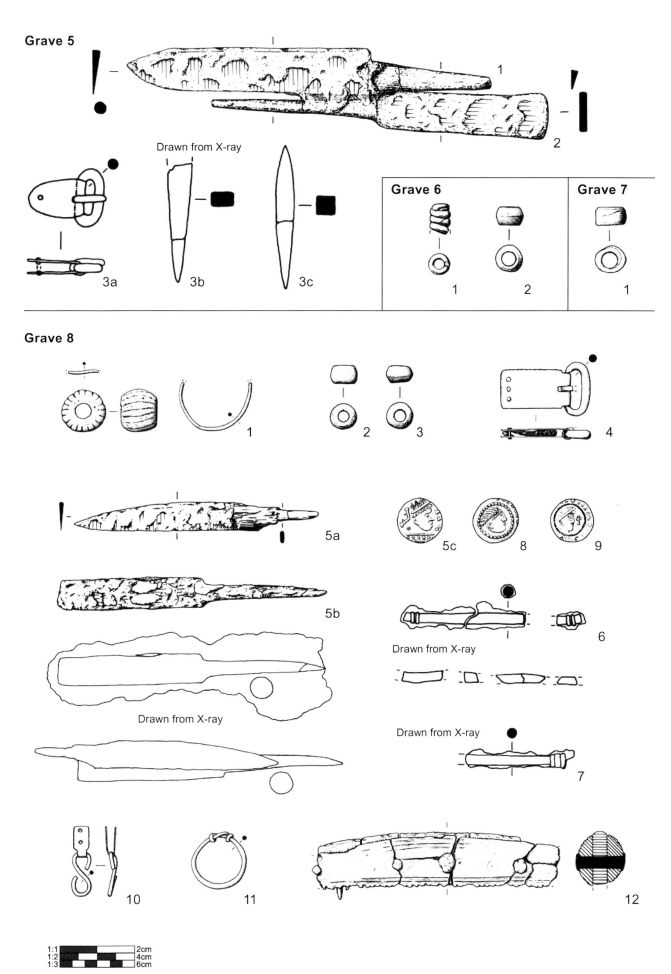

Figure 91 Graves 5–8, grave-goods. Scale 1:1, except 5/1 and 2; 8/5a, b at 1:2

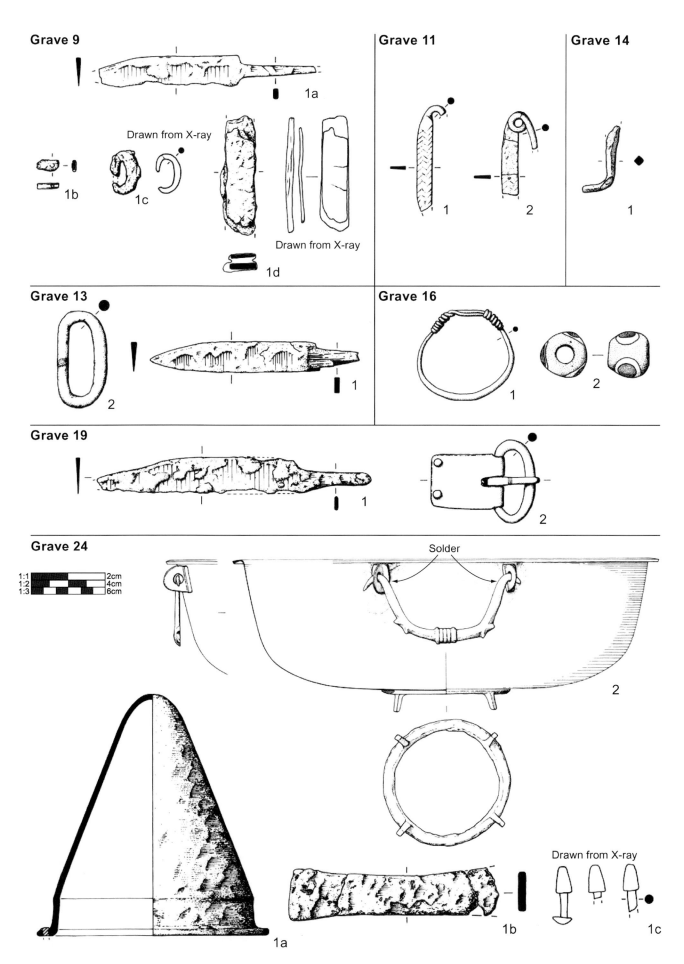

Figure 92 Graves 9, 11, 13–14, 16, 19 and 24, grave-goods. Scale 1:1, except 9/1a, 13/1, 19/1, 24/1a, b at 1:2; 24/2 at 1:3

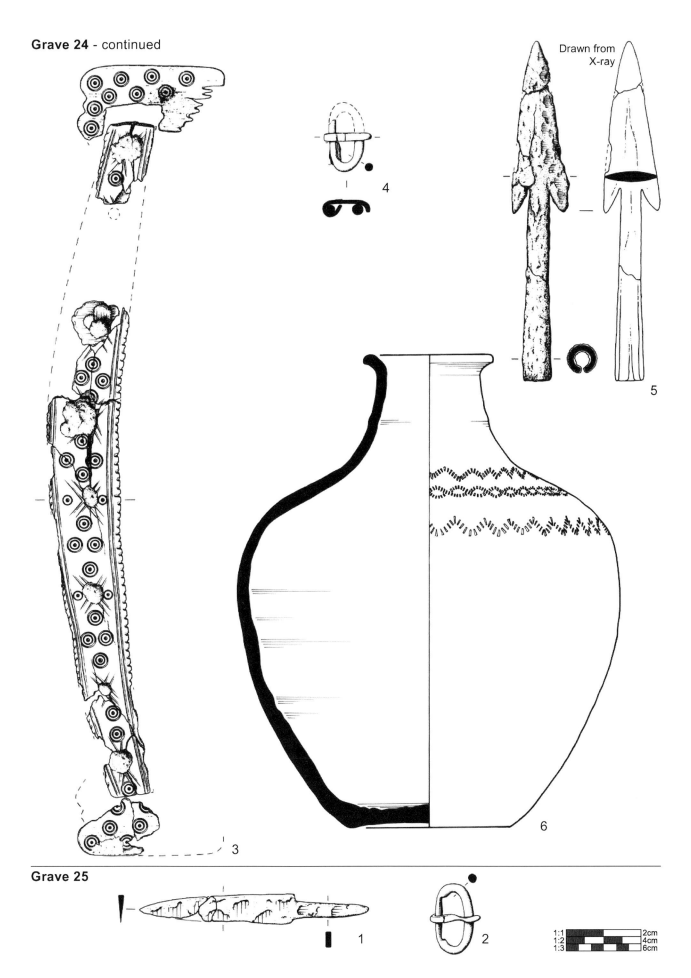

Drawn from X-ray

Grave 25

Figure 93 Graves 24 and 25, grave-goods. Scale 1:1, except 24/5, 25/1, 24/6 at 1:2

Grave 26

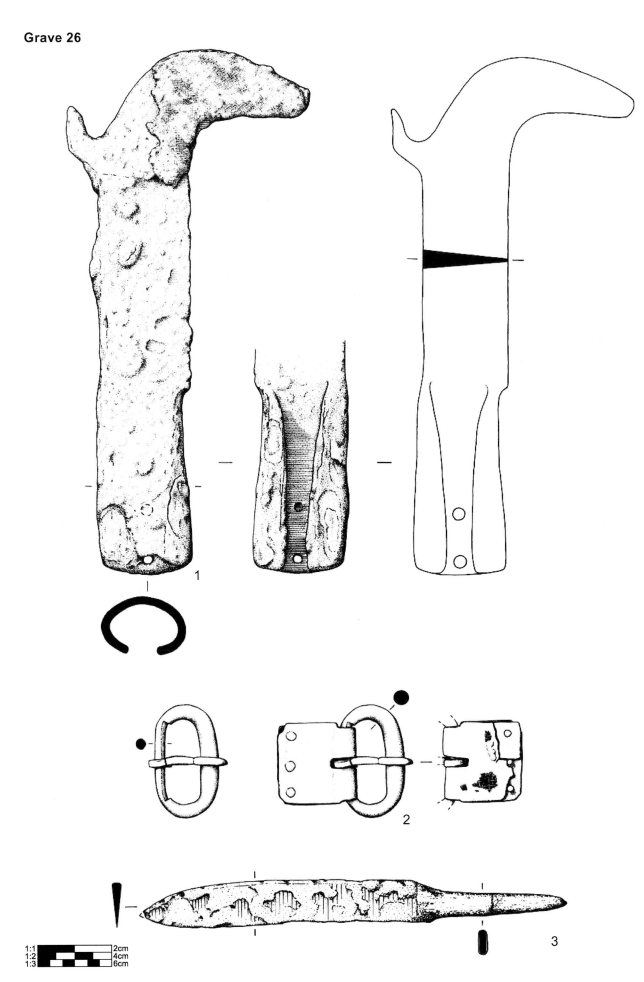

Figure 94 Grave 26, grave-goods. Scale 1:1, except 26/1 and 26/3 at 1:2

Grave 30

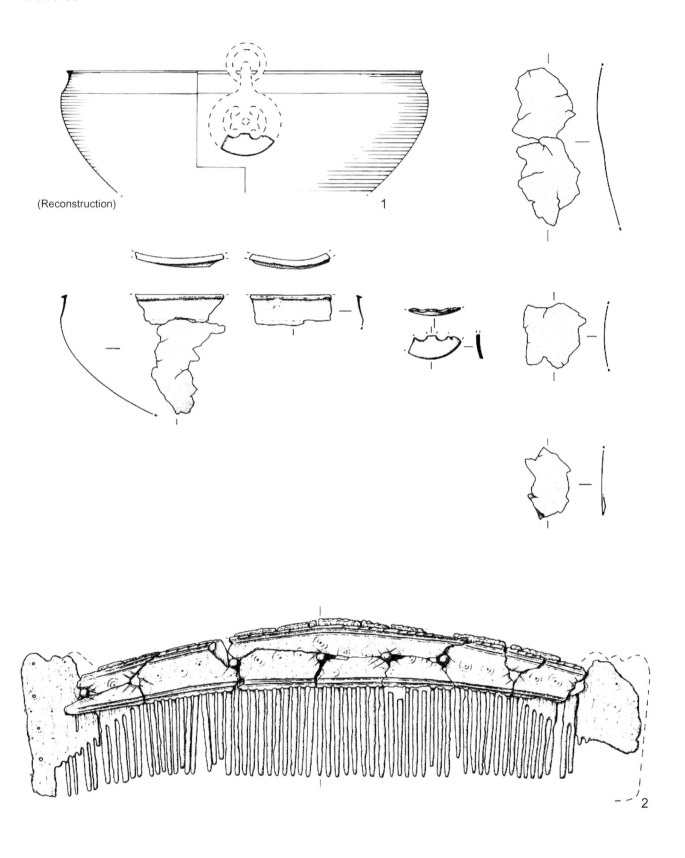

(Reconstruction)

1

2

Figure 95 Grave 30, grave-goods. Scale1:1, except 30/1 at 1:2

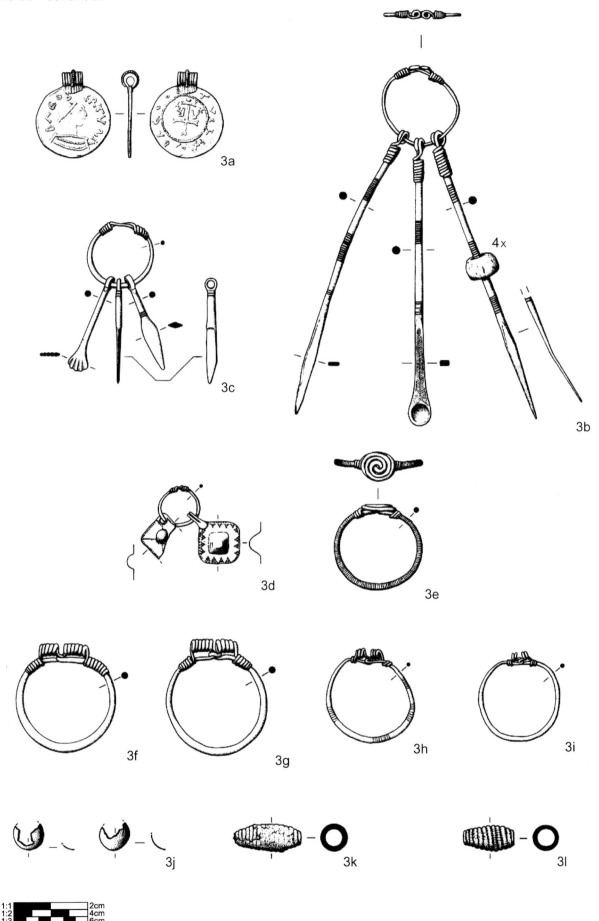

Figure 96 Grave 30, grave-goods. Scale 1:1

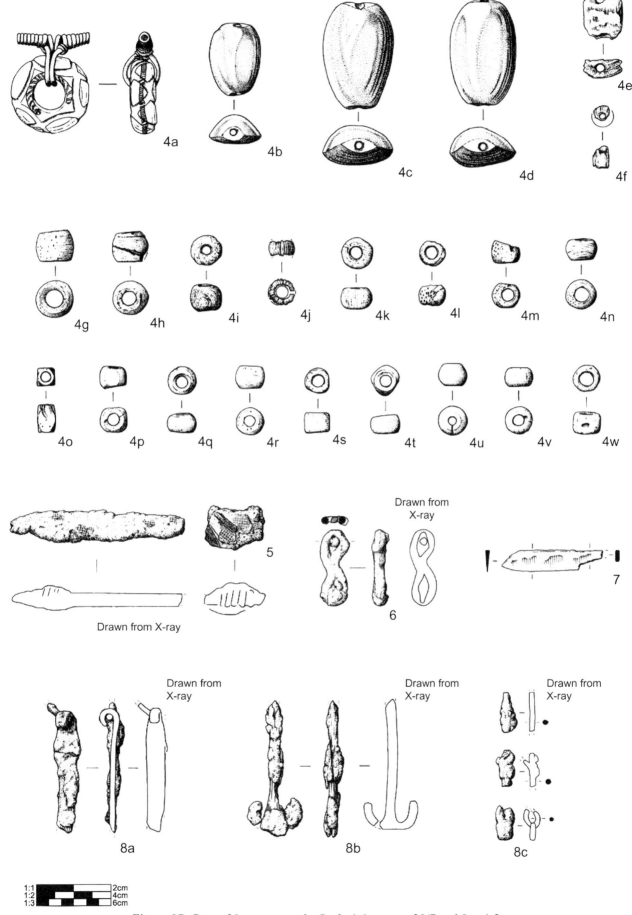

Figure 97 Grave 30, grave-goods. Scale 1:1, except 30/7 and 8 at 1:2

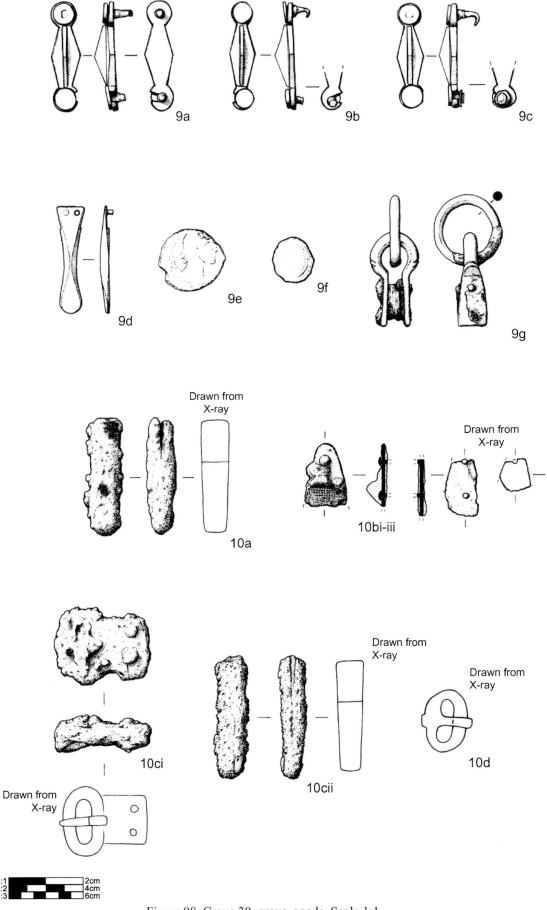

Figure 98 Grave 30, grave-goods. Scale 1:1

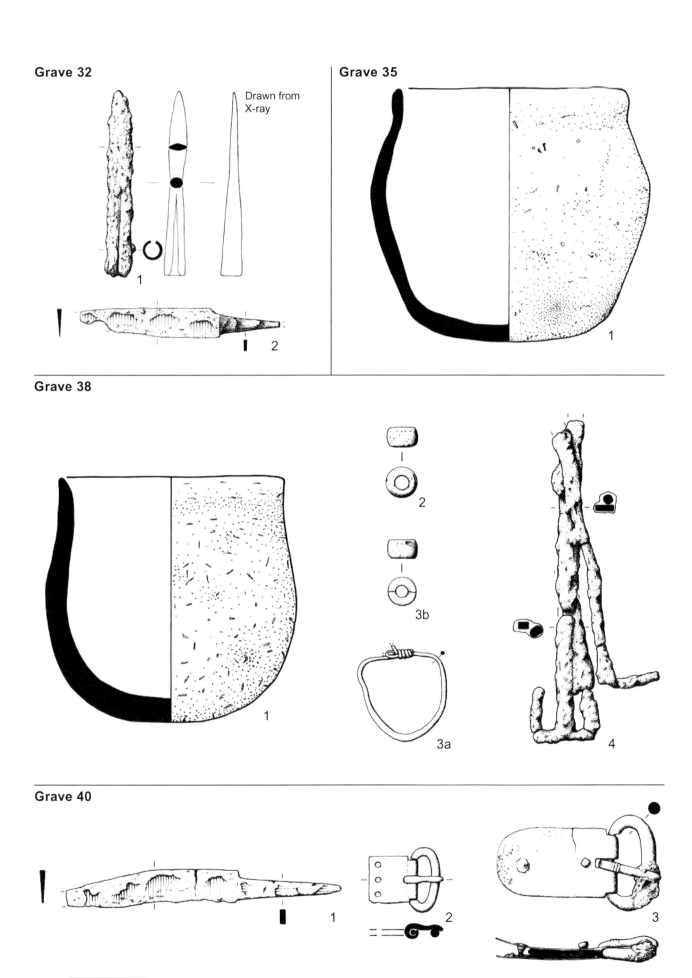

Grave 32

Drawn from X-ray

1

2

Grave 35

1

Grave 38

1

2

3b

3a

4

Grave 40

1

2

3

1:1   2cm
1:2   4cm
1:3   6cm

Figure 99 Graves 32, 35, 38 and 40, grave-goods. Scale 1:1, except 32/1, 32/2, 35/1, 35/2, 38/1, 38/4 at 1:2

Grave 44

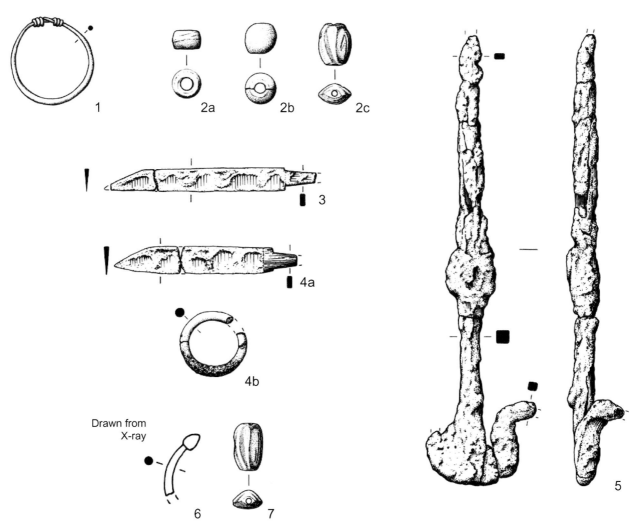

Drawn from X-ray

Grave 45

Grave 46

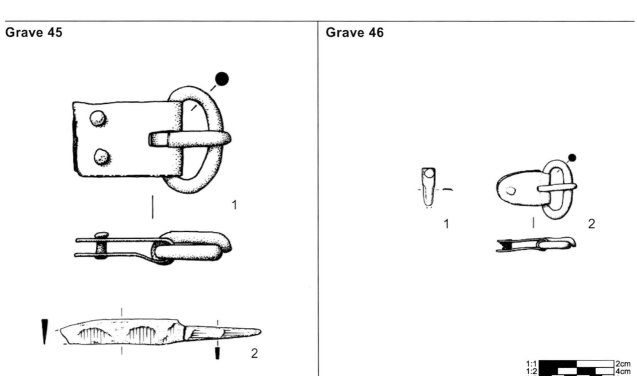

1:1 2cm
1:2 4cm
1:3 6cm

Figure 100 Graves 44–6, grave-goods. Scale 1:1, except 44/3, 44/4, 44/5, 45/2 at 1:2

120

Grave 47

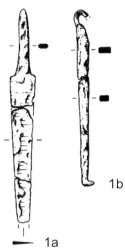

1b

1a

Grave 48

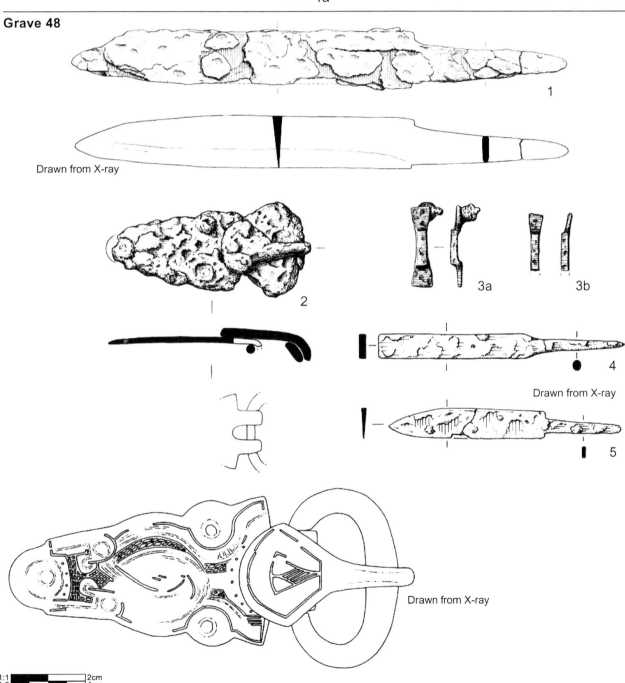

1

Drawn from X-ray

3a

3b

2

4

Drawn from X-ray

5

Drawn from X-ray

1:1 2cm
1:2 4cm
1:3 6cm

Figure 101 Graves 47, 48, grave-goods. Scale 1:2, except 48/1 at 1:3

Grave 50

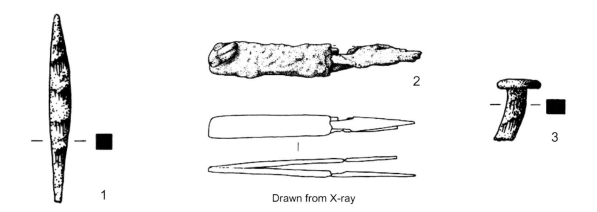

1

2

Drawn from X-ray

3

Other objects

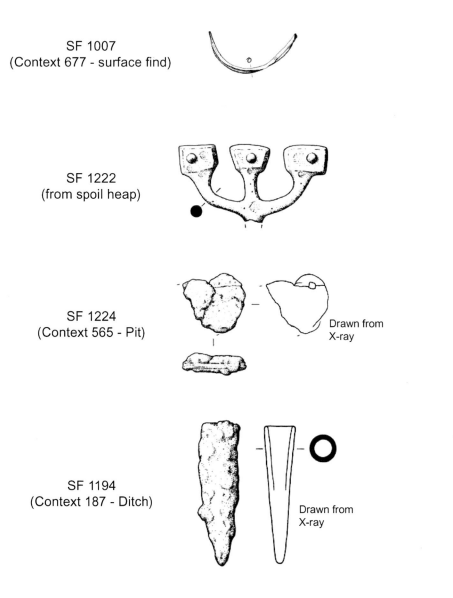

SF 1007
(Context 677 - surface find)

SF 1222
(from spoil heap)

SF 1224
(Context 565 - Pit)

Drawn from
X-ray

SF 1194
(Context 187 - Ditch)

Drawn from
X-ray

1:1   2cm
1:2   4cm
1:3   6cm

Figure 102 Grave 50, grave-goods, and unstratified finds. Scale 1:2, except 50/3 at 1:1

Bibliography

Cartographic Sources

SRO HD 1467/1   'A map of the Glebelands belonging to the Vicarage of Coddenham' 1773
(Glebe land in several places situated in those Enclosures part of the Shrubland Estate Nov 1812)

SRO HD 1467/2   A map showing the extent of the Parish of Coddenham and the Hamlet of Crowfield 1785

SRO P 461/66   Tithe map 1839

Bibliography

Ager, B., 1989   'The Anglo-Saxon cemetery', in Stead, I. and Rigby, V., (eds), *Verulamium: The King Harry Lane Site*, English Heritage Archaeol. Rep. 12, 219–239

Anderson, S., 1990   *The Human Skeletal Remains from Staunch Meadow, Brandon, Suffolk*, English Heritage Ancient Monuments Lab. Rep. 99/90

Anderson, S., 1991   *The Human Skeletal Remains from Caister-on-Sea, Norfolk*, English Heritage Ancient Monuments Lab. Rep. 7/91

Anderson, S., 1993   'The Human Skeletal Remains from Caister-on-Sea', in Darling, M.J. with Gurney, D., *Caister-on-Sea Excavations by Charles Green, 1951–55*, E. Anglian Archaeol. 60, 261–8

Anderson, S., 2002   *Assessment and Updated Project Design: Smye's Corner, Shrublands Quarry, Coddenham, Suffolk Site CDD 050*, Suffolk County Council Archaeological Service Report 02/81

Anderson, S., 2007   'The human population', in Daniels, R., *Anglo-Saxon Hartlepool and the Foundations of English Christianity: An Archaeology of the Anglo-Saxon Monastery*, Tees Archaeology Monogr. 3

Anderson, S. and Birkett, D., 1991   *The Human Skeletal Remains from Burgh Castle, Norfolk, 1960 Addendum*, English Heritage Ancient Monuments Lab. Rep. 6/91

Anderson, S. and Birkett, D., 1993   'The Human Skeletal Remains from Burgh Castle', in Darling, M.J. with Gurney, D., *Caister-on-Sea Excavations by Charles Green, 1951–55*, E. Anglian Archaeol. 60, 256 260

Anon; 2005   Woodworking in the Viking Age, http://www.vikinganswerlady.com/wood.htm/ (accessed 14.10.2005)

Archibald, M.M., 1975   'Medieval and modern hoards: British and Irish', *Coin Hoards* I, 85–108

Archibald, M.M, 1995   *Coins from the Boss Hall Grave 93*, (unpublished note)

Bass, W., 1971   *Human Osteology*, (Missouri Archaeol. Soc.)

Birbeck, V. with Andrews, P. and Stoodley, N., 2005   *The Origins of Mid-Saxon Southampton: Excavations at the Friends Provident St Marys Stadium 1998–2000*, Wessex Archaeology Monograph

Blair, J., 2005   *The Church in Anglo-Saxon Society*, (Oxford)

Blair, I., Barham, E. and Blackmore, L., 2004   'My Lord Essex', *British Archaeology* (May 2004), 10–17

Blinkhorn, P., 1999   'Of cabbages and kings: production, trade and consumption in middle saxon England' in Anderton, M., (ed.), *Anglo-Saxon Trading Centres: Beyond the Emporia,* (Glasgow), 4–23

Blockley, K., Blockley, M., Blockley, P., Frere, S.S. and Stow, S., 1995   *Excavations in the Marlowe Car Park and Surrounding Areas*, The Archaeology of Canterbury 5 (Canterbury Archaeological Trust)

Böhme, H,W., 1974   *Germanische grabfunde des 4. bis 5. Jahrhunderts zwischen unterer Elbe und Loire*, Münchner Beiträge zur Vor und Frühgeschichte 19, 2 vols (Munich)

Böhner, K., 1958   *Die fränkischen Altertümer des Trier Landes*, Germ. Denkmäler Volkerswanderungszeit B, 1 (Berlin)

Boulter, S., 1993   *Archaeological Evaluation: Shrubland Park, Coddenham,* Suffolk County Council Archaeological Service Report 93/5

Bouts, W. and Pot, T., 1989   'Computerized recording and analysis of excavated human dental remains', in Roberts, C.A., Lee, F. and Bintliff, J. (eds), *Burial Archaeology: current research, methods and developments*, Brit. Archaeol. Rep. Brit. Ser. 211 (Oxford)

Boyle, A., Jennings, D., Miles, D. and Palmer, S., 1998   *The Anglo-Saxon Cemetery at Butler's field, Lechlade, Gloucestershire, Vol.1: Prehistoric and Roman Activity and Anglo-Saxon Grave Catalogue*, Thames Valley Landscapes Monograph 10 (Oxford Archaeological Unit)

Bradley, R., 1987   'Time regained: The creation of continuity', *J. Brit. Archaeol. Assn.* 140, 1–17

Brenan, J., 1984–5   'Assessing social status in the Anglo-Saxon cemetery at Sleaford', *Bull. Institute Archaeol.* 21–22, 125–131

Brenan, J., 1991   *Hanging bowls and their contexts; An archaeological survey of their socio-economic significance from the fifth to the seventh centuries*, Brit. Archaeol. Rep. Brit. Ser. 220 (Oxford)

Brookes, S., 2007   'Boat-rivets in graves in pre-Viking Kent: reassessing Anglo-Saxon boat-burial traditions', *Medieval Archaeol.* 51, 1–19

Brothwell, D., 1981   *Digging up Bones,* (London: British Museum Natural History)

Brown, G.B., 1903   *The Arts in Early England*, 1

Bruce-Mitford, R.L., 1975   *The Sutton Hoo Ship Burial Volume One*, (Trustees of the British Museum)

Bruce-Mitford, R.L. and Raven, S., 2005   *A Corpus of Late Celtic Hanging Bowls* (Oxford)

Brugmann, B., 2004   *Glass beads from Anglo-Saxon Graves* (Oxbow Monographs: Oxford)

Buckberry, J., 2007   Missing, presumed buried? Bone diagenesis and the under-representation of Anglo-Saxon children', Research Article, www.ads.ahds.ac.uk/catalogue/adsdata/assemblage/htmcl/5/ (accessed 08.10.2008)

Bullough, D., 1983   Burial, Community and Belief', in Wormald, P., (ed), *Ideal and Reality in Frankish and Anglo-Saxon Society* (Oxford), 177–201

Burzler, A., Höneisen, J., Leicht, J. and Ruckstuhl, B., 2002   *Das frühmittelalterliche Schleitheim — Siedlung, Gräberfeld und Kirch*, Schaffhausener Archäologie 5 (Schaffhausen)

Cam, H.M., 1944   *Liberties and Communities* (Manchester)

Cameron, E., 1991   'Identification of skin and leather preserved by iron corrosion products', *J. Archaeol. Science* 18, 25–33

Cameron, E., 2000   *Sheaths and Scabbards in England AD 400–1100,* Brit. Archaeol. Rep. Brit. Ser. 301

Care Evans, A. and Galloway, P., 1983   'The Combs', in Bruce-Mitford, R.L., (ed) *The Sutton Hoo Ship Burial Volume Three pt ii,* (British Museum Press), 813–32

Caruth, J., 1996   'Archaeology in Suffolk', *Proc. Suffolk Inst. Archaeol.* 38(iv), 476–7

Carver, M., 1998   *Sutton Hoo: Burial Ground of Kings?* (British Museum Press)

Carver, M., 2002   'Reflections on the Meaning of Monumental Barrows in Anglo-Saxon England', in Lucy, S., and Reynolds, A., (eds), *Burial in Early Medieval England and Wales*, Soc. Medieval Archaeol. Monograph 17, 137–143

Carver, M., 2005   *Sutton Hoo: a seventh-century princely burial ground and its context*, Rep. Res. Comm. Soc. Antiq. 60 (British Museum Press)

Cessford, C. and Dickens, A., 2005   'The manor of *Hintone*: the origins and development of Church End, Cherry Hinton', *Proc. Cambridge Antiq. Soc.* 94, 51–72

Coin Register   Coin Register: Fitzwilliam Museum Early Medieval Corpus of Coin Finds

Cook, J., 2004   *Early Anglo-Saxon Buckets*, Oxford University School of Archaeology Monograph 60

Copinger, W.A., 1909   *The Manors of Suffolk* (Vol. 2)

Cotta, H., 1978   *Orthopaedics, a brief textbook*, (Stuttgart: Georg Thiem Verlag)

Cowell, M., 1979   'Appendix 3: Report on the analysis of some sixth- and seventh-century pottery from sites in southern Britain and northern Europe', in Evison, V., *A Corpus of Wheel-thrown pottery in Anglo-Saxon Graves*, 96–99 (London: Royal Archaeological Institute)

Cox, M., 1990   *The Human Bones from West Heslerton, North Yorkshire*, English Heritage Ancient Monuments Lab. Rep. 112/90

Cox, D., 2001   *Smye's Corner (Shrublands Quarry), Coddenham, Suffolk: Report on the controlled excavation of Soil Block 0345, from Grave 0308*, English Heritage Research Dept. Rep. 4.10.2001

Crawford, S., 1993   'Children, Death and the Afterlife in Anglo-Saxon England', *Anglo-Saxon Studies Archaeol. Hist.* 6, 83–91

Crowfoot, E., 1967   'The textiles' in Davidson, H.R.E. and Webster, L., 'The Anglo-Saxon burial at Coombe (Woodnesborough), Kent', *Medieval Archaeol.* 11, 37–9

Crowfoot, E., 1973   'Appendix A, Textile', pp53–4 in West, S.E. and Owles, E., 'Anglo-Saxon cremation burials from Snape', *Proc. Suffolk Inst. Archaeol.* 33(i), 47–57

Crowfoot, E., 1976   'The textiles and leather', in Barfoot, J.F. and Price-Williams, D., 'The Saxon Barrow at Gally Hills, Banstead Down, Surrey', *Surrey Archaeol. Soc.* 3, 68–71

Crowfoot, E., 1983   'The Textiles' in Bruce-Mitford, R.L., (ed), *The Sutton Hoo Ship Burial Volume Three pt. i,* 409–479

Crowfoot, E., 1989   'The textiles', pp170–171 in Adams, B. and Jackson, D., 'The Anglo-Saxon cemetery at Wakerley, Northamptonshire', *Northants Archaeol.* 22, 69–178

Crowfoot, E., 1998   'Textiles associated with metalwork' in Malim, T. and Hines, J., *The Anglo-Saxon Cemetery at Edix Hill (Barrington A), Cambridgeshire*, Counc. Brit. Archaeol. Res. Rep. 112, 235–246

Crowfoot, E., 2000   'The textiles' in Penn, K., *Excavations on the Norwich Southern Bypass, 1989–91 Pt II: The Anglo-Saxon Cemetery at Harford Farm, Caistor St Edmund, Norfolk*, E. Anglian Archaeol. 92, 82–91

Crowfoot, E., 2001   'The textiles' in Filmer-Sankey, W. and Pestell, T., *Snape Anglo-Saxon Cemetery: Excavations and Surveys 1824–1992*, E. Anglian Archaeol. 95, 114–9 and 207–212

Dallas, C., 1993   *Excavations in Thetford by B. K. Davison between 1964 and 1970*, E. Anglian Archaeol. 62

Darling, M. with Gurney, D., 1993   *Caister-on-Sea: Excavations by Charles Green, 1951–55*, E. Anglian Archaeol. 60

Davis, R.H.C., 1954   *The Kalendar of Abbot Samson of Bury St Edmunds,* Camden Soc. Series 84 (Roy. Hist. Soc.)

Dickens, A., Mortimer, R. and Tipper, J., 2005   'The Early Anglo-Saxon settlement and cemetery at Bloodmoor Hill, Carlton Colville, Suffolk: a preliminary report', *Anglo-Saxon Stud. Archaeol. Hist.* 13, 63–79

Dickinson, T.M., 1993   'An Anglo-Saxon 'cunning woman' from Bidford-on-Avon', in Carver, M., (ed.), *In Search of Cult*, (Boydell: Woodbridge), 45–54

Dickinson, T.M. and Härke, H., 1992   *Early Anglo-Saxon Shields*, Archaeologia 110, (Society of Antiquaries of London)

Dodwell, N., Lucy, S. and Tipper, J., 2004   'Anglo-Saxons on the Cambridge Backs: the Criminology Site settlement and King's Garden Hostel cemetery', *Proc. Cambridge Antiq. Soc.* 93, 95–124

Döppelfeld, O., 1960   'Das fränkische Frauengrab unter dem Chor des Kölner Domes', *Germania* 38, 89–113

Drinkall, G. and Foreman, M., 1998   *The Anglo-Saxon cemetery at Castledyke South, Barton-upon-Humber*, Sheffield Excavation Reports 6

Duhig, C., 1998   'The human skeletal material', in Malim, T. and Hines, J., *The Anglo-Saxon Cemetery at Edix Hill (Barrington A), Cambridgeshire*, Counc. Brit. Archaeol. Res. Rep. 112, 154–196

Duncan, H., Duhig, C. and Phillips, M., 2003
'A late Migration/Final Phase cemetery at Water Lane, Melbourn', *Proc. Cambridge Antiq. Soc.* 92, 57–134

East, K., 1983
'Review of the evidence for drinking-horns and wooden cups from Anglo-Saxon sites', in Bruce-Mitford, R.L., (ed), *The Sutton Hoo Ship Burial Volume Three pt. i*, (British Museum Press), 385–391

Ellis-Davidson, H. and Webster, L., 1967
'The Anglo-Saxon Burial at Coombe (Woodnesborough), Kent', *Medieval Archaeol.* 11, 1–41

Ellmers, D., 1990
'The Frisian monopoly of coastal transport in the 6th–8th centuries AD', in McGrail, S., (ed.), *Maritime Celts, Frisians and Saxons*, Counc. Brit. Archaeol. Res. Rep. 71, 91–2

Everett, L., Anderson, S., Powell, K. and Riddler, I., 2003
Vicarage Farm, Coddenham CDD 022 An Archaeological Evaluation, 2003, Suffolk County Council Archaeological Service Report 03/66

Evison, V.I., 1956
'An Anglo-Saxon cemetery at Holborough, Kent', *Archaeol. Cantiana* 70, 84–141

Evison, V.I., 1961
'The Saxon objects' in Hurst, J.G., 'The kitchen area of Northolt Manor, Middx.', *Medieval Archaeol.* 5, 226–30

Evison, V.I., 1963
'Sugar-loaf shield bosses', *Antiq. J.* 43, 38–96

Evison, V.I., 1969
'Note on the seax and bronze belt-fititng, Laverstock', in Musty, J., 'Excavations of two barrows', *Antiq. J.* 49, appendix 1, 98–117

Evison, V.I., 1974
'The Asthall type of bottle', in Evison, V.I. and Hurst, J.G. (eds.), *Medieval Pottery from Excavations: Studies presented to Gerald Clough Dunning, with a bibliography of his works*, (London: John Baker), 77–94

Evison, V.I., 1979
A Corpus of Wheel-thrown Pottery in Anglo-Saxon Graves, (London: Royal Archaeological Institute)

Evison, V.I., 1987
Dover: The Buckland Anglo-Saxon Cemetery, English Heritage Archaeol. Rep. 3, (London)

Faull, M., 1977
'British Survival in Anglo-Saxon Northumbria' in Laing, L. (ed.), *Studies in Celtic Survival*, Brit. Archaeol. Rep. 37, 1–55, (Oxford)

Faussett, B., 1856
Inventorium Sepulchrae, C.R. Smith (ed.), (London)

Fern, C., 2007
Sutton Hoo Visitors' Centre, Tranmer House, Bromeswell, Suffolk, Suffolk County Council Archaeological Service Report 07/116

Filmer-Sankey, W. and Pestell, T., 2001
Snape Anglo-Saxon Cemetery: Excavations and Surveys 1824–1992, E. Anglian Archaeol. 95

Fryer, V., n.d.
Plant macrofossils from environmental sampling (Project Archive Report)

Gale, D., 1989
'The seax', in Hawkes, S.C., (ed.) *Weapons and Warfare in Anglo-Saxon England*, Oxford University Comm. Archaeol. Monograph 21, 71–83

Geake, H., 1994
'Anglo-Saxon double-tongued buckles', *Medieval Archaeol.* 38, 164–7

Geake, H., 1997
The Use of Grave-Goods in Conversion-Period England, c. 600–c. 850, Brit. Archaeol. Rep. Brit. Ser. 261, (Oxford)

Geake, H., 1999a
'When were hanging bowls deposited in Anglo-Saxon graves?' *Medieval Archaeol.* 43, 1–18

Geake, H., 1999b
'Invisible kingdoms: the use of grave-goods in seventh-century England', *Anglo-Saxon Stud. Archaeol. Hist.* 10, 203–215

Geake, H., 2002
'Persistent problems in the Study of Conversion-period Burials in England', in Lucy, S. and Reynolds, A., (eds), *Burial in Early Medieval England and Wales*, Soc. Medieval Archaeol. Monograph 17, 144–155

Geake, H., 2003
'The Control of Burial Practice in Anglo-Saxon England', in Carver, M., *The Cross Goes North: Processes of Conversion in Northern Europe, AD 3000–1100*, (York Medieval Press), 259–269

Geijer, A., 1938
Birka III: Die Textilfunde aus den Gräbern, (Uppsala, Sweden: Almqvist & Wiksells)

Golding, B., 1982
'The coming of the Cluniacs', *Anglo-Norman Studies* 4 (Proc. Battle Conference 1981), 65–77

Graham, K., 2001a
Smye's Corner (Shrublands Quarry), Coddenham, Suffolk: Conservation report on the excavation of a soil block from Grave 0308 (Block 1140), English Heritage Research Dept. Report

Graham, K., 2001b
Smye's Corner (Shrublands Quarry), Coddenham, Suffolk: Grave 0141. Report on the controlled excavation of a comb, English Heritage Research Dept. Report

Graham, K. and Cox, D., 2001
Smye's Corner (Shrublands Quarry), Coddenham, Suffolk: report on the excavation of the bone comb soil block, English Heritage Research Dept Report

Green, B. and Rogerson, A., 1978
The Anglo-Saxon Cemetery at Bergh Apton, Norfolk, E. Anglian Archaeol. 7

Green, B. and Rogerson, A., 1987
The Anglo-Saxon Cemetery at Morning Thorpe, Norfolk, E. Anglian Archaeol. 36

Gregory, A., 1986
'An Enclosure of the First Century AD at Thornham', in Gregory, A. and Gurney, D., *Excavations at Thornham, Warham, Wighton and Caistor, Norfolk*, E. Anglian Archaeol. 30, 1–13

Guðjónsson, E.E., 1962
Forn röggvarvefnaður, *Árbók hins Íslenzka Fornleifáfélags (Reykjavik)*, 12–71

Haith, C., 1997
Buckland II, Dover, Anglo-Saxon cemetery: a provisional list of the gravegoods, (unpublished report for the British Museum)

Hamerow, H., 1991
'Settlement mobility and the "Middle Saxon Shift": rural settlement and settlement patterns in Anglo-Saxon England', *Anglo-Saxon England* 20, 1–17

Hamerow, H., 1993
Excavations at Mucking Volume 2: The Anglo-Saxon settlement, (London: English Heritage/ British Museum Press)

Hamerow, H., 1999
'Angles, Saxons and Anglo-Saxons', *Studien zur Sächsenforschung* 13, 189–206

Hamerow, H., 2002
Early Medieval Settlements. The Archaeology of Rural Communities in North-West Europe 400–900, (Oxford)

Härke, H., 1989
'Knives in early Saxon burials; blade lengths and age at death', *Medieval Archaeol.* 33, 144–8

Hawkes, S.C., 1973
'The Dating and Social Significance of the Burials in the Polhill Cemetery', in Philp, B., *Excavations in West Kent 1960–1970*, (Dover), 186–201

Hawkes, S.C., 1981 'Recent finds of inlaid iron buckles and belt-plates from seventh-century Kent', in *Anglo-Saxon Studies in Archaeology and History*, Brown, D., Campbell, J. and Hawkes, S.C., (eds), Brit. Archaeol. Rep. Brit. Ser. 92, 49–70

Hills, C.M., Penn, K.J. and Rickett, R., 1984 *The Anglo-Saxon Cemetery at Spong Hill, North Elmham Part III: Catalogue of Inhumations*, E. Anglian Archaeol. 21

Hillson, S., 1996 *Dental Anthropology*, (Cambridge University Press)

Hines , J., 1984 *The Scandinavian Character of Anglo-Saxon England in the Pre-Viking Period*, Brit. Archaeol. Rep. Brit. Ser. 124 (Oxford))

Hines, J., 1999 'Angelsächsische Chronologie: Probleme und Aussichten', in von Freeden, U., Koch, U. and Wieczorek, A., (eds) *Volker an Nord-und Ostsee und die Franken*, (Akten des 48. Sachsensymposiums in Mannheim vorm 7. Bis 11. September 1997. Kolloq. Vor- and Fruhgesch. 3 (Bonn)), 19–30

Hinton, D.A., 2000 *A Smith in Lindsey: The Anglo-Saxon Grave at Tattershall Thorpe, Lincolnshire*, Soc. Medieval Archaeol. Monograph 16

Hirst, S., 1985 *An Anglo-Saxon Cemetery at Sewerby, Yorkshire*, York University Archaeological Publications 4

Hoffman, M., 1983 'Beds and bedclothes in medieval Norway', in Harte, N.B. and Ponting, K.G., (eds) *Cloth and Clothing in Medieval Europe: Essays in memory of Professor E.M. Carus Wilson*, (London) 351–367

Huggett, J.W., 1988 'Imported gravegoods and the Early Anglo-Saxon economy', *Medieval Archaeol.* 32, 63–96

Hyslop, M., 1963 'Two Anglo-Saxon cemeteries at Chamberlain's Barn, Leighton Buzzard, Bedfordshire', *Archaeol. J.* 120, 161–200

James, E., 1988 *The Franks*, (Blackwell: Oxford)

Johnson, S., 1983 *Burgh Castle: excavations by Charles Green, 1958–61*, E. Anglian Archaeol. 20

Koch, U., 1987 *Der Runde Berg bei Urach IV. Die Glas- und Edelsteinfunde aus den Plangrabungen 1967–1983*, Heidelberger bAkad. Wiss. Komm. Alamannische Alterkumskde 12 (Sigmaringen)

Koch, U., 1990 *Das fränkische Gräberfeld von Klepsau im Hohenlohekreis*, Forschungen und Berichte zur Vor- und Frühgeschichte in Baden-Württemberg 38 (Stuttgart)

Krogman, W., 1978 *The Human Skeleton in Forensic Medicine*, (Illinois)

Lasko, P., 1971 *The Kingdom of the Franks*, (Thames and Hudson)

Layard, N., 1907 'An Anglo-Saxon cemetery at Ipswich', *Archaeologia* 60, 325–352

Leeds, E.T., 1923 'A Saxon village near Sutton Courtenay, Berkshire', *Archaeologia* 72, 147–192

Leeds, E.T., 1936 *Early Anglo-Saxon Art and Archaeology*, (Oxford)

Lethbridge, T.C., 1926–7 'The Anglo-Saxon cemetery at Burwell, Cambs. part III', *Proc. Cambridge Antiq. Soc.* 29, 84–94

Lethbridge, T.C., 1931 *Recent Excavations in Anglo-Saxon Cemeteries in Cambridgeshire and Suffolk*, Cambridge Antiq. Soc. Quarto Publications ns 3

Lethbridge, T.C., 1936 *A cemetery at Shudy Camps, Cambridgeshire*, Cambridge Antiq. Soc. Quarto Publications ns 5, 9–12

Lloyd-Jones, J., 1997 'Calculating bio-distance using dental morphology', in Anderson, S. and Boyle, K. (eds.), *Computing and Statistics in Osteoarchaeology*, (Oxford: Oxbow Books)

Lucy, S., 1999 *The Early Anglo-Saxon Cemeteries of East Yorkshire: An Analysis and Reinterpretation*, Brit. Archaeol. Rep. Brit. Ser. 272 (Oxford)

Lucy, S. and Reynolds, A., (eds) 2002 *Burial in Early Medieval England and Wales*, Soc. Medieval Archaeol. Monograph 17

Lucy, S., Tipper, J. and Dickens, A., 2009 *The Anglo-Saxon Settlement and Cemetery at Bloodmoor Hill, Carlton Colville, Suffolk*, E. Anglian Archaeol. 131

McCormac, F.G.H., Bayliss, A, Baillie, M.G.L. and Brown, D.M., 2004 'Radiocarbon calibration in the Anglo-Saxon period: AD 495–725', *Radiocarbon* 46, 1123–5

McCormac, F.G.H., Bayliss, A, Brown, D.M., Reimer, P.J. and Thompson, M.M, forthcoming 'Extended radiocarbon calibration in the Anglo-Saxon period, AD 395–485', *Radiocarbon*

MacGregor, A., 1992 'Bone and Antler Objects', in Milne, G. and Richards, J.D.,(eds) *Wharram: a Study of Settlement on the Yorkshire Wolds, VII. Two Anglo-Saxon Buildings and Associated Finds*, University of York Archaeological Publications 9 (York), 54–8

MacGregor, A., 1997 *A Summary Catalogue of the Continental Archaeological Collections*, Brit. Archaeol. Rep. Int. Ser. 674 (Oxford)

MacGregor, A., 2000 'Bone and Antler Objects', in Stamper, P.A. and Croft, R.A., *Wharram. A Study of Settlement on the Yorkshire Wolds, VIII. The South Manor Area*, York University Archaeological Publications 10 (York), 148–54

Malim, T. 1990 *Barrington Anglo-Saxon cemetery Edix Hill: Interim Report*, (Cambridgeshire County Council)

Malim, T. and Hines, J., 1998 *The Anglo-Saxon Cemetery at Edix Hill (Barrington A), Cambridgeshire*, Counc. Brit. Archaeol. Res. Rep. 112

Manley, J., 1985 'The archer and the army in the late Anglo-Saxon period', *Anglo-Saxon Stud. Archaeol. Hist.* 4, 223–235

Marlow, C.A., 1992 'The population', in Sherlock, S.J. and Welch, M.G., *An Anglo-Saxon Cemetery at Norton, Cleveland*, Counc. Brit. Archaeol. Res. Rep. 82, 107–17 (London)

Martin, M., 1984 'Weinsiebchen und Toilettgerät', in Cahn, A. und Kauffmann-Heinimann, A., *Der spätrömische Silberschatz von Kaiseraugst*, (Derendingen), 97–132

Martin, M., 1990 *Bemerkungen zur Ausstattung der Frauengräber und zur Interpretation der Doppelgräber und Nachbestattungen im frühen Mittelalter*, in Affeldt, W., (ed.), *Frauen in Spätantike und*

Frühmittelalter. Lebensbedingungen — Lebensnormen — Lebensformen, (Siegmaringen)

Marzinzik, S, 2003 — *Early Anglo-Saxon Belt Buckles (late 5th to early 8th centuries AD): their Classification and Context,* Brit. Archaeol. Rep. Brit. Ser. 357 (Oxford)

Meaney, A., 1964 — *A Gazetteer of Early Anglo-Saxon Burial Sites,* (London)

Meaney, A.L., 1981 — *Anglo-Saxon Amulets and Curing Stones,* Brit. Archaeol. Rep. Brit. Ser. 96 (Oxford)

Meaney, A.L. and Hawkes, S.C., 1970 — *Two Anglo-Saxon Cemeteries at Winnall,* Soc. Medieval Archaeol. Monograph 4

Metcalf, D.M., 1984 — 'Twenty-five notes on sceatta finds', pp193–4 in Hill, D. and Metcalf, D.M., (eds), *Sceattas in England and on the Continent,* Brit. Archaeol. Rep. Brit. Ser. 128, 193–205

Metcalf, D.M., 1993 — *Thrymsas and sceattas in the Ashmolean Museum, Oxford 1,* Royal Numismatic Society Special Publications 27a (London)

Miles, D. and Palmer, S., 1986 — *Invested in Mother Earth: The Anglo-Saxon Cemetery at Lechlade,* (Oxford)

Mills, A.D., 1991 — *A Dictionary of English Place-names* (Oxford)

Moore, I.E., Plouviez, J. and West, S., 1988 — *The Archaeology of Roman Suffolk* (Suffolk County Council)

Mortimer, R., 2000 — *Bloodmoor Hill, Carlton Colville, Suffolk: Excavation of the Early Anglo-Saxon Settlement,* (Cambridge: Cambridge Archaeological Unit)

Murphy, P., 2001 — 'Plant Macrofossils', in Flitcroft, M., *Excavation of a Romano-British Settlement on the A149 Snettisham Bypass, 1989,* E. Anglian Archaeol. 93, 77

Myres, J., 1977 — *A Corpus of Anglo-Saxon Pottery of the Pagan Period,* (Cambridge University Press)

Newman, J., 1992 — 'The Late Roman and Anglo-Saxon Pattern in the Sandlings of Suffolk' in Carver, M., (ed.), *The Age of Sutton Hoo: The Seventh Century in North-Western Europe,* (Woodbridge: Boydell), 25–38

Newman, J., 1993 — 'The Anglo-Saxon cemetery at Boss Hall, Ipswich', *Bulletin Sutton Hoo Res. Comm.* 8, 32–35

Newman, J., 1996 — 'New light on old finds — Bloodmoor Hill, Gisleham, Suffolk', *Anglo-Saxon Stud. Archaeol. Hist.* 9, 75–9

Newman, J., 1999a — *Project Design for archaeological monitoring excavation and archive/assessment report for site at Shrubland Quarry, Coddenham (CDD 050),* Suffolk County Council Archaeological Service Report (unpublished)

Newman, J., 1999b — 'Wics, trade and the hinterlands — the Ipswich region', in Anderton, M., (ed.), *Anglo-Saxon trading centres: beyond the emporia* (Glasgow: Cruithne Press), 32–47

Newman, J., 2003 — 'Exceptional Finds, Exceptional sites? — Barham and Coddenham, Suffolk', in Pestell, T. and Ulmschneider, K., *Markets in early medieval Europe: trading and productive sites, 650–850* (Macclesfield: Windgather Press), 97–109

Newman, J., 2004 — 'Coddenham', *Medieval Settlement Research Group Annual Report* 19, 36

Newman, J., 2005 — 'Survey in the Deben Valley', in Carver, M., 2005 *Sutton Hoo: a seventh-century princely burial ground and its context,* Rep. Res. Comm. Soc. Antiq. 60 (London: British Museum Press), 477–487

Newman, J., 2006 — 'Coddenham, Suffolk (NGR TM 133542)', *Medieval Settlement Research Group Annual Report* 21, 42

Newman, J., 2007 — 'Coddenham, Suffolk (NGR TM 1335452)', *Medieval Settlement Research Group Annual Report* 22, 54–5

Nieveler, E. and Siegmund, F., 1999 — 'The Merovingian Chronology of the Lower Rhine Area: results and problems', in Hines, J., Høilund Nielsen, K. and Siegmund, F., (eds) *The Pace of Change: Studies in Early Medieval Chronology,* (Oxford: Cardiff Studies in Archaeology), 3–22

O'Brien, E., 1999 — *Post-Roman Britain to Anglo-Saxon England: Burial Practices Reviewed,* Brit. Archaeol. Rep. Brit. Ser. 289 (Oxford)

Ortner, D. and Putschar, W., 1981 — *Identification of Pathological Conditions in Human Skeletal Remains,* (Washington: Smithsonian Institute)

Owen-Crocker, G.R., 2004 — *Dress in Anglo-Saxon England,* (revised edition, Woodbridge: Boydell)

Ozanne, A., 1962 — 'The context and date of the Anglian cemetery at Ipswich', *Proc. Suffolk Inst. Archaeol.* 29, 208–212

Parfitt, K. and Anderson, T., forthcoming — *Buckland Anglo-Saxon Cemetery, Dover: Excavations in 1994* (Canterbury Archaeol. Trust/British Museum Press)

Parfitt, K. and Brugmann, B., 1997 — *The Anglo-Saxon Cemetery on Mill Hill, Deal, Kent,* Soc. Medieval Archaeol. Monograph 14

Paulsen, P., 1992 — *Die Holzfunde aus dem Gräberfeld bei Oberflacht und ihre kulturhistorische Bedeutung,* (Theiss: Forschungen und Berichte zur Vor- und Frühgeschichte in Baden-Wüttemberg, 41/2: Stuttgart)

Penn, K., 2000 — *Excavations on the Norwich Southern Bypass, 1989–91. Part 2: The Anglo-Saxon Cemetery at Harford Farm, Markshall, Norfolk,* E. Anglian Archaeol. 92

Penn, K.J. and Brugmann, B., 2007 — *Aspects of Anglo-Saxon Inhumation Burial: Morning Thorpe, Spong Hill, Bergh Apton and Westgarth Gardens,* E. Anglian Archaeol. 119

Penn, K.J. and Whitmore, D., 2007 — 'A seventh-century burial at Bayfield, *Norfolk Archaeol.* 45, 212–21

Perkins, D.R.J., 1985 — 'The Monkton Gas pipeline: Phases III and IV, 1983–84', *Archaeol. Cantiana* 102, 43–70

Pestell, T., 2003 — 'The afterlife of "productive" sites in East Anglia', in Pestell, T. and Ulmschneider, K., (eds), *Markets in early medieval Europe: trading and productive sites, 650–850* (Macclesfield: Windgather Press), 122–137

Pestell, T. and Ulmschneider, K., (eds) 2003 — *Markets in early medieval Europe: trading and productive sites, 650–850* (Macclesfield: Windgather Press)

Piton, D. 1985 — *La Necropole de Nouvion-en-Ponthieu,* Dossiers archeologiques, historiques et culturels du Nord et du Pas-de-Calais 20, (Berck-sur-Mer)

Plunkett, S., 2001 — 'Some Recent Metalwork Discoveries from the Area of the Gipping Valley, and their Local Context', in Binski, P. and Noel, W., (eds) *New*

Offerings, Ancient Treasures: Studies in Medieval Art for George Henderson, (Sutton: Stroud), 61–87

Plunkett, S., 2005 — *Anglo-Saxon Suffolk* (Stroud: Tempus)

Putnam, G., 1978 — 'The human bone', in Huggins, P.J., 'Excavations of Belgic and Romano-British farms with Middle Saxon cemetery and churches at Nazeingbury, Essex, 1975–6', *Essex Archaeol. Hist.* 10, 29–117

Richards, P.J., 1980 — *Byzantine Bronze Vessels in England and Europe: The origins of Anglo-Saxon trade,* (unpublished PhD thesis, University of Cambridge)

Riddler, I.D., 2001 — 'The Spatial Organisation of Bone and Antler Working in Trading Centres', in Hill, D. and Cowie, R., (eds), *Wics, The Early Medieval Trading Centres of Northern Europe,* (Sheffield), 61–6

Riddler, I.D. and Trzaska-Nartowski, N.T.N., forthcoming — 'The Anglo-Saxon Material Culture', in Wrathmell, S., *Wharram: A Study of Settlement on the Yorkshire Wolds XIII. Overall Synthesis,* University of York Archaeological Publications, (York)

Riddler, I.D., Trzaska-Nartowski, N.T.N. and Hatton, S., forthcoming — *An Early Medieval Craft. Antler and Boneworking from Ipswich Excavations 1974–1994,* E. Anglian Archaeol.

Rigold, S.E., 1960 — 'The two primary series of sceattas', *Brit. Numis. J.* 30, 6–53

Rigold, S.E., 1966 — 'The two primary series of sceattas: addenda and corrigenda', *Brit. Numis. J.* 35, 1–6

Rigold, S.E. and Metcalf, D.M., 1984 — 'A revised check-list of English finds of sceattas', in Hill, D. and Metcalf, D.M., (eds) *Sceattas in England and on the Continent,* Brit. Archaeol. Rep. Brit. Ser. 128, 245–266

Riha, E., 1986 — *Römisches Toilettgerät und medizinische Instrumente aus Augst und Kaiseraugst,* (Forschungen in Augst, 6: Augst)

Rogers, N.S.H., 1993 — *Anglian and other Finds from 46–54 Fishergate,* The Archaeology of York 17/9 (Counc. Brit. Archaeol./York Archaeol. Trust)

Rumble, A., 1986 — *Domesday Book: Suffolk,* (Chichester: Phillimore)

Scarfe, N., 1999 — 'Domesday Churches', in Dymond, D. and Martin, E., (eds) *An Historical Atlas of Suffolk* (Suffolk County Council/Suffolk Institute of Archaeology and History), 52–3

Scarfe, N., 2002 — *The Suffolk Landscape,* (Chichester: Phillimore)

Scull, C.J., 1990 — 'Scales and weights in early Anglo-Saxon England', *Archaeol. J.* 147, 183–215

Scull, C.J., 2009 — *Early Medieval (late 5th–early 8th centuries AD) cemeteries at Boss Hall and Buttermarket, Ipswich, Suffolk,* Soc. Medieval Archaeol. Monograph 27

Shephard, J.F., 1979 — 'The social identify of the individual in isolated barrows and barrow cemeteries in Anglo-Saxon England', in Burnham, B.C. and Kingsbury, J. (eds), *Space, Hierarchy and Society,* Brit. Archaeol. Rep. Int. Ser. 59, 47–79

Sherlock, S., 2008 — 'The lost royal cult of Street House, Yorkshire', *British Archaeol.* May/June 2008, 30–37

Simmons, M., forthcoming — 'A bed burial from an Anglo-Saxon cemetery at Street House, Loftus, Redcar and Cleveland', *Medieval Archaeol.*

Smith, R.A., 1912 — 'An Anglo-Saxon cemetery at Uncleby, East Riding of Yorkshire', *Proc. Soc. Antiq. Ser 2,* 24, 146–158

Speake, G., 1970 — 'A seventh-century coin pendant from Bacton, Norfolk, and its ornament', *Medieval Archaeol.* 14, 1–16

Speake, G., 1989 — *A Saxon bed burial on Swallowcliffe Down,* English Heritage Archaeol. Rep. 10 (London)

Stevenson, R.B.K., 2005 — 'Appendix 2. Note on the dating of openwork hanging bowl escutcheons', in Bruce-Mitford, R.L. and Raven, S., *A Corpus of Late Celtic Hanging Bowls* (Oxford)

Stoodley, N., 1999 — *The Spindle and the Spear,* Brit. Archaeol. Rep. Brit. Ser. 288 (Oxford)

Stoodley, N., 2002 — 'Multiple Burials, Multiple Meanings? Interpreting the Early Anglo-Saxon Multiple Interment', in Lucy, S. and Reynolds, A., (eds) *Burial in Early Medieval England and Wales,* Soc. Medieval Archaeol. Monograph 17, 103–121

Swanton, M.J., 1973 — *The Spearheads of the Anglo-Saxon Settlements,* (London)

Swanton, M.J., 1974 — *A Corpus of Pagan Anglo-Saxon Spear-Types,* Brit. Archaeol. Rep. 7 (Oxford)

Teague, S., 2005 — 'Manor Farm, Monk Sherborne, Hampshire: archaeological investigations in 1996', *Proc. Hants Field Club Archaeol. Soc.* 60, 64–135

Theune, C., 1999 — 'On the Chronology of Merovingian grave goods in Alamannia', in Hines, J., Høilund Nielsen, K. and Siegmund, F., (eds) *The Pace of Change: Studies in Early Medieval Chronology,* (Oxford: Cardiff Studies in Archaeology), 23–33

Topham-Smith, C. and Anderson, S., 2000 — *Smye's Corner (Shrublands Quarry), Coddenham, Suffolk (Site CDD 050) Project Design for Assessment,* Suffolk County Council Archaeological Service Report 00/06

Trenteseau, B., 1966 — *La Damasquinure Merovingiennne en Belgique,* De Tempel: Dissertationes Archaeologicae Gandenses Vol. 9 (Bruges)

Trotter, M., 1970 — 'Estimation of stature from intact long limb bones', in Stewart, T.D. (ed), *Personal Identification in Mass Disasters* (Washington: Smithsonian Institute)

Ubl, H., 1989 — 'Was trug der Römische Soldat unter dem Cingulum?', in van Driel-Murray, C., (ed), *Roman Military Equipment: the Sources of Evidence (Proceedings of the fifth Roman Military Equipment Conference)* Brit. Archaeol. Rep. Int. Ser. 476, 61–74

VCH *Victoria County History. A History of the County of Hertford vol 4,* (1971 reprint)

Van de Noort, R., 1993 — 'The context of Early Medieval barrows in western Europe', *Antiquity* 67, 66–73

Waldron, A.W., 1994 — 'The human remains', in Evison, V., *An Anglo-Saxon Cemetery at Great Chesterford, Essex,* Counc. Brit. Archaeol. Res. Rep. 91, (London)

Walton Rogers, P., 2003 — 'Textiles' pp91–5 in McKinley, J.I., 'The early Saxon cemetery at Park Lane, Croydon', *Surrey Archaeological Collections* 90, 1–116

Walton Rogers, P., 2005 — *Textiles from the Anglo-Saxon Cemetery at Shrublands Quarry, Coddenham, Suffolk, CDD 050,* (The Anglo-Saxon Laboratory, York)

Walton Rogers, P., 2007 — *Cloth and Clothing in Early Anglo-Saxon England, AD 450–700,* Counc. Brit. Archaeol. Res. Rep. 145 (York)

Walton Rogers, P., forthcoming — 'Costume and textiles', in Parfitt, K. and Anderson, T., *Buckland Anglo-Saxon Cemetery, Dover: Excavations in 1994* (Canterbury Archaeol. Trust/British Museum Press)

Walton Rogers, P., 1997 — *Textile Remains on the Boar's-crest Helmet (the 'Pioneer Helmet') from Wollaston, near Wellingborough, Northamptonshire,* Textile Research Report 30 December 1997, (The Anglo-Saxon Laboratory, York)

Warner, P., 1996 — *The Origins of Suffolk,* (Manchester)

Watson, J., 1995 — 'Wood usage in Anglo-Saxon shields', *Anglo-Saxon Stud. Archaeol. Hist.* 7, 35–48

Watson, J., 2005–6 — 'Laid to Rest — two Anglo-Saxon chambered graves reconstructed', *Research News* 2 (Newsletter of the English Heritage Research Department), Winter 2005–6, 6–12

Watson, J., 2006a — *Smye's Corner (Shrublands Quarry), Coddenham, Suffolk: The examination and reconstruction of an Anglo-Saxon bed burial,* English Heritage Research Dept. Report 60/2006

Watson, J., 2006b — *Smye's Corner (Shrublands Quarry), Coddenham, Suffolk: The identification of organic material associated with metalwork from the Anglo-Saxon cemetery,* English Heritage Centre for Archaeology Report 27/2006

WEA, 1980 — 'Recommendations for age and sex diagnoses of skeletons', *J. Human Evolution* 9, 517–49

Webster, L. and Backhouse, J., 1991 — *The Making of England: Anglo-Saxon Art and Culture AD 600–900,* (British Museum Exhibition Catalogue)

Webster, L. and Brown, M., 1997 — *The Transformation of the Roman World AD400–900,* (British Museum Press)

Welch, M., 1983 — *Early Anglo-Saxon Sussex,* Brit. Archaeol. Rep. Brit. Ser. 112

Werner, J., 1964 — 'Frankish royal tombs in the cathedrals of Cologne and Saint-Denis', *Antiquity* 38, 201–16

Werner, J., 1992 — 'A review of *The Sutton Hoo Ship Burial Volume 3:* Some remarks, thoughts and proposals', *Anglo-Saxon Stud. Archaeol. Hist.* 5, 1–24

West, S.E., 1985 — *West Stow. The Anglo-Saxon Village,* E. Anglian Archaeol. 24

West, S.E., 1998 — *A Corpus of Anglo-Saxon Material from Suffolk,* E. Anglian Archaeol. 84

Wheeler, R.E.M., 1930 — *London in Roman Times,* (London Museum Catalogue, No 3)

White, R., 1988 — *Roman and Celtic Objects in Anglo-Saxon Graves,* Brit. Archaeol. Rep. Brit. Ser. 191 (Oxford)

Whitwell, J.B., 1990 — 'Excavation of the Anglo-Saxon cemetery, Castledyke South, Barton-upon Humber', *Lincolnshire Hist. Archaeol.* 25, 51–3

Wieczorek, A., Perin, P. and von Welck, K., 1996 — *Die Franken-Wegbereiter Europas.Vor 1500 Jahren: Konig Chlodwig und seine Erben,* (Mainz)

Williams, H., 1997 — 'Ancient landscapes and the dead: the reuse of prehistoric and Roman monuments as early Anglo-Saxon burial sites', *Medieval Archaeol.* 41, 1–32

Williamson, T., 1988 — 'Settlement chronology and regional landscapes: the evidence from the claylands of East Anglia and Essex', in Hooke, D., (ed.), *Anglo-Saxon Settlements* (Oxford: Blackwell), 153–175

Wilson, D.M., 1956 — 'The initial excavation of an Anglo-Saxon cemetery at Melbourn, Cambridgeshire', *Proc. Cambridge Antiq. Soc.* 49, 29–41

Youngs, S., 2008 — 'Anglo-Saxon, Irish and British Relations: Hanging Bowls Reconsidered', *Proc. British Academy* 157, 205–230

Index

Illustrations are denoted by page numbers in *italics*.

131

East Anglian Archaeology

is a serial publication sponsored by ALGAO EE and English Heritage. It is the main vehicle for publishing final reports on archaeological excavations and surveys in the region. For information about titles in the series, visit **www.eaareports.org.uk**. Reports can be obtained from:

Oxbow Books, 10 Hythe Bridge Street, Oxford OX1 2EW

or directly from the organisation publishing a particular volume.

Reports available so far:

No.1, 1975 Suffolk: various papers
No.2, 1976 Norfolk: various papers
No.3, 1977 Suffolk: various papers
No.4, 1976 Norfolk: Late Saxon town of Thetford
No.5, 1977 Norfolk: various papers on Roman sites
No.6, 1977 Norfolk: Spong Hill Anglo-Saxon cemetery, Part I
No.7, 1978 Norfolk: Bergh Apton Anglo-Saxon cemetery
No.8, 1978 Norfolk: various papers
No.9, 1980 Norfolk: North Elmham Park
No.10, 1980 Norfolk: village sites in Launditch Hundred
No.11, 1981 Norfolk: Spong Hill, Part II: Catalogue of Cremations
No.12, 1981 The barrows of East Anglia
No.13, 1981 Norwich: Eighteen centuries of pottery from Norwich
No.14, 1982 Norfolk: various papers
No.15, 1982 Norwich: Excavations in Norwich 1971–1978; Part I
No.16, 1982 Norfolk: Beaker domestic sites in the Fen-edge and East Anglia
No.17, 1983 Norfolk: Waterfront excavations and Thetford-type Ware production, Norwich
No.18, 1983 Norfolk: The archaeology of Witton
No.19, 1983 Norfolk: Two post-medieval earthenware pottery groups from Fulmodeston
No.20, 1983 Norfolk: Burgh Castle: excavation by Charles Green, 1958–61
No.21, 1984 Norfolk: Spong Hill, Part III: Catalogue of Inhumations
No.22, 1984 Norfolk: Excavations in Thetford, 1948–59 and 1973–80
No.23, 1985 Norfolk: Excavations at Brancaster 1974 and 1977
No.24, 1985 Suffolk: West Stow, the Anglo-Saxon village
No.25, 1985 Essex: Excavations by Mr H.P.Cooper on the Roman site at Hill Farm, Gestingthorpe, Essex
No.26, 1985 Norwich: Excavations in Norwich 1971–78; Part II
No.27, 1985 Cambridgeshire: The Fenland Project No.1: Archaeology and Environment in the Lower Welland Valley
No.28, 1985 Norfolk: Excavations within the north-east bailey of Norwich Castle, 1978
No.29, 1986 Norfolk: Barrow excavations in Norfolk, 1950–82
No.30, 1986 Norfolk: Excavations at Thornham, Warham, Wighton and Caistor St Edmund, Norfolk
No.31, 1986 Norfolk: Settlement, religion and industry on the Fen-edge; three Romano-British sites in Norfolk
No.32, 1987 Norfolk: Three Norman Churches in Norfolk
No.33, 1987 Essex: Excavation of a Cropmark Enclosure Complex at Woodham Walter, Essex, 1976 and An Assessment of Excavated Enclosures in Essex
No.34, 1987 Norfolk: Spong Hill, Part IV: Catalogue of Cremations
No.35, 1987 Cambridgeshire: The Fenland Project No.2: Fenland Landscapes and Settlement, Peterborough–March
No.36, 1987 Norfolk: The Anglo-Saxon Cemetery at Morningthorpe
No.37, 1987 Norfolk: Excavations at St Martin-at-Palace Plain, Norwich, 1981
No.38, 1987 Suffolk: The Anglo-Saxon Cemetery at Westgarth Gardens, Bury St Edmunds
No.39, 1988 Norfolk: Spong Hill, Part VI: Occupation during the 7th–2nd millennia BC
No.40, 1988 Suffolk: Burgh: The Iron Age and Roman Enclosure
No.41, 1988 Essex: Excavations at Great Dunmow, Essex: a Romano-British small town in the Trinovantian Civitas
No.42, 1988 Essex: Archaeology and Environment in South Essex, Rescue Archaeology along the Gray's By-pass 1979–80
No.43, 1988 Essex: Excavation at the North Ring, Mucking, Essex: A Late Bronze Age Enclosure
No.44, 1988 Norfolk: Six Deserted Villages in Norfolk
No.45, 1988 Norfolk: The Fenland Project No. 3: Marshland and the Nar Valley, Norfolk
No.46, 1989 Norfolk: The Deserted Medieval Village of Thuxton
No.47, 1989 Suffolk: West Stow: Early Anglo-Saxon Animal Husbandry
No.48, 1989 Suffolk: West Stow, Suffolk: The Prehistoric and Romano-British Occupations

No.49, 1990 Norfolk: The Evolution of Settlement in Three Parishes in South-East Norfolk
No.50, 1993 Proceedings of the Flatlands and Wetlands Conference
No.51, 1991 Norfolk: The Ruined and Disused Churches of Norfolk
No.52, 1991 Norfolk: The Fenland Project No. 4, The Wissey Embayment and Fen Causeway
No.53, 1992 Norfolk: Excavations in Thetford, 1980–82, Fison Way
No.54, 1992 Norfolk: The Iron Age Forts of Norfolk
No.55, 1992 Lincolnshire: The Fenland Project No.5: Lincolnshire Survey, The South-West Fens
No.56, 1992 Cambridgeshire: The Fenland Project No.6: The South-Western Cambridgeshire Fens
No.57, 1993 Norfolk and Lincolnshire: Excavations at Redgate Hill Hunstanton; and Tattershall Thorpe
No.58, 1993 Norwich: Households: The Medieval and Post-Medieval Finds from Norwich Survey Excavations 1971–1978
No.59, 1993 Fenland: The South-West Fen Dyke Survey Project 1982–86
No.60, 1993 Norfolk: Caister-on-Sea: Excavations by Charles Green, 1951–55
No.61, 1993 Fenland: The Fenland Project No.7: Excavations in Peterborough and the Lower Welland Valley 1960–1969
No.62, 1993 Norfolk: Excavations in Thetford by B.K. Davison, between 1964 and 1970
No.63, 1993 Norfolk: Illington: A Study of a Breckland Parish and its Anglo-Saxon Cemetery
No.64, 1994 Norfolk: The Late Saxon and Medieval Pottery Industry of Grimston: Excavations 1962–92
No.65, 1993 Suffolk: Settlements on Hill-tops: Seven Prehistoric Sites in Suffolk
No.66, 1993 Lincolnshire: The Fenland Project No.8: Lincolnshire Survey, the Northern Fen-Edge
No.67, 1994 Norfolk: Spong Hill, Part V: Catalogue of Cremations
No.68, 1994 Norfolk: Excavations at Fishergate, Norwich 1985
No.69, 1994 Norfolk: Spong Hill, Part VIII: The Cremations
No.70, 1994 Fenland: The Fenland Project No.9: Flandrian Environmental Change in Fenland
No.71, 1995 Essex: The Archaeology of the Essex Coast Vol.I: The Hullbridge Survey Project
No.72, 1995 Norfolk: Excavations at Redcastle Furze, Thetford, 1988–9
No.73, 1995 Norfolk: Spong Hill, Part VII: Iron Age, Roman and Early Saxon Settlement
No.74, 1995 Norfolk: A Late Neolithic, Saxon and Medieval Site at Middle Harling
No.75, 1995 Essex: North Shoebury: Settlement and Economy in South-east Essex 1500–AD1500
No.76, 1996 Nene Valley: Orton Hall Farm: A Roman and Early Anglo-Saxon Farmstead
No.77, 1996 Norfolk: Barrow Excavations in Norfolk, 1984–88
No.78, 1996 Norfolk:The Fenland Project No.11: The Wissey Embayment: Evidence for pre-Iron Age Occupation
No.79, 1996 Cambridgeshire: The Fenland Project No.10: Cambridgeshire Survey, the Isle of Ely and Wisbech
No.80, 1997 Norfolk: Barton Bendish and Caldecote: fieldwork in south-west Norfolk
No.81, 1997 Norfolk: Castle Rising Castle
No.82, 1998 Essex: Archaeology and the Landscape in the Lower Blackwater Valley
No.83, 1998 Essex: Excavations south of Chignall Roman Villa 1977–81
No.84, 1998 Suffolk: A Corpus of Anglo-Saxon Material
No.85, 1998 Suffolk: Towards a Landscape History of Walsham le Willows
No.86, 1998 Essex: Excavations at the Orsett 'Cock' Enclosure
No.87, 1999 Norfolk: Excavations in Thetford, North of the River, 1989–90
No.88, 1999 Essex: Excavations at Ivy Chimneys, Witham 1978–83
No.89, 1999 Lincolnshire: Salterns: Excavations at Helpringham, Holbeach St Johns and Bicker Haven
No.90, 1999 Essex:The Archaeology of Ardleigh, Excavations 1955–80
No.91, 2000 Norfolk: Excavations on the Norwich Southern Bypass, 1989–91 Part I Bixley, Caistor St Edmund, Trowse
No.92, 2000 Norfolk: Excavations on the Norwich Southern Bypass, 1989–91 Part II Harford Farm Anglo-Saxon Cemetery
No.93, 2001 Norfolk: Excavations on the Snettisham Bypass, 1989
No.94, 2001 Lincolnshire: Excavations at Billingborough, 1975–8
No.95, 2001 Suffolk: Snape Anglo-Saxon Cemetery: Excavations and Surveys
No.96, 2001 Norfolk: Two Medieval Churches in Norfolk
No.97, 2001 Cambridgeshire: Monument 97, Orton Longueville